THACKERAY: *A Critical Portrait*

THACKERAY
FROM A CRAYON DRAWING BY SAMUEL LAURENCE

Thackeray: A CRITICAL PORTRAIT

By JOHN W. DODDS

OXFORD UNIVERSITY PRESS
NEW YORK   LONDON   TORONTO
1941

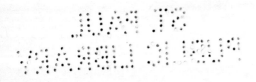
Printed in the United States of America

TO
M. K. D.

TO
M. K. D.

Preface

THIS BOOK is neither a critical biography nor an effort merely to analyse Thackeray as a novelist. It is, rather, criticism with some biographical infiltration—an attempt to trace the growth of a mind and at the same time to identify the quality of an art in fiction. Anything that will help to illuminate this has been grist for the mill, for Thackeray's writings are the reflection of a rich and intricate personality. Their moods are honest, transparent, but behind them lies always the sharp edge of a brooding and perceptive mind. A part of the real Thackeray, compounded of many simples, peers from every page he wrote—acid or benevolent, wistful or sprightly, gloomy or gay.

It is because he reveals so much of himself that some people have found him baffling. Deep as the reach of his understanding often is, he has no philosophical or sociological system to propound, nor does he turn to the world a carefully draped and judiciously spotlighted portrait of himself. By reason of his transparency he seems often paradoxical and inconsistent. But to those aware of the walking paradoxes that most men are to themselves, Thackeray is the more human because the less calculated. He is, however, no creature of artistic whim: his reading of life has its own symmetry. This it is the purpose of this book to trace, and much of it deals with the years before *Vanity Fair,* because in the early writings the development of his dominant ideas and the fixing of his artistic manner can best be seen. Incidentally, the quality of some of that early work is better than one who has never explored it might expect.

The great novels, from *Vanity Fair* through *The Newcomes,* must of course be the centre of any such study as this. There one enters a world which seems at first distant and Victorian, as indeed it is in many respects, for Thackeray was a man of his time, subject to its confusions and its certainties. Yet as one lives with his characters and discovers not only the geography of the fictional world which they inhabit but also the cool light which their creator turns on them, he realizes that the measure of Thackeray's creative intellect is to no small extent the distance that it is separated from what we have come to bracket easily as 'typically Victorian.' That division narrowed his range. It made him less popular in his own day than the more 'typical' Dickens. But it will always keep for him an audience fit, and not too few.

I am grateful to the Thackeray heirs for permission to quote certain portions of Thackeray's unpublished letters, and to Mr. Gordon N. Ray for his good offices in this connection. Two other debts among many I am happy to mention here: that to Mr. Hardin Craig for his careful reading of the manuscript and his many excellent suggestions; and to Mr. Howard F. Lowry for his constant and generous enthusiasm ever since the idea for this book began to grow.

J. W. D.

Stanford University,
10 *September* 1941.

Contents

THACKERAY: *A Critical Portrait*

CHAPTER ONE

Young Man in Search of a Profession

On Monday, the 2nd of March 1829, a tall, thin, ruddy-faced freshman of Trinity College, Cambridge, was writing to his mother. 'I have some thoughts of writing, for a college prize,' he said, 'an English essay on "The Influence of the Homeric Poems on the Religion, the Politics, the Literature and Society of Greece," but it will require much reading, which I fear I have not time to bestow on it.' Presumably young William Makepeace Thackeray never got around to writing his Homeric monograph. There were so many more pleasant things to occupy his time—wine parties at his tutor's, sketching tours through the neighbouring countryside, long talks with his new friends, John Allen and Edward FitzGerald, even a comfortable lying abed of a morning. 'Today has been an idle day with me rather,' he wrote on 16 April. 'But a little idleness doth one good.' Thackeray was no dullard, but neither was he one to unhinge his mind by too much study. And if his academic record to date had been undistinguished there was some reason for it. Never the blithe scholar, he had suffered under what seemed to him ever afterward the cold brutalities of an educational system which was supposed to 'breed manhood,' 'strengthen the fibres of the race,' and make possible the winning of future Waterloos, but which was as likely to inhibit dangerously the development of a shy and sensitive youth.

He had been born near Calcutta on the 18th of July 1811, the son of Richmond Thackeray, a civil servant in Bengal, who, at the time of his death, was Collector of the Twenty-four Parganas. Richmond Thackeray died when William Makepeace was five years of age, and in 1817 the boy's mother sent him to England to begin his education. There an aunt took charge of him. He was sent to a variety of preparatory schools, first to one in Hampshire and then, because he hated the place, to a school at Cheswick where he was but little happier. Years later he wrote: 'We Indian children were consigned to a school of which our deluded parents had heard a favourable report, but which was governed by a horrible little tyrant, who made our young lives so miserable that I remember kneeling by my little bed of a night, and saying "Pray God, I may dream of my mother." ' [1] In the meantime his mother had married a Major Carmichael-Smyth, and in 1821, to the small boy's great delight, the Smyths returned to England. The next year Thackeray entered Charterhouse School, to continue there until 1828.

Retrospectively, Thackeray recorded conflicting memories of his Charterhouse days. He revisited the place often, trying always to be present on Founder's Day, and delighting to talk both to the boys and to the old Pensioners. 'The oldest of us,' he said, 'grow young again for an hour or two as we come back into these scenes of childhood.' [2] He wrote Charterhouse into *Pendennis* and *The Newcomes* as 'Grey Friars' and sent his heroes there. In the *Roundabouts* he writes: [3] 'Men revisit the old school, though hateful to them, with ever so much kindness and sentimental affection.' 'Though hateful to them'—and indeed his direct references to his school days are filled with memories of uncomfortable boarding houses, blustering and unsympathetic masters, unmerited floggings, and the general bullying of boys trained according to 'the good old English system.' Thackeray fell foul of Dr. Russell, the headmaster, who pursued him systematically with sarcastic abuse. 'I was made so miserable by a

[1] *Roundabout Papers:* 'On Letts's Diary.'
[2] Ibid.: 'On a Joke I once heard from the late Thomas Hood.'
[3] Ibid.

classical education,' said Thackeray, 'that all connected with it is disagreeable in my eyes; and I have the same recollection of Greek in youth that I have of Castor oil.'[4] He spent a good deal of his time drawing sketches, and he filled the margins of his school books with lively caricatures. From early childhood he had shown remarkable facility with the pencil.

From this 'banishment of infernal misery' he was released in 1828. That summer and autumn he spent with his mother and stepfather, who were now living at Larkbeare, near Ottery St. Mary. There Major Carmichael-Smyth tutored him for entrance to Cambridge (Thackeray had made something less than a brilliant record at Charterhouse), and the following February he entered Trinity College, in the same college generation with Alfred Tennyson and his brothers Charles and Frederick, Arthur Hallam, Edward FitzGerald, Mitchell Kemble, John Allen (later Archdeacon), William Brookfield, Monckton Milnes, James Spedding, John Sterling, and William Kinglake. All of these Trinity men Thackeray came to know; FitzGerald and Brookfield became his closest friends. At Jesus College, too, was Thackeray's old Charterhouse classmate George Venables, who had in a fight broken the Thackerayan nose, Thackeray winning from the combat both a permanent disfigurement and a permanent friendship.

In this Cambridge atmosphere the Carthusian incubus seemed to roll from his shoulders. In the flush of his first month's residence he wrote to his mother that he hoped to learn 'to think in Greek.' We hear nothing more of this.

And as for the literary exercise, there were many possibilities more provocative than essays on Greek culture. Thackeray's fellow student, W. G. Lettsom, had established a little weekly paper called *The Snob: A Literary and Scientific Journal, Not Conducted by Members of the University.*[5] The journal was neither literary nor scientific, of course—just a compendium of rather feeble undergraduate humour and satire, which ran its

[4] *Cornhill to Cairo.*
[5] 'Snob,' in this connection, meant simply townsman rather than gownsman.

little day of eleven issues, died an end-of-the-term death, and
was resuscitated for a few months the following year under the
title of *The Gownsman*. To No. 4 of *The Snob* Thackeray contributed his poem 'Timbuctoo,' a burlesque on the subject set
for the prize contest of the year. The Chancellor's Medal was
won that year by Alfred Tennyson, with a poem much more
meritorious and much duller than Thackeray's. No one would
have forecast a great career for Thackeray on the basis of this
poem, but even here there is a tenuous hint of the future Titmarsh. 'Timbuctoo' is in its broad way a parody of all undergraduate prize poems and is perhaps the most reasonable treatment of such an esoteric subject.

Part of it runs:

THE SITUATION	In Africa (a quarter of the world) Men's skins are black, their hair is crisp and curl'd; And somewhere there, unknown to public view, A mighty city lies, called Timbuctoo.
THE NATURAL HISTORY	There stalks the tiger,—there the lion roars, Who sometimes eats the luckless blackamoors; All that he leaves of them the monster throws To jackals, vultures, dogs, cats, kites, and crows; His hunger thus the forest monarch gluts, And then lies down 'neath trees called cocoa nuts.

* * *

Desolate Afric! thou art lovely yet!!
One heart yet beats which ne'er shall thee forget.
What though thy maidens are a blackish brown,
Does virtue dwell in whiter breasts alone?
Oh no, oh no, oh no, oh no, oh no!
It shall not, must not, cannot, e'er be so.

Not the least amusing device of the poem is its machinery of
mock-pedantic footnotes. 'Line 13.—"Pop goes the musketoons."
A learned friend suggested "Bang" as a strong expression, but
as African gunpowder is notoriously bad, the Author thought
"Pop" the better word.'

About this time Thackeray wrote to his mother: 'A poem of

mine hath appeared in a weekly periodical here published, and
called *The Snob* . . . Young had a pleasant wine party, at which
for a short time I attended. "Timbuctoo" received much laud. I
could not help finding out that I was very fond of this same
praise. The men knew not the author, but praised the poem;
how eagerly I sucked it in! "All is vanity!"' How much of
Thackeray there is in those last three sentences! Not only the
'vanitas vanitatum' theme, which was to be dominant in so
much of his later writing, but also that tone of curious, amused
self-inspection, that first candid and disarming recognition and
confession that he, like most men, could tolerate praise. Much
of his inclination, in his maturity, to temper his probing of man's
folly with a benign understanding of human frailty stems from
this same quality of honest self-examination. It is a long step,
artistically as well as geographically, from 'Timbuctoo' to Vanity
Fair. But thus early we get a reasonable suggestion that the
transition is possible.

One of Thackeray's literary indiscretions at this time was
writing for *The Snob* a series of 'Ramsbottom Papers,' interesting
now only because they show the delight he took in the humour
of misspelling and because they point forward to the more mature
Yellowplush Papers. These epistles of Dorothea Julia Ramsbottom are imitations of the popular Ramsbottom papers of the
egregious Theodore Hook, which ran in *John Bull* between 1822
and 1831 and which consisted, like Thackeray's, chiefly of grotesque misspellings and incredible puns, with some pure mala-
propisms. Hook speaks of the 'laws of the Maids and Parsons'
and of 'the Vacuum at Rome'; Thackeray of knowing 'many
extinguished persons,' and of 'exorcising' his pen. It is all pretty
sad and bad. One realizes with a shock that Hook, who was
spending part of his time editing libellous slander for the political
paper, *John Bull,* was perhaps the most popular novelist writing
at the time. Certainly the vineyard needed new labourers.

After a residence of a year and a half, Thackeray ended his
Cambridge career in the spring of 1830. He had taken a fourth
in the May examination, and it seemed fruitless to continue a

course that gave little promise of distinguished achievement. So at nineteen years of age he was turned loose to hunt for a career.

The problem was not a pressing one, however. In the meantime, he thought, why not finish his education by making a trip to the Continent? July found him in Coblenz looking with the keen eye of an artist at the beauties of the Rhine and at picturesque natives, and sketching, always sketching. He wondered about his gifts and thought that he might do something with them. By September he was in Weimar, settling down with his friend, Norman Macleod, for a winter in the gay Duchy—studying German, falling merrily into love and out again, meeting the great Goethe and writing small poems for Ottilie von Goethe's weekly literary magazine, *Chaos,* attending the theatre, and playing around the fringes of court life. He was living the carefree life of a good-natured, high-spirited young man, no more solemn than young men should be at twenty, but drinking in all the time unwittingly those scenes and characters which were to appear later in the novels. The education of a novelist was proceeding outside of academic cloisters.

With the return of spring, however, Thackeray began to think a little self-consciously about a profession. He was nearly twenty; his father, he realized, had at that age been engaged in his profession for nearly five years. The law seemed safe and suitable and (at that distance) not unattractive; and so by fall he was reading law in Hare Court, Temple.

But sitting on a stool reading Blackstone was so much duller than drawing pen portraits of pretty girls at Weimar. 'The lawyer's preparatory education is certainly one of the most coldblooded, prejudiced pieces of invention that ever a man was slave to,' he wrote. 'The sun won't shine into Taprell's chambers, and the high stools don't blossom and bring forth buds.' He didn't know it, but he was getting material for a novel to be called *Pendennis.* Just then, however, spring had her way with him and in June 1832 he shook the dust of the Temple from his feet to go down into Cornwall and make speeches in the political campaign of his friend, Charles Buller. He wrote with great gusto to his mother and to FitzGerald about his experiences. At Liskeard before the election he discovered the town in an uproar and made a triumphal entry with Buller amid waving flags and saluting guns. For the cause of liberal politics he offered himself freely on the altar of teas and dances, all the while pledging Buller to reforms in politics and religion —reforms of which Thackeray admitted he knew nothing himself. It was all great fun—exciting and not too profound.

That summer Thackeray turned twenty-one, came into a fortune of some £500 a year, and bade farewell to the law for ever. He went immediately to Paris, there to read widely, study the language, and, incidentally, gamble away a good share of his patrimony. Thackeray at twenty-one was bubbling over with kindness and good humour; life seemed good, but it was good living rather than the good life which appealed to him. Something of the literary Bohemian always clung to Thackeray and in these days, with a debonair light-heartedness, he penetrated well beyond the seacoast of that legendary country. There he was found, and plucked, by the man later to be the original of his Deuceace.

About this time his stepfather, who lived in an atmosphere of unworldliness much like that of Colonel Newcome, lost in the failure of an Indian bank not only a good share of his own fortune but also part of Thackeray's. Within a year of receiving his inheritance, Thackeray faced the necessity of earning some money. The Young Man in Search of a Profession became really serious about it.

An opportunity came to Thackeray and Major Smyth to buy with part of their remaining capital a weekly paper called *The National Standard and Journal of Literature, Science, Music, Theatricals, and Fine Arts*. This paper had been founded in January 1833 by F.W.N. ('Alphabet') Bayley, a former henchman of Theodore Hook's on *John Bull* and one of the half-lights of journalistic London. With the issue of 11 May Thackeray assumed the editorship and flung himself energetically into the Gilbertian *mélange* of functions indicated in the title of the journal. He made woodcuts; he wrote verses, dramatic criticisms, editorials, book reviews, and stories; he made translations. In July he hurried across to Paris: 'It looks well to have a Parisian correspondent,' he wrote his mother; but he was back in town in September. For some reason people refused to buy this weekly compendium of wit and wisdom. And with the issue of 1 February 1834, the *National Standard* was hauled down for ever. For its Parisian correspondent, both income and occupation were gone.

The *National Standard* was an honest journalistic attempt, and its level of accomplishment was not so low as its short life might indicate. Yet for one interested in tracing the development of Thackeray's mind and art there is little in this beginning to lay hold upon. Amid the potpourri of his identified contributions there are, however, a few indications if not of literary power at least of attitudes that were to be typically Titmarshian. A satirical sketch of King Louis Philippe with umbrella and high hat ('pretty good,' Thackeray wrote his mother) is the first expression of the scorn which Thackeray was to retain for that monarch. A review of Mlle Taglioni's ballet 'Flore et Zephyr' is a lively discourse on one of Thackeray's pet antipathies: the grotesqueness of the mythological ballet performed by 'persons of most unprepossessing physiognomies and unclassical figures tricked out in such extraordinary costumes.' [6]

The comments on French life and character in 'Foreign Correspondence' are in satiric vein; Thackeray pillories Napoleon and Louis Philippe, mocks the French fondness for revolutions, holds his nose at their horror fiction and at Victor Hugo's 'bombastic claptrap,' and stands aghast at their lack of taste in drama. There is a not too subtle ironic power here, and a satiric relish

[6] Professor H. S. Gulliver's identification of this review as Thackeray's seems most probable. (*Thackeray's Literary Apprenticeship,* Valdosta, Georgia, 1934, pp. 41-2.) Thackeray's first published volume, in 1836, was a series of nine caricatures entitled *Flore et Zephyr, Ballet Mythologique,* a burlesque of the violent exercise rather than of the art of the ballet.

as well as an insularity which remind one of the later Thackeray. Of the tales printed here, *The Devil's Wager* was the only one which Thackeray thought worthy of republication.[7] It is a story of Sir Rollo's cheating the devil, told in burlesque romantic manner. It adds little to his reputation.

There is a review here, brief but pungent, which in spite of its lack of subtlety is so much in Thackeray's later devastating style that it is worthy of special notice. One can almost hear him sharpening his teeth for Bulwer. The book was Robert Montgomery's poem *Woman: the Angel of Life*. Thackeray annihilates the florid sentimentality of the poem and then perpetrates successfully the astounding trick of printing its last fourteen lines backward to show that the poem makes as much sense read backward as forward.[8]

In this first helter-skelter attempt at journalism, Thackeray tried his hand at a wide variety of literary forms. None of it is of enduring literary value, but it is important in so far as it enables us to see Thackeray spreading his first literary wings and making tentative satiric flights.

The last issue of the *National Standard* appeared on 1 February 1834. For the next two and a half years we see Thackeray somewhat dimly. Although it is difficult to identify any of his contributions, it is probable that during this period he began to write reviews for *Fraser's*. But we can be sure that he was not giving his days and nights to the literary discipline. Art and the Bohemian life of the artist in Paris were at the time much

---

[7] In *The Paris Sketch Book*.

[8] An interesting footnote to this review is contained in a letter of Thackeray's to Montgomery, now in the manuscript collection of the Huntington Library. Writing on 3 August [1850] Thackeray says, referring no doubt to Macaulay's slashing review (*The Edinburgh Review*, April 1830) of Montgomery's *The Omnipresence of Deity: a Poem*, and *Satan: a Poem:* 'It was not fair to judge of you or any man by his works at nineteen, though many men would be proud to have been able to write as you did then, at any period of their lives.' Macaulay had recently reprinted his early review in his collected edition of the essays in 1850. One wonders if Thackeray remembered what he himself had said in his own youthful article.

closer to his heart. After the failure of his first journalistic venture he turned seriously to art as a profession.

During the summer of 1833, when he had been grinding out
'foreign correspondence' for the *National Standard,* he had written to his mother from Paris: 'I have been thinking very seriously of turning artist. I think I can draw better than do anything else, and certainly I like it better than any other occupation; why shouldn't I? It requires a three years' apprenticeship,
however, which is not agreeable, and afterwards the way is
clear and pleasant enough.' With the demise of the paper he
scuttled across to Paris, there to settle down with his pencil and
brush amid a cloud of tobacco smoke and the merry choruses
of the *ateliers.* He returned frequently to London (all his life he
shuttled back and forth at frequent intervals across the Channel), but most of the time he was taking lessons from the painter
John Brine, haunting the art galleries, copying pictures, and fill-
ing notebooks with drawings.

Thackeray's subsequent reviews of art exhibitions showed
that he held lively and often discerning opinions on contemporary painting. But here it is important to note his progressive
disillusionment about his ability as painter and at the same time
to recognize the native urge which led him all his life to fill
with sketches his letters to his friends, to draw some hundreds
of illustrations for *Punch,* and, when he at last turned author,
to make designs for many of his books.

After a year's study he recorded his discouragement in a letter to Frank Stone, writing under date of 20 April 1835. Stone
was already a well-known painter, exhibiting at the Royal Academy.

As for myself—I am in a state of despair—I have got enough torn-up
pictures to roast an ox by—the sun riseth upon my efforts and goeth
down on my failures, and I have become latterly so disgusted with
myself and art and everything belonging to it, that for a month past
I have been lying on sofas reading novels, and never touching a
pencil. In these 6 months, I have not done a thing worth looking at.
O God when will Thy light enable my fingers to work, and my

colours to shine?—if in another 6 months, I can do no better, I will arise and go out and hang myself.[9]

The dream died hard, and Thackeray dwindled reluctantly from painter into illustrator. A year later, married, and embarked by force of financial necessity on his second newspaper venture, he was still trying to sell through various channels his pen-and-ink drawings. He climbed the stairs of Furnival's Inn to present a few tentative drawings to a young man who, flushed with the success of *Sketches by Boz,* was looking for an illustrator for *Pickwick Papers.* Thackeray's offer was turned down. And on 20 January 1837 he wrote again to Stone:

I have sent some drawings to London, which I want to be submitted to your Committee . . . I fear very much that my skill in the art is not sufficiently great to entitle me to a place in your Society, but I will work hard and, please God, improve. Perhaps also the waggish line which I have adopted in the drawings may render them more acceptable for variety's sake . . . I wish I had more time to work, but the newspaper [*The Constitutional*] takes up most part of my time, and carries off a great deal of my enthusiasm.[10]

Here is suggested the eventual compromise: Why should not a waggish artist who is also a waggish author illustrate his own letter-press?

Thackeray's drawings, therefore, have an interest beyond themselves; he is the only great novelist who was also his own illustrator, and his pictures serve as admirable commentaries on the text. Through their strength and weakness one often gets a clue to his conception of character. But it is foolish to say, as has been said, that he ranks almost with Leech and Cruikshank. Thackeray himself knew better. He would have smiled (and have been pleased) at what Charlotte Brontë wrote of him in the early days of her idolization: 'He can render, with a few black lines and dots, shades of expression so fine, so real; traits of character so minute, so subtle, so difficult to seize and fix, I

[9] Lady Ritchie: *From Friend to Friend,* London, 1920, p. 107.
[10] Ibid.

cannot tell—I can only wonder and admire . . . he is a wizard of a draughtsman.' [11]

Now draughtsmanship, in the strict sense, was just what Thackeray lacked. Trollope said that Thackeray never learned to draw. There are, among his unpublished sketches, some charming pen and watercolour studies of landscape and architecture, possessing a fresh delicacy of line, but in his drawings of people he shows a lack of technical skill. This is most apparent in his more serious pictures. There one finds his mature and completely incredible children and his vacuous maidens (always brunettes, by the way) who, with faces uncreased by any marks of intelligence, simper from the page like the females whose images one used to find stamped on the sides of prune boxes.[12]

No, when Thackeray is at his best he is more than a little the caricaturist, in which vein he was often delightful. He could be engagingly absurd and nonsensical, as in the illustrations to *The Rose and the Ring* and in the innumerable sketches for *Punch*. More frequently he was satirical with a lusty but inoffensive Hogarthian gusto. Bleary vulgarity, perky insolence, stuffy respectability, egotistical asininity—all felt the point of his pencil. His splay-footed butlers and his debonairly conceited bucks are drolly humorous. He could do to a turn the fat smugness of a Jos Sedley. For grotesque female ugliness he had no mercy, and his pages are sprinkled with hideous harridans any one of whom might have been the Campaigner. Particularly lively are his ingenious initial letters and tail-pieces; Thackeray moved easily in the realm of pure inventive nonsense.

One wonders, however, if he saw the characters of his novels in his mind quite as he reduced them to the copper plate. The Cruikshank vein does very well for the *Yellowplush Papers,* just as it did well for Dickens, where the distortions of line reinforce and give point to the broad eccentricities of character. 'Phiz' is

[11] Letter of 11 March 1848, to W. S. Williams. Shakespeare Head Press edition, II, 197.

[12] A simile used by Professor Beers, I believe, in reference to the heroines of the Gothic novel.

keyed perfectly to the *Pickwick Papers*. But in the some 40 etch-
ings and 150 woodcuts to *Vanity Fair* one feels that the illustrations are in a sense contradicting the text, broadening down
subtleties and making caricatures of very human people. Certainly Becky was more than a vixenish Mona Lisa, and Amelia,
however dull, deserved better than the imbecilic prettiness which
her artist gave her.

Not infrequently, however, Thackeray's drawings interpret
and reinforce his criticism of life, which, in its larger reaches,
is the ironist's point of view. Such is the familiar self-portrait in
Vanity Fair—the amusing caricature of the flat-nosed bespec-
tacled jester in fool's uniform, with the humorous mask in his
lap and on his face an expression of wistful melancholy. Such is
the drawing of 'Ludovicus Rex' in the *Paris Sketch Book,* where
in three little sketches Thackeray gives the equivalent of a whole
chapter of Carlyle's clothes-philosophy. And malapropos as some
of Thackeray's more serious attempts are, we should be unwill-
ing to lose the hundreds of unpretentious illustrations which he
dashed off with technical incompetence, perhaps, but with a vigorous and enduring good humour. Thackeray rose to literature
across the stepping stones of his baffled artistry, and no one who
is unaware of that can understand fully either the man or the
pictorial tact with which, in the text of his novels, he seizes always upon just the right characterizing detail.

In 1836, however, art had unfortunately to be its own reward,
and the artist had to cast about for some more remunerative
employment. Major Carmichael-Smyth, with a hopefulness reminiscent again of Colonel Newcome, helped to float a new daily
paper, which was to be radical in politics and which secured the
support of such men as Charles Buller, Joseph Hume, and Sir
William Molesworth. Laman Blanchard was made editor and
Thackeray became Paris Correspondent with a salary of £400
a year. On such excellent prospects he married Miss Isabella
Shawe and went to Paris to live in such state as his salary might
afford. Years later he wrote to a young friend who was contemplating early marriage:

My dear J.[ohn] E.[liot]

This letter, so far as the printed extract,[13] was begun who knows how many days ago?—whilst you were in the bliss of your honeymoon. The delicate subject of early and imprudent marriages is touched also in the ensuing number of a periodical which you read. I made such a marriage myself. My means being

> 8 guineas a week (secured on a newspaper which failed 6 months after.)
>
> My wife's income 50£ a year promised by her mother, and paid for 2 quarters, since which (1837) I have received exactly 10£ on account.

And with this fortune, I have done so well, that, you see, I am not a fair judge of early marriages, but always look upon them, and upon imprudent young people *qui s'aiment* with a partial eye.

In the first 6 months, *I saved money.*

I hope J.E. may do likewise; and as to the struggle, and ups and downs of life that are before him, that he may bear them with a cheerful heart. How to set to work? How to confront the baker and butcher with an unconcerned face? How to pay that Doctor's fees at that period when he must be called in? These, and a hundred other such questions, you will have to solve. As I think of my own past, and what happened, I say Laus Deo with a very humble grateful heart. May your voyage end prosperously too, I sincerely hope and—I am going to say, pray;—for I can't see a friend and his young wife setting forth on a journey which I have made myself, and in which I have undergone disaster, grief, and immense joys and consolations, without the most serious thoughts and a prayer to God Almighty for his welfare.

But the *Constitutional* proved an even feebler child than the *National Standard*. It declined visibly after a few months; Thackeray was called over from Paris to become manager and

[13] From the unpublished manuscript in the Huntington Library. Thackeray had pasted at the head of the first page a newspaper clipping reading as follows: 'There is at the present moment, somewhere in the West End of London, a young barrister, who is highly connected, but in a dreadful dilemma owing to his recent marriage.' The letter is dated '36 Onslow Square, S.W., June 28 [1859].' The 'periodical' mentioned later was *The Virginians,* the 'marriage' that of George Warrington and Theo Lambert.

to apply artificial respiration; the stockholders were assessed £1 a share; and on 1 July 1837, with the number announcing the death of the king, the paper passed away. With its collapse went the rest of Major Carmichael-Smyth's fortune. Laman Blanchard even pawned his watch to get the last number out.

Thackeray contributed to the *Constitutional* some fifty letters from Paris signed 'T.T.' They were hack work, dealing chiefly with French politics and bringing heavy guns to bear upon the tyranny of Louis Philippe, the 'citizen king.' [14] They add little or nothing to our knowledge of Thackeray; much less, in fact, than the work of the earlier *National Standard*. The importance of the episode in any history of Thackeray's development, therefore, is purely external; once again his occupation was gone, his family was beginning to grow by small additions (his eldest daughter was born 9 June), and he faced the necessity of earning a living by whatever means. It was no question of creating great literature; it was a matter of getting ahead. Through the Sterlings he got the chance to write with reasonable regularity book reviews for *The Times* and for *Fraser's*. And in addition to his reviews he began to explore his first really creative comic vein—the adventures of the fantastic Yellowplush. The work for these two journals carried him through 1838 and 1839. It was hard work, but they were reasonably happy years.

[14] Although Thackeray could not have known it, the *Constitutional* goaded the thin-skinned Leopold, King of the Belgians, into one of his complaining outbursts. On 18 November 1836, he wrote to his niece, Queen Victoria: 'An infamous Radical or Tory-Radical paper, the *Constitutional,* seems determined to run down the Coburg family. I don't understand the meaning of it; the only happiness poor Charlotte knew was during her short wedded existence, and there was but one voice on that subject, that we offered a bright prospect to the nation.' (*Letters of Queen Victoria,* I, 53. Quoted by Edith Sitwell in *Victoria of England,* Boston, 1936, p. 45.)

CHAPTER TWO

Critical Beginnings: Book Reviews; *Catherine*

WHEN THACKERAY wrote his first review for *The Times,* in April 1837, he was in his twenty-sixth year. At that age Dickens, of Thackeray's contemporaries, had published *Pickwick* and *Oliver Twist;* Disraeli, *Vivian Grey;* Bulwer, three novels, including *Pelham.* But Thackeray was to struggle through eleven years of miscellaneous journalism under a dozen pseudonyms before reaching his first great success with *Vanity Fair.* Various explanations have been offered for this delayed success: Thackeray lacked assurance; he was lazy; he failed to put his best foot foremost; the multiplicity of his *noms-de-plume* (Michael Angelo Titmarsh, Charles Yellowplush, Ikey Solomons, Major Gahagan, Fitz-Boodle, and many others) operated against him. Undoubtedly there is something to be said for this last point of view, since the public could hardly follow concertedly a literary will-o'-the-wisp who changed his shape with each new publication. Even the *Snob Papers,* a striking success, were anonymous. Undoubtedly, too, there is justice in the claim that Thackeray refused to compromise his intellectual standards and, hungry as he was for success, would not write down to the public. This helps to explain why Thackeray had not in his own day, and never will have, the popularity of Dickens. The ironist, sharply intellectual, who goes about puncturing bubbles of pretension with however humorous a melancholy, will never enjoy the following of the man who guffaws loudly and weeps riotously with his characters. As Thackeray himself put it: 'Mere satiric wit is addressed to a class of readers quite different to those simple souls who laugh and weep over the novel.' [1] But this does not take us far into an understanding of Thackeray's delayed success. To be sure, there is a mellowing in the later novels which might attract some who would find unpleasant the harder surfaces of the earlier work. A combination of elements worked against Thackeray, but to discover the underlying reasons for the slow acceptance of his work we shall have to penetrate more deeply into his writings before *Vanity Fair*.

The explanation begins on a paradox: Thackeray's art matured slowly, yet some of the best things he did are little read today. The point is that those good things are often done in snatches, on a small canvas. Not until he reached *Barry Lyndon* (which after all is a superb *tour de force*) did Thackeray attempt anything which had the amplitude and resonance of which he was capable. He had thought of himself as a *Punch* man, a critic, a satirist, an urbane and observant writer of travel books, a creator of edged farce; but never, except briefly in *The Great Hoggarty Diamond,* as a creator of character and incident in the integrated form we find in the great novels. Indeed there is a letter on record to show that he thought of *Vanity Fair* as fundamentally a 'humorous' work.[2] The sub-title on the yellow cover of the first monthly part would indicate that it grew into a novel unawares: 'Pen and Pencil Sketches of English Society.' All in all, Thackeray came slowly into the conception of the novel on a broad, deliberate scale, incorporating the histories of families as well as of individuals, and penetrated with a humanity which gave gentleness as well as authority to his perception of life's cruelties and ironies—a humanity which increased, at the same time, his appreciation of men's lovable ridiculousness. The art of Thackeray's novels is an intensely personal art; more than most authors he impregnated his stories with his own personal-

---

[1] *Lectures on the English Humourists.*
[2] See the discussion of *Vanity Fair*, pp. 128-9.

ity. It is our good fortune that he had matured so fully before he came to *Vanity Fair* and *Pendennis* and *Henry Esmond* and *The Newcomes*.

The great body of Thackeray's work before *Vanity Fair* makes the tracing of his ideas and attitudes a fruitful task and gives a special significance to a consideration of his apprentice work. Many points of view, many typical moods and perceptions which are given superior body and form in the novels appear in the reviews, burlesques, and narratives which make up the bulk of his early journalism. Thackeray did not change much from early to late; there is no sudden break in the stream of development. He did mature, however, and the process of that growth is worth following.

In Thackeray's early book reviews we can trace not only the sharpening of his style but also the fixing of definite attitudes towards the art and function of prose fiction. His post-*Constitutional* journalism is closely tied in with the early history of *Fraser's Magazine* and its editorship under Dr. William Maginn, the gadfly of the London literary world.[3] The bent of Thackeray's early literary career, perhaps even his relish for a plethora of pseudonyms, was determined in no small part by this brilliant, witty Irishman who flashed across the literary scene, kept pompous humbugs ever in tremulous expectation of his next devastating attack, and who, in 1842, at the age of 49, finally succeeded in drinking himself to death. Maginn, writing under the name of 'Ensign O'Doherty,' had been one of the principal supports of the young *Blackwood's* and had perhaps collaborated with John Wilson in instituting the 'Noctes Ambrosianae.' He could not confine his efforts to one magazine, however, and made wide excursions into scurrility with the notorious *John Bull* and the worse *Age*. About 1829 he severed his connection with *Blackwood's* and the next year, with Hugh Fraser, established *Fraser's Magazine*. For ten years this was the most brilliant and

---

[3] See Malcolm Elwin's *Victorian Wallflowers*, London, 1934, for an excellent short discussion of this interesting and neglected person.

provocative of the London magazines. Maginn was a perpetuator of the old hang-draw-and-quarter school of criticism in which the *Edinburgh Review,* the *Quarterly Review,* and *Blackwood's* had excelled. Himself an incisive and dexterous writer, he insisted upon and maintained for the magazine a high literary standard, and in its heyday *Fraser's* impaled its literary enemies (most frequently mediocrity and pretension) upon the barbed spikes of its relentless satire. It was to this school of indefatigable vivacity and truculence and Toryism that Thackeray, the future manager of a Radical weekly, came. As an advanced left-wing liberal he had to swallow his political creed for the time, and doubtless the complete absence of any political allusions in his contributions, amid the Tory drum-fire of the other writers, can be traced to this necessity.

Thackeray had met Maginn as early as 1832 and was at first fascinated by him. Later he loaned Maginn money, probably to enlist his efforts on behalf of the *National Standard.* Upon the failure of that paper, it must have been Maginn's influence that landed him a position on *Fraser's.* Just when he joined the staff of that publication it is difficult to determine; very little of his material is identifiable before *Yellowplush.* Yet certainly he was a member of the circle late in 1834, when Maclise included him in his drawing of the Fraserians seated convivially about the editorial table. It was not, however, until late in 1837, with the first *Yellowplush Paper,* that Thackeray began his steady contribution of stories, literary reviews, and art criticisms.[4]

---

[4] Any discussion of Thackeray's earliest contributions to *Fraser's* involves the authorship of the burlesque *Elizabeth Brownrigge,* a not unlively satire on Bulwer's *Eugene Aram.* Because the theme of the story (i.e. that the way to become a successful author is to make virtue and vice indistinguishable) is similar to Thackeray's treatment of the same idea in *Catherine,* the story has been attributed to Thackeray. Each of Thackeray's biographers and bibliographers has had an opinion to offer; they disagree with remarkable unanimity. I cannot find Thackeray's hand in this piece. The style does not seem to me to be his, although it is true that in 1832 one would not expect his style to be fully formed. His *Catherine,* published in the same magazine in 1839-40, is a superior treatment of the same theme, but it appears to me improbable that Thackeray at twenty-one years of age would have been capable of *Elizabeth Brownrigge.* It is

When Thackeray began to write for *Fraser's* the magazine
had for several years been carrying on a satirical attack upon
the currently popular 'fashionable novelists'—the 'silver-fork
school'—with Bulwer bearing the brunt of the attack. Thackeray was by temperament hostile to the intellectual dishonesty,
the spongy and inflated sentimentality, the drooling gush and
pomposity of this kind of fiction. Always it was his delight to
pillory shallow conventionalities and snobbish elegance. So he
joined the hunt with the *Fraser* pack and began his pursuit of
Bulwer, and later of Disraeli, with a relentless vigor—a pursuit
not to end until the banalities of the fashionable novelists had
been embalmed in *Punch's* 'Prize Novelists' of 1847. Looking
back on it later, Thackeray was sorry for what seemed to him
then the unnecessary ferociousness of his attacks. Cruel he was,
to be sure, but except for an occasional injudicious personal reference, cruel with a sort of cauterizing cruelty, serving a definite
therapeutic purpose. At this distance most of it seems healthy
and justifiable. It is futile to complain, as some of Bulwer's de-
fenders have done, that Thackeray was jealous of Bulwer's popular success. Thackeray's later apologies for his severity indicate
no softening of his fundamental dislike for hollow pretentious-
ness. His record on that point, however charitable he may have
grown, is all of a piece from beginning to end.

The first *Yellowplush Paper* appeared in November 1837.
'Fashionable Fax' is a review of Skelton's *Anatomy of Conduct,*
a book of rules for fashionable deportment. Thackeray has high
fun with this absurd and stilted guide to high life, the general
temper of which may be inferred from the following quota-
tion: 'When the finger-glass is placed before you, you must not
drink the contents, or even rinse your mouth, and spit it back;

in the vein which Maginn encouraged in his contributors and it is possible, as
has been suggested, that he himself, or perhaps Douglas Jerrold, wrote it. There
is a letter of Thackeray's quoted in the catalogue for the Goodyear Sale in
1926 which helps to clear up this vexed question: '. . . a comic story called
"The Professor" was I think my first regular appearance as a paid author, in
Bentley's *Miscellany* 1837 I think, but about dates I am not certain.' He was
right about the date.

although this has been done by some inconsiderate persons.'

The next month Thackeray went after 'a parcel of gilded books,' the season's Annuals—a form of sentimental keepsake which achieved an astounding popularity during the 'thirties and early 'forties. The titles give the clue: 'Flowers of Loveliness,' 'Friendship's Offering,' 'Gems of Beauty.' Thackeray's review is concerned chiefly with the pictorial aspects of the books, which seem to him a prostitution of the painter's art. They are all of the same character:

A large weak plate, done in what we believe is called the stipple style of engraving, a woman badly drawn, with enormous eyes—a tear, perhaps, upon each cheek, and an exceedingly low-cut dress—pats a greyhound, or weeps into a flower-pot . . . Miss Landon, Miss Mitford, or my Lady Blessington, writes a song upon the opposite page, about water-lily, chilly, stilly, shivering beside a streamlet, plighted, blighted, love-benighted, falsehood sharper than a gimlet, lost affection, recollection, cut connection, tears in torrents, true-love token, spoken, broken, sighing, dying, girl of Florence, and so on. The poetry is quite worthy of the picture, and a little sham sentiment is employed to illustrate a little sham art.

Thackeray approaches the fashionable novel first in a review in *The Times*[5] of Lady Charlotte Bury's *Love*. He dwells upon the absurd plot and the still more absurd manners, quotes to show the pseudo-elegant style, and makes clear that the details of the novel are dull and the morals faulty. The same month in *Fraser's* he discusses 'Our Batch of Novels for Xmas, 1837.' Mrs. Trollope's *Vicar of Wrexhill* is condemned for its religious bigotry. Of Miss Landon's *Ethel Churchill* he says: 'It is not written in a healthy and honest tone of sentiment; there is a vast deal too much tenderness and love-making, heart-breaking and repining, for persons in this every-day world.' All the heroes and heroines are either consumptive or crossed in love. 'Oh,' he cries out, 'for a little manly, honest, God-relying simplicity—cheerful, unaffected, and humble!'

[5] 11 January 1838.

The most interesting part of this review is devoted to a dissection—Thackeray's first—of Bulwer. The book is *Ernest Maltravers*. Thackeray points out that the morality which Bulwer
has acquired in his researches, political and metaphysical, is of
the most extraordinary nature.

For one who is always preaching of Truth, of Beauty, the dulness
of his moral sense is perfectly ludicrous. He cannot see that the hero
into whose mouth he places his favourite metaphysical gabble—his
dissertations upon the stars, the passions, the Greek plays, and what
not—his eternal whine about what he calls the good and the beautiful, is a fellow as mean and paltry as can be imagined . . . He
wishes to paint an amiable man and he succeeds in drawing a scoundrel: he says he will give us the likeness of a genius, and it is only
the picture of a *humbug*. [Ernest seduces the girl.] . . . After a
deal of namby-pamby Platonism, the girl, as Mr. Bulwer says, 'goes
to the deuce.' The expression is as charming as the morality, and
appears amidst a quantity of the very finest writing about the good
and the beautiful, youth, love, passion, nature, and so forth.

He goes on to praise Bulwer's descriptions and some of his minor
characterizations, but ends by advising him that his *forte* lies in
the humorous and the sarcastic rather than in the sublime.

This illustrates the tone of amused irritation that Thackeray
was to take with Bulwer, except that he allowed himself, on a
few occasions, to become more personal. In his review in *The
Times* [6] of *Alice: or, the Mysteries,* he says:

The Bond-street dandy, Mr. Pelham, is by no means so offensive
as the philosophical dandy, Mr. Maltravers; the former's affectations
and egotism are far more natural than the sickly cant of the latter
. . . We are not going to press the point that this character [the
hero] is neither more nor less than Mr. Edward Earle Lytton Bulwer. That gentleman expressly declares that all men are 'fools' who
see in this windy declaimer of bad morals, this vain spouter of
pompous twaddle, only the morals and egotism of the author himself . . . [But] the hero appears upon the stage, and straightway
the style becomes intolerably bloated and pompous; the genius of Mr.

[6] 24 April 1838.

Bulwer, the ill-usage which has been shown to Mr. Bulwer, the self-love of Mr. Bulwer, the piques of Mr. Bulwer, appear in every line.

This is the sort of attack which Thackeray later deplored, but he was yet to pursue Bulwer even more devastatingly in burlesque. In 'Yellowplush's Ajew' [7] Bulwer ('Sawedwadgeorge-earllittnbulwig') dines at the house of Yellowplush's master. He gives in long learned periods an extensive, exclamatory description of the misery, desolation, and jealousy that surrounds the successful literary man. He says that because he is unrivalled on the throne of literature he is to be made a baronet, and Yellow-plush decides that he will write a novel in the style of Bulwig.

In another Yellowplush paper [8] he takes Bulwer to task for his painful puling and piping about the unjust criticism that his play *The Sea Captain* had received. This is a relentless piece of criticism. Not ill-tempered, and filled with a certain good humour, the tone is one of kindly reprimand. But it lays pitilessly bare Bulwer's weaknesses both as man and author—his sensitiveness which makes him assume the martyr's pose under criticism and the artistic shoddiness both in sentiment and diction which is revealed in his inflated bombast, his mixed metaphors, his whining sentiment. It was a thorough job of demolition that must have made Bulwer writhe. There is a certain sleek savagery about it, the more effective because it is cushioned with a good-will for Bulwer's future and an admission of his undoubted abilities.

In more dignified tone, Thackeray took issue with Bulwer once more when he wrote for *Fraser's* in March 1846 an article on the recently deceased Laman Blanchard, and on the chances of the literary profession. He pays tribute to Blanchard, 'generous, honest, gay, gentle, and amiable.' Bulwer-Lytton's kind biographical notice of Blanchard had lamented that he had neglected his talents, frittering away in fugitive publications time and genius which might have led to the production of a great

[7] *Fraser's*, August 1838.
[8] 'Epistles to the Literati,' *Fraser's*, January 1840.

work. Thackeray's comments on this are significant as giving his attitude towards the profession in which he himself had laboured with reasonable success but without any great acclaim. *Vanity Fair,* we must remember, was still to be written.

Thackeray takes the frankly practical point of view that all men are labouring for daily bread, sometimes reaping reputation along with profit,

> . . . but Bread, in the main, is the incentive . . . If only men of genius were to write, Lord help us! how many books would there be? How many people are there even capable of appreciating genius? . . . To do your work honestly, to amuse and instruct your reader of today, to die when your time comes, and go hence with as clean a breast as may be; may these be all yours and ours, by God's will. Let us be content with our *status* as literary craftsmen, telling the truth as far as may be, hitting no foul blow, condescending to no servile puffery, filling not a very lofty, but a manly and honorable part.

Thackeray is here working out his own philosophy of the literary profession, and his own status in it, as much as he is defending Blanchard. 'And after all,' he says, 'what is this Reputation, the cant of our trade, the goal that every scribbling penny-a-liner demurely pretends that he is hunting after? Why should we get it? Why can't we do without it? We only fancy we want it.' Why, he goes on to ask, should admiration of other men's works be the test of friendship? So he thinks that Blanchard would *not* have produced, in other circumstances, a work of the highest class. He had a duty—to get his family their dinner.

At this point in Thackeray's career this is a very illuminating utterance, a realistic conception of the writer's trade and a dignified defence of journalism. Thackeray's muse was always a humble one, clinging close to the realities of everyday life. Therein lies its peculiar sweetness and strength.

Few men were more simply and buoyantly pleased by success than Thackeray, but often, even when his rival Dickens was outselling him five to one, he protested against the complaints of authors that their profession was neglected. At the conclusion of his 1852 lectures in the United States, at a Literary Fund dinner, and in *Sketches and Travels in London* he reiterates his belief that literary men receive their just due. If their calling is ever sneered at, it is only because it is not well paid. 'The world has no other criterion for respectability.' In the future, perhaps, the writer's social rank will rise; he will be getting what they call 'honours,' and dying in the bosom of the genteel.

For Bulwer's bleats, then, he had no more respect than for his early novels. In the late 'thirties and 'forties other fashionable novelists, too, fell foul of his pen. Mrs. Trollope's *Widow Barnaby* he praised, but of her *Romance of Vienna* he asked, 'What shall we say of this picture of fashionable German life? The silver-fork school of novels has long been admired; but what is it compared to Mrs. Trollope's branch academy, which may be called the *German* silver-fork school?' The Austrian noblemen 'talk even worse French than our own noblemen do in novels; they are more insufferably dull . . .'[9]

Disraeli had to wait for the *Prize Novelists* to receive proper parody, but in 1844 Thackeray reviewed his *Coningsby* in both the *Morning Chronicle* and the *Pictorial Times.* He saw the book as the fashionable novel 'pushed to its extremest verge,' and was offended by the pompous foppery of its style. In the latter review he says:

Coningsby possesses all the happy elements of popularity. It is personal, it is witty, it is sentimental, it is outrageously fashionable, charmingly malicious, exquisitely novel, seemingly very deep, but in reality very easy of comprehension, and admirably absurd; for you do not only laugh at the personages whom the author holds up to ridicule, but you laugh at the author too, whose coxcombries are incessantly amusing.

Thackeray's paper *The Fashionable Authoress*[10] gives a generic picture, in Lady Fanny Flummery, of the fecund female

[9] *The Times,* 4 September 1838. (Gulliver, op. cit., p. 217.)
[10] Kenny Meadows' *Heads of the People,* 1840.

who spawns scores of incurably sentimental novels of high life; and in Timson, the publisher, a picture of the sycophant who cringes at her feet and compares her with Shakespeare. Thackeray manages here an effectively humorous burlesque, ironically disdainful of frippery and froth and namby-pamby beauty. He longs for the Golden Age when there will be no more fiddle-faddle novels, no more 'Blossoms of Loveliness.'

In Thackeray's concern with these literary inanities of his time one senses something of a Fraserian delight in satire for its own sake—the bear-cub stretching its claws because they are so sharp and pretty—but there is also much of the wholesome realist who was to retain, in his prime, a steady aversion for shoddy writing, not because it was merely second-rate, but because it pretended to be something it was not. Thackeray did not waste all of his reviewer's ammunition, however, on the fashionable novel.

Any one whose task it has ever been to go down the byways of early Victorian fiction cannot escape a melancholy recognition of its congenital feebleness. Booksellers were making their living from the stories of high jinks and buffoonery poured out by Pierce Egan and Theodore Hook and from the early rattling, rollicking, hard-drinking, hard-riding tales of Charles Lever; from sentimental glittering trash about fashionable society by those who were in it and those who aspired to it—the Bulwers, Gores, Burys, Blessingtons, *et al;* and from equally sentimental stories of crime and low life, which blended the appearance of a tell-all realism with an actual meretricious idealization of the criminal. Thackeray's early concern with the Newgate novel is important, for it leads him into his stories which begin to approach the novel in form—first *Catherine,* the crime novel planned to end all crime novels, and later *Barry Lyndon,* where the record of depravity reaches a kind of artistic translation.

In 1830 Bulwer published *Paul Clifford,* the first of the picaresque-romantic stories of criminals, in part an indictment of the existing penal code. This was followed in 1832 (the year of *Elizabeth Brownrigge*) by *Eugene Aram,* attempting to analyse the mind of a murderer, but padded with a kind of maudlin sympathy of just the kind to set Thackeray's teeth on edge. The next person to achieve eminence in the Newgate novel was the brisk and handsome Harrison Ainsworth, whose *Rookwood* (1834) and *Jack Sheppard* (1840) took the town by storm. Even Maginn reviewed *Rookwood* not unfavourably in *Fraser's*. These stories were romantic and bustling, mingling brutal realism with a kind of unreal Gothic terror, and spraying the whole with sentimental rhetoric.

By 1834 Thackeray had begun to protest against this idealization of criminals. Writing in the March *Fraser's* he said: 'Hitherto the English criminal has been exhibited amidst the incidents of a novel, or his personal beauty lauded, and his untimely fate deplored in the stanzas of a song. It would be well to have him at last displayed as he really is in action and in principle . . . [to] exclude poetic adornment and speculative reverie.[11]

By 1839 Thackeray was able to include Dickens's *Oliver Twist* in his strictures upon the false representation of criminal life. He protests against the 'sham low . . . which amateurs delight to write and read, and which is altogether different from the honest, hearty vulgarity, which it pretends to represent.'[12] He speaks of Bulwer's

ingenious inconsistencies, and Dickens's startling, pleasing, unnatural caricatures . . . when either of these writers has descended from his natural sphere to indulge the public with pictures of low life— of the ways of cut-throats, burglars, women of bad life, Jew old-clothesmen, and others, who are introduced as talking the most exquisite slang and bad grammar under circumstances the most profoundly tragic—it has always been our opinion that the scenes so sketched are perfectly absurd and unreal . . .

He softens his criticism here, however, by admitting that he waits eagerly for the new instalments of *Nicholas Nickleby* and *Jack Sheppard*.

[11] 'Hints for a History of Highwaymen,' a review of Whitehead's *Lives and Exploits of English Highwaymen*, etc.
[12] 'Horae Catnachianæ,' *Fraser's*, April 1839.

But a few months later he declares of *Jack Sheppard* (even though Ainsworth was his friend and was on the staff of *Fraser's*): 'We like not this gallows school of literature.' [13] Sheppard's metamorphosis from a vulgar villain into a melodramatic hero offended Thackeray. The novel is agreeably written, he admits, and his review of it is given in sorrow rather than in anger, but he reprehends Ainsworth's subject and his treatment of that subject. Later he contrasts Ainsworth unfavourably with Fielding. 'Ainsworth dared not paint his hero as the scoundrel he knew him to be; he must keep his brutalities in the background, else the public morals will be outraged, and so he produces a book quite absurd and unreal, and infinitely more immoral than anything Fielding ever wrote. "Jack Sheppard" is immoral actually because it is decorous.' [14]

This was written shortly after Thackeray had concluded in *Fraser's* [15] his attempt to achieve the morality of indecorum. *Catherine* was the result of his quixotic and fruitless attempt to write a crime novel so revolting that the public would in the future turn in disgust from anything of the sort. A few people liked it—Carlyle called it 'wonderful'—but there is no evidence that it proved the moral cathartic for the public which Thackeray meant it to be. It fails to revolt us today, and, in spite of itself, interests us. It is a story of selfish and rapacious criminality, dealing with as unlovely a set of rogues as an author could invent. Certainly by doctrine and by precept he makes his point against the sentimental treatment of crime. Brock is a thoroughgoing villain who seems even more evil in his later days of retirement than in his earlier, more picaresque days. Galgenstein is throughout completely base—a dull-witted bore and seducer, cruel and predatory. Billings, Catherine's son, is an insolent brat. Hayes, the husband, is a poor weak thing, but completely unsympathetic and mean. Yet Thackeray, polemic as his purpose is, makes these characters live, and unrelievedly black or impo-

[13] A review in *Fraser's*, February 1840.
[14] A review of Fieldings' *Works*, *The Times*, 2 September 1840.
[15] May 1839—February 1840.

tent and crawling as they are, they live in an atmosphere so real and are themselves so coherent that it is easy to believe in them. Nor does Thackeray shrink from the frank exposition of ugly passions, brutal immorality, and blunt language.

Thackeray meant that in this story 'no man shall mistake virtue for vice, no man shall allow a single sentiment of pity or admiration to enter his bosom for any character of the piece: it being, from beginning to end, a scene of unmixed rascality performed by persons who never deviate into good feeling.' He begins with a mock apology for introducing the public to characters so utterly worthless, against the prevailing taste and the general manner of authors:

The amusing novel of *Ernest Maltravers,* for instance, opens with a seduction; but then it is performed by people of strictest virtue on both sides; and there is so much religion and philosophy in the heart of the seducer, so much tender innocence in the soul of the seduced, that—bless the little dears!—their very peccadilloes make one interested in them; and their naughtiness becomes quite sacred, so deliciously is it described. Now, if we *are* to be interested by rascally actions, let us have them with plain faces, and let them be performed, not by virtuous philosophers, but by rascals.

One feels, however, a curious uncertainty of tone in the story. For one thing, Thackeray's manner of telling it is touched with felicitous allusion and not a little humour. He assumes a lightness of manner which ought, perhaps, to make the episodes more cold-blooded and horrible, but which has quite an opposite effect, and interests us for itself. Thus, of Corporal Brock: 'Not seven cities, but one or two regiments, might contend for the honour of giving him birth; for his mother, whose name he took, had acted as camp-follower to a Royalist regiment; had then obeyed the Parliamentarians.' And of Hayes's hopeless early love for Catherine: 'It was still a kind of dismal satisfaction to be miserable in her company.'

Thackeray might say at the time, 'It is a disgusting subject, and no mistake. I wish I had taken a pleasanter one . . . ,' and might write to his mother, 'It is very ingenious in you to find beauties in "Catherine," which was a mistake all through.' But try as he might to whip himself into a rage with his characters, let him exclaim that here no one is going to die a whitewashed saint 'like poor "Biss Dadsy" in "Oliver Twist",' let him tell his readers that they 'ought to be made cordially to detest, scorn, loathe, abhor, and abominate all people of this kidney'—nevertheless in spite of his declared purpose he makes us interested in them. The character of 'Cat' herself, the author's interest in her as a human being, is perhaps the chief reason for Thackeray's failure to realize his purpose. He himself understood this when he wrote to his mother: '. . . the triumph of it would have been to make readers so horribly horrified as to cause them to give up or rather throw up the book and all its kind; whereas you see the author had a sneaking kindness for his heroine, and did not like to make her quite worthless.'

In the history of Thackeray's growth as a novelist the book has a value beyond its subject, for it is the first of his stories which approaches the novel in form. To begin with, there is the prose style itself. It is almost as smooth and clear and controlled as it was to be later in the great novels. And it is, even in its more realistic scenes, filtered through irony. The hand may be the hand of the propagandist against the Newgate novel, but the voice is the voice of the ironist-realist-humorist of *Vanity Fair*.

Here too appears the tendency to digress and philosophize which was to become so much a part of his later manner. He writes little pessimistic essays on Fate and the dark ways of destiny. He picks up a 110-year-old copy of the *Daily Post* telling of Hayes's murder and of the execution of the culprits and, thinking himself back into the eighteenth century, he contemplates the evanscence of life and the common lot of all to go into the darkness.

Think of it! it has been read by Belinda at her toilet, scanned at 'Button's' and 'Will's,' sneered at by wits, talked of in palaces and cottages, by a busy race in wigs, red heels, hoops, patches, and rags of all variety—a busy race that hath long since plunged and vanished in the unfathomable gulf towards which we march so briskly.

Where are they? 'Afflavit Deus'—and they are gone! Hark! is not the same wind roaring still that shall sweep us down? and yonder stands the compositor at his types who shall put up a pretty paragraph some day to say how, 'Yesterday, at his house in Grosvenor Square,' or 'At Botany Bay, universally regretted,' died So-and-So.

Thus is the author of the future *Roundabouts* discernible, in 1839, in his story of calculated horror and brutality.

Thackeray's literary reviews (to which *Catherine* relates closely) were not all attacks on the fashionable or on the Newgate school of novels. Some of them were written for the *Foreign Quarterly Review* (1842-4) on Hugo, Dumas, Sue, Scribe, and others.[16] In 1840 he wrote for *The Times* a review of Fielding's novels of which we shall see more later. In 1844, under the title 'A Box of Novels,' he praises Lever's *Tom Burke of Ours,* Samuel Lover's *Treasure Trove,* and waxes ecstatic over Dickens's *Christmas Carol.*[17] By this time Thackeray had worked beyond the influence of Maginn and he indicates that his cut-and-slash days of reviewing are over. He reminisces in mellow vein about how they have all grown mild in *Fraser's* since the mid-'thirties, when young and ardent geniuses used 'to belabour with unmerciful ridicule almost all the writers of this country of England, to sneer at their scholarship, to question their talents, to shout with fierce laughter over their faults historical, poetical, grammatical, and sentimental; and thence leave the reader to deduce our (the critic's) own immense superiority in all the points which we questioned in the world beside.' To be sure, the very pertinent parody of *Punch's Prize Novelists* was yet to come, which made no less havoc because it was good humoured, but the 'thirties marked the close of Thackeray's corrosive journalism. Experience and sorrow did not blunt the edge of his perceptive faculties or the keenness of his irony, but they did take him away from his

[16] See R. S. Garnett: *The New Sketch Book,* London, 1906.
[17] *Fraser's,* February.

youthful savagery into a world of more universal and less personal satire. Nevertheless we are able to see in the reviews of this apprentice period a setting of literary signals which helps us to understand his more mature work.

It might be noted here that on two occasions Thackeray reviewed at length books by Carlyle, who became his good friend and for whom he had a great liking. The first of these was the *French Revolution*.[18] It is a thoughtful appreciation of Carlyle's genius, praising him for his learning, observation, and humour, for his hatred of cant and for his 'sound, hearty philosophy.' But Thackeray is much distressed, as one would expect him to be, about Carlyle's style. The eccentric prose, the grotesque conceits and images, the 'choking double words, astonishing to the admirers of simple Addisonian English,' repel him, although he can admire 'that gloomy rough Rembrandt-kind of reality which is Mr. Carlyle's style of rhetoric painting.' [19]

Later he reviewed the *Life of John Sterling* less favorably.[20] He views the wrath of God's angry gentleman with a mock terror and hastens to scramble out of the way. In this work of Carlyle's, which is in many ways the quietest and gentlest thing he ever did, Thackeray seizes upon those portions of gloomy prophecy and violent cavorting-about which form only a small portion of the whole. One gets the impression that Thackeray is reviewing the Carlyle of the *Latter Day Pamphlets* as much as the *John Sterling*. He is particularly incensed by what seems to him Carlyle's attack upon Christianity. When brought beside the fire-breathing Carlyle, the 'cynic' and 'pessimist' Thackeray seems a blooming optimist defending, if not the best of all possible worlds, at least one much more satisfactory than the fulminating Carlyle would admit.

We shall see more of Thackeray's literary criticism, from *Punch* to the *Lectures* to the *Roundabouts*. Here it will be sufficient to indicate the remarkably high quality of his best criticism

18 *The Times*, 3 April 1837.
19 *The Times*, 3 April 1837.
20 Ibid., 1 November 1851.

from early to late. He could be wrong-headed at times, for he suffered from the limitations of his temperament and of his time. When he was wrong he was so with a satisfying complete-ness, as in the case of Swift; and where he liked (or disliked, sometimes) he could be soundly revealing and discriminating. He had no body of critical statutes to which he was bound, nor was he warped, as many of his contemporaries were, by violent political prejudices. His standards were those of common sense penetrated by a tact for the really excellent. He wanted honesty and simplicity and clarity and good humour, and within the limits of his surprisingly catholic taste he was both astute and sound.

CHAPTER THREE

The Early Humorist and Story-Teller:
1838-40

AFTER THE EVENT, it is easy to see in Thackeray's first ventures into fiction the traces of the mind and the outlook upon life which, refined, developed, and enriched, were to lead to *Vanity Fair* and *Pendennis*. But the reader of *Bentley's Miscellany* who picked up the issue of September 1837 to read *The Professor, A Tale of Sentiment,* Thackeray's first appearance as a paid author, might have been excused for failing to find even an embryonic genius in this tale by 'Goliah Gahagan.' Thackeray began authorship in this story, in *Yellowplush, Cox's Diary, Fitz-Boodle's Confessions,* and in many other early sketches, with the vein of broad caricature and boisterous satire which he had struck as early as *The Snob*. There were, to be sure, certain additions of his own, but superficially he wrote in the extravagantly facetious manner made popular by the buffoonery of Pierce Egan and carried into ludicrous realism by Theodore Hook. It was an age when humour made its point by sound and fury, by horseplay and perspiration. People held their sides with laughter over the antics of Lever's Harry Lorrequer and Lover's Handy Andy. Albert Smith, with a pawky wit, made a great reputation on wretched novels; Tom Hood was thriving on bad puns; Douglas Jerrold, with a superior equipment, made his greatest success in the low humour of *Mrs. Caudle's Curtain Lectures*. Thus Thackeray, with a nice eye for the ridiculous and with a natural tendency towards burlesque, plunged into the broad stream of contemporary fun. *The Professor* by its pseudo-romantic manner makes the most of a very thin point which might have come out of Hook: 'Professor' Dandolo, dancing master in a girls' school, woos Miss Grampus until, when he is invited to an oyster dinner at her father's, he is revealed as a traitorous, deceptive wretch— Dando the oyster eater. The mock moral: the vice of gluttony. Not, by and large, a very edifying beginning.

The Yellowplush Papers were very popular, sufficiently so to enable the author, after the first three instalments, to strike for higher pay from *Fraser's*. The *Yellowplush Correspondence* began in November 1837. At this time Thackeray was still hot on the trail of the 'fashnabble novvles,' and as we have already seen, the best part of the papers is devoted to the baiting of Bulwer. Yet there is more to them than that, and more, too, than the grotesque orthography *à la* Smollett and Hook, which, although it lends a certain amusing characterizing flavour, no longer seems very uproarious. Yellowplush spells by ear: 'consquints,' 'sellybrated,' 'suckmstance,' 'lucksry,' 'leading the bride to the halter,' etc. The satire in places is elementary; we learn that servants listen at keyholes, that they ape their masters and are likely to be the most snobbish of snobs, that there is no honour among thieves. Yellowplush, however, is an engaging rascal with no small perception and with an inoffensive moral obliquity. His origins are somewhat obscure, for his mother, who called herself Miss Montmorency, had 'wrapped up my buth in a mistry.' Yellowplush is naïvely proud of his fine uniforms, and early developed a longing for fashionable life.

Some of Yellowplush's amusingly haughty observations show Thackeray flushing for the first time objects of satire which he was to pursue later. The servant says of his master, a gambler, 'If he had been a common man, you'd have said he was no better than a swinler. It's only rank and buth that can warrant such singularities as my master show'd . . . My master, being a more fashionabble man than Mr. B., in course he owed a deal more money.' Again, 'I've always found through life that if you wish to be respected by English people, you must be insalent to them, especially if you are a sprig of nobiliaty. We *like* being insulted by noblemen—it shows they're familiar with us . . . I've known many and many a genlmn about town who'd rather be kicked by a lord than not noticed by him.' Already Thackeray is sharpening his scent for snobs.

There are other indications, too, of the Thackeray we know later. To begin with one of the slightest: Thackeray always found seasickness (at least in print) funny. Yellowplush gets sick on the Channel crossing, and ever afterwards Thackeray is constitutionally incapable of mentioning boats and ocean voyages without a staple reference to stewards hurrying with basins. More significantly, some of the characterizations in the *Yellowplush Correspondence,* although lacking the delicacy of light and shade they were to have in later incarnations, are recognizable prototypes. Deuceace himself, gambler and crook, is the first of Thackeray's characters to live in lazy luxury on nothing a year. His father, the Earl of Crabs, is a study in gross malevolent selfishness, about whom there lingers, nevertheless, a sort of malicious good-cheer. His son, whom he hates and upon whom he preys, is even more depraved than he, so that the old man's amiability is perhaps a relative thing.

There are also in these stories two characters of the kind for which Thackeray was always to have a fearful relish and whom he was to portray with an almost intolerable vividness—his termagant women, most frequently stepmothers or mothers-in-law. The first is found in the initial *Yellowplush* story, *Miss Shum's Husband*—a story which turns upon the attenuated idea of a young man whose chief concern is to hide from his young wife the nature of the profession in which he makes a very good living; he is a crossing-sweeper. Mrs. Shum, the stepmother, rules despotically her meek husband (who finds solace in a steady, dull intoxication) and her large family of daughters. In spite of the fact that they live in a beggarly hole, she puts on airs, and blusters about the celebrity and antiquity of her family. She is an earlier and coarser Campaigner, given to shrieks, hysterics, and mean and miserable hatreds. The other insufferable female is Lady Griffin, with whom Deuceace becomes embroiled. 'She hated, in her calm quiet way, almost every one else who came near her . . . She never got into a passion, not she—she never said a rude word; but she'd a genius—a genius which many women have—of making a *hell* of a home, and tort'ring the poor creatures of her family, until they were wellnigh drove mad.'

These Yellowplush stories are well told, in the lucid style and with some of the strength if not the subtlety of characterization which Thackeray was to show later. But their total impression is unsatisfying, and it comes, I think, from their author's failure to recognize that he is trying to blend two incompatible themes, the humorous and the cruelly realistic. The result of this attempt, one might suppose, would be the grotesque. It fails to reach that, however. There is the superficial humour lent by the misspelling; there is the passing irony about fashionable affectations; but if the story is stripped of its comic framework it is a sinister, bitter record of selfishness and revenge. Deuceace is cruel as well as selfish; the Earl of Crabs, with his breezy corruption and his savage revenge on his own son, with his ironic platitudes, his cold-blooded heartlessness, is a living but far from savoury figure.

The story ends with a scene of ruthless Hogarthian realism. Crabs meets in a park the tattered, unshaven Deuceace and his ragged wife whom Crabs had tricked Deuceace into marrying. Crabs bursts into peals of laughter, and Deuceace strikes his wife to the ground with his handless wrist. The whole narrative is a gruesome scavenger-hunt in low passions and greed, and over it all is this gloss of comic spelling and humorous incidental observations. Thackeray had still much to learn about his art. His somewhat fumbling efforts to blend his instinctive play of the comic spirit and his aptitude for the probing of human weakness are one of the signs of his artistic immaturity.

The mutation of Charles Yellowplush, Esq., of 1838 into the

C. Jeames de la Pluche of 1845-6 is an interesting phenomenon. The Jeames of the later *Punch* papers, footman and 'nice deranger of epitaphs' though he is, is quite a different person from the earlier Charles. The change marks one phase of Thackeray's growth. For one thing, the bitter realism has dropped out; the social satire has become more generic though none the less pointed; and Jeames, though even more subject than his predecessor to the afflatus of social success, is more genial if less cunning. The satire on the fashionable novels is still there—Jeames reads *Pelham* six times to learn what a gentleman is—but it is less pervasive, while the satire on social snobbery has expanded until it dominates the scene. The tone of broad farce is maintained merrily throughout.

The footman comes into £30,000 through railway speculation and is then fawned upon by his employer, who encourages Jeames's attentions to his daughter. Plans for an elaborate wedding are thwarted by the girl's elopement with the man she loves. About this time the market collapses (Thackeray himself had been caught in the great Railway boom of 1845-6 and its subsequent bursting). Jeames's head had been turned by wealth, but at heart he has always been a footman; in the days of his success he never turns on his poor relations or on his old friends. He is openly happy when sudden poverty makes it possible for him to marry Mary Hann, the kitchen maid of his heart. The humour of the episodes, as well as their social criticism, arises from Jeames's becoming a burlesque type of the *nouveau riche*. Amid the fireworks of hearty burlesque, snobbery and greed are thwacked with resounding if not crippling blows. Jeames suddenly discovers that he is of ancient lineage (Hugo de la Pluche came over with the Conqueror); he takes apartments in the Albany; he becomes a director in thirty-three railroads; he plans to stand for Parliament; he rides a horse in wistful discomfort; he learns dancing, and goes shooting in an elegant outfit. Here Thackeray's sense of the absurd is running at full tilt and carries his satire easily along with it.

On the heels of the first *Yellowplush Correspondence* came

the unbuttoned burlesque of the *Historical Reminiscences* of the astounding Major Gahagan.[1] Thackeray is thoroughly enjoying himself here, and if he had an eye on extravagant Eastern tales and the breezy exploits of such military heroes as Harry Lorrequer, such criticism is incidental and negligible. The egregious Major lives in his own right as a nineteenth-century Münchausen, relating with a straight face and an air of indisputable veracity such incredible adventures in love, war, and high society as transcend mere egotism. Gahagan is the distilled essence of lying braggadocio. 'I have been,' he says modestly, 'at more pitched battles, led more forlorn hopes, had more success among the fair sex, drunk harder, read more, been a handsomer man than any officer now serving Her Majesty.' Sabre in hand, he leaps with the greatest of ease over six-foot walls into the mouths of roaring cannon. Thackeray sprinkles the pages with ludicrous near-Indian names which, presumably, give the final touch of veracity to the Major's impossible feats. It is all good fun and no heads are broken—except those of the Major's enemies.

In the same vein of broad caricature is *Cox's Diary*, published in the *Comic Almanac for* 1840, the text of which is a proper commentary on Cruikshank's illustrations. It is the old theme: a barber inherits money and under his wife's influence woos society; the Coxes attend the opera; the Coxes hold a tournament; the Coxes go to the circus. The central idea is Thackerayan enough; the slapstick humour and the puns are typical of Thackeray's lusty comic-strip manner; but the situations are the broadest possible, and the satire, when it does come in, is obvious and perfunctory. The whole thing might have been by Hook out of Dickens. It is when Thackeray tries this sort of thing that it is clear how much wiser he was to feed in other literary pastures and leave Dickens to his.

During the time that Thackeray was writing *Catherine* for *Fraser's* he was prone to divide the world into two categories: dupes and rogues. *Captain Rook and Mr. Pigeon*[2] is a story of

[1] *New Monthly Magazine*, 1838-9.
[2] First published in *The Corsair*, New York, September 1839.

this ilk, an exposition of the idea that Nature, by a sort of compensation, has created fools for rogues to gull. 'Wherever shines the sun,' says Thackeray, being possessed for the time with a species of fixed idea, 'you are sure to find Folly basking in it; and Knavery is the shadow at Folly's heels . . . Especially there is no cheat like an English cheat.' In all likelihood Thackeray put his own tenderly sore recollections into the story of Freddy, the amiable green youth plucked by Captain Rook. About the same time he published in the *Comic Almanac for 1839,* with twelve illustrations by Cruikshank, *Stubbs's Calendar: or, The Fatal Boots,* a kind of companion piece for *Catherine,* or for the earlier Deuceace stories. Here again is a professed piece of humour, but it is of the grimmest kind, the humour of a Swift or a Hogarth, with all the gaiety of the chapters on the Houyhnhnms and the merry frolicsomeness of *The Rake's Progress.* For there is no real humour here, not even humanity, only a study in sordid depravity. Stubbs, the 'hero,' is completely ugly in disposition, selfish, cowardly, willing to cheat any one, and in the end completely gulled himself. From the first, when he extorts money from his schoolfellows, his evil disposition is the dominant element, indeed the only element, in the story. Thackeray had to work himself clear of this sort of thing. Its weakness lies not so much in its being poorly done (it is not convincing and is far from being his best writing even at the time), but in its not being, under any conceivable critical canon, worth doing.

Thackeray's next story, *The Bedford-Row Conspiracy,*[3] is a good example of what he could do well and what not so well in 1840. It is an adaptation of a story from the French of Charles de Bernard, wherein Thackeray has a little difficulty getting under way. It opens with a not-too-convincing love passage and then goes rather stiffly into the intricate problem of the lovers' backgrounds, their ancestry, their present prospects. The tale is one of politico-family intrigues such as Thackeray delighted in.

[3] *New Monthly Magazine,* January, March, April, 1840.

Against a background of conventionally enthusiastic young love he throws the story of the fatuous Gorgons (Tory) and the time-serving Scully (Whig)—all of them willing to sell for political advancement such shreds of honour as they have. Not too savoury a story, filled with easy corruptibility, it leads to a somewhat implausible climax which enables two of the characters to listen at the door while Scully makes impassioned love to the wife of his political enemy. But then the whole thing is done in broad strokes which, for once, blend in with the materials of the story itself, and the ultimate deflation of that pompous and corrupt pair, Gorgon and Scully, is complete and satisfying.

Thackeray is in his best comic vein as he anatomizes the political enmities of the families and sketches in the portrait of Sir George Grimsby Gorgon—small, very military, swears fearfully, regular at church, regularly reads to his family and domestics the morning and evening prayer.

He bullied his daughters, *seemed* to bully his wife, who led him whither she chose; gave grand entertainments, and never asked a friend by chance; had splendid liveries, and starved his people; and was as dull, stingy, pompous, insolent, cringing, ill-tempered a little creature as was ever known. With such qualities you may fancy he was generally admired in society and by his country. So he was.

In spite of the fact that *The Bedford-Row Conspiracy* verges frequently upon the farcical and is primarily a dissection of vulgarity, both proud and mean, it does show Thackeray's strengthening power in characterization and his unerring facility for puncturing stuffed shirts of whatever variety.

The year 1840 is a convenient pausing place in the study of Thackeray's literary apprenticeship, not because it marks any sudden transition in his development, but because it was the year of his domestic tragedy. From that year on, too, there is, amid a quality of unlicked stuff, a perceptible steady deepening of his art. There remains, for 1840, first a review of Fielding's works which is of first importance; then a bit of realistic news reporting which is yet more than that and is of interest too because it was the first time that Thackeray had signed an article with his own initials; then his first published volume, *The Paris Sketch Book;* and one remaining story, the unfinished *Shabby Genteel Story,* broken off during the days of his great distress.

The development of Thackeray's narrative art is the gradual coalescing and purification of two divergent points of view which, in his earlier work, can be studied almost independently. Their stratification is distinct even though he baffles us by attempting to superimpose them. On the one hand there is the professional funny man with a true and native sense of the ludicrous and the grotesque, and with a nice feeling for bathos. On the other hand, is the man with a clinical interest in blackguards, searching among the seams of the social fabric for the *pediculi* which infest them; never cheaply cynical or misanthropic, but focusing his vision with a painful intensity upon shabby and vulgar motives, ferreting out meanness and cruelty, and isolating without pity, in its chemically pure form, not heroic sin but scurvy and malignant rascality. To this end his gallery of Deuceaces, Earls of Crabs, Mrs. Shums, Captain Rooks, Stubbses, Catherines, Gorgons, and Scullys. These are the more painful because they are not melodramatic Dickensian villains smelling of grease paint and false whiskers. They are brutally real.

Knowing Thackeray, we know him capable of a supreme tenderness, and we are aware that he came to show for the human race not only a lacerated pity but also a pervasive relish and enjoyment. Even his sordidness has a prophylactic purpose. His concern is to strip the pretence from life and, without sneering at frailty, to scrutinize human motives wherever they might lead him. The mistake in art, in these early years, was not merely in his tortured preoccupation with cynical sinners—even that could be creative—but in his frequent attempts to immerse them in a bath of burlesque. Far from tempering the satire, this makes it seem more than a little hideous. Thackeray retained always his gift for probing beneath the surface and exposing sham; he retained, too, his essentially humorous appreciation of men and events. But as he grew in wisdom both of these fused into a new molecular combination; out of the lion came forth sweetness. He could always take the button off the foil when it seemed necessary, yet for the most part sympathy blended with satire to make the irony which is the most striking quality of his best work.

In the unfinished *Shabby Genteel Story,* which was to be continued years later, with a difference, in *Philip,* he is still fascinated by the spectacle of fools and knaves. He is a bit gentler with the fools, however, if no less severe on the knaves.

There is a precision of detail in Thackeray's backgrounds of decayed pseudo-gentility for which he has not always received credit. The respectable vulgarity of Mrs. Gann—fat, damp, living in an atmosphere of smelling-bottles and cheap finery; the boozy vulgarity of Gann himself, most of the time gently in his gin cups, fleeing periodically to the neighbouring pubs to escape the sharp tongue of his wife, sensitive about his Cockney accent, radiating a sort of hearty, ineffectual cordiality—these are vividly realized. The fat and predatory Widow Carrickfergus is a creature of pure farce, but we see little of her. Andrea Fitch, the painter, is also presented in terms of broad comedy—a fantastic youth, all art and whiskers and a naïvely harmless and affected romanticism. Curiously enough, he is credible in a strange way and Thackeray has given him, as he so often gives his people of weak head and warm heart, a simple honesty and lack of guile which makes the reader fond of him. We could wish better for him than the Widow Carrickfergus.

Caroline, the Cinderella daughter of the Gann *ménage,* is one of Thackeray's first studies of the warm-sweet-abused-sentimental type, simple and unhappy, who, before the story breaks off, is the victim of an attempted seduction and a mock marriage. In spite of the not unkindly tolerance with which Thackeray depicts his shabby-genteel characters, the fragmentary plot is conceived in terms of unrelenting tragedy. Here again is a tale fundamentally sordid, in spite of the fact that it is crossed this time by humane humour rather than cruel farce.

For the knaves who descend upon this island of harmless vulgarity Thackeray has no mercy. Attempting, one feels, to be fair, he gives George Brandon, the idle, conceited villain of the story, a few moments of tolerable decency. This bragging roué is not, says Thackeray, 'altogether a bad man.' On the other hand, Brandon's friend, Lord Cinqbars, that foppish and feeble sprig of seedy aristocracy, is laid open with a merciless scalpel. In perspective against Thackeray's other narratives, *A Shabby Genteel Story* is mildly transitional in nature. The stuff of the story itself is still refractory, but it shows Thackeray strengthening his hand in characterization and approaching in narrowing circles the goal of the comico-satirico-sympathetic upon which he was to lay his distinctive mark. *A Shabby Genteel Story* points forward to *The Great Hoggarty Diamond*.

Thackeray's 1840 midsummer piece for *Fraser's* 'Going to See a Man Hanged,' is of special importance to our understanding of the early Thackeray; not because of its unreasoning revolt against capital punishment, an attitude which Thackeray later reversed, nor because of its attack upon public executions, which he hated as long as he lived; but rather because it shows in small space some of the dominant qualities of his personality and art.

This article on the execution of Courvoisier is an excellent piece of straightforward objective reporting, with sociological overtones. Here Thackeray is the intent observer, drinking in sights and sounds and then describing them with an acute perception of their relative significance. He is eager to watch the effect of a public execution on the persons who see it. How do they view all the phenomena connected with it? What induces them, in the first instance, to attend? How are they moved by it afterwards?

More important, however, is his impulse to turn his eye inward and to analyse, without exaggeration, his own reaction to the scene. Thus he gets a shock when he first sees the gallows, but 'presently you examine the object before you with a certain feeling of complacent curiosity.' Parenthetically he wonders why it is that he has always been delighted at the sight of a clown getting flogged on his backside. 'What is there so ridiculous in the sight of one miserably-rouged man beating another on the breech?' For this he has no answer, but he does trace in himself the growth of a shame for the 'brutal curiosity' which took him to the hanging. His reaction to the whole thing is one of terror and a feeling of degradation. The hanging itself is a 'sickening, ghastly, wicked scene,' and he comes down Simon Hill that morning disgusted with the murder he saw done. This candid, analytical probing of his own mind is typically Thackerayan and is in part the key to his sympathetic understanding of men and women, just as it is the clue, also, to his own nervous suscepti-bility and to the poignancy of his recurring recognition that all men are ultimately secrets unto themselves.

The year 1840, and the first stage of Thackeray's novitiate, close with the appearance of his first published volume, *The Paris Sketch Book*,[4] a miscellaneous potpourri of tales and articles of varying quality. It is chiefly important to us in so far as it leads us into an understanding of his attitude towards the French and towards foreigners in general. Here Thackeray is a strange blend of British insularity and cosmopolitan tolerance. He likes the French; he dislikes the French. He shares the ineffable British feeling of superiority to the rest of the world, but not infrequently he is aware of his prejudices and shadow-boxes manfully with himself in a sort of wistful attempt to clear his mind of the parochial twist which he reprehends in others. At the same time he has a shrewd insight into the palpable extravagances in Gallic life and literature.

The Paris Sketch Book was signed by 'Mr. Titmarsh,' and, incidentally, made very little money for that gentleman. Many of the criticisms and stories had been published previously either in *Fraser's* or in N. P. Willis's New York weekly, *The Corsair,* or in both. The stories are very uneven in quality, retellings of

[4] *The Paris Sketch Book* was published by Macrone, who had also published Dickens's first book, *Sketches by Boz.*

feeble legends of the marvellous with humorous trick endings, or thin realistic sketches which have little excuse for being except the commendable one of putting shillings into their author's pocket. *The Case of Peytel* is an interesting-enough retelling of a French *crime célèbre*, with a humanitarian obbligato; *Cartouche*, a thumb-nail history of a more depraved Villon; *Little Poinsenet*, a disagreeable story about practical jokes played upon a half-wit dwarf. The rather obvious rook-and-pigeon story, *A Citation for Travellers*, Thackeray reworked later in *Pendennis*; as an author he was thrifty and wasted nothing he could decently save. The opening sketch, *An Invasion of France*, is one of the best things in the book, dealing in a lively, bustling, almost Dickensian manner with the embarkation, the passengers, the voyage, the inevitable seasickness (at some length), and the landing. There is much verve here and a facetious good humour, as well as a typical wry lamentation over the antics of the Englishman abroad.

The expository articles in the book, particularly as they give Thackeray's attitude towards the French, are more important than the stories. That attitude varies with the subjects he treats. To the end of his life Thackeray made frequent trips to France —as art student; as 'foreign correspondent' for the *National Standard* and the *Constitutional;* to see his mother, who, with his stepfather, lived much of the time in Paris; or merely for holiday visits. Ever since his early Bohemian adventures as an art student he had liked Parisian life; and he had a sturdy appreciation of many aspects of French civilization, which he saw as a strange mixture of 'nature and affectation, exaggeration and simplicity.' He believed the French common people superior in taste and manners to Englishmen of the same class. The innocent gaiety of a French crowd at a festival, he says, shows 'a very pleasing contrast to the coarse and vulgar hilarity which the same class would exhibit in our country—at Epsom race course, for instance, or Greenwich Fair.'[5]

He never tires of declaring the superiority of the French over

[5] *The Fêtes of July.*

the English in matters of art. In France, he says, good painters are better understood and better paid than in England. Some of his best pages here are unassuming yet sensible criticisms of French art. He finds, too, the taste of the French middle-classes superior to that of the English, who, in an attempt to dissipate the gloom of the British Sunday, have seized upon the ribaldry and scandal of the Sunday paper as their amusement. In general, French society is better than the English: 'how much better is social happiness understood; how much more manly equality is there between Frenchman and Frenchman, than between rich and poor in our own country, with all our superior wealth, instruction, and political freedom! There is, among the humblest, a gaiety, cheerfulness, politeness, and sobriety, to which in England no class can show a parallel.' [6]

Thackeray could never escape, however, the uneasy conviction that the French hate the English. In the article 'Napoleon and his System' he attributes this to natural vanity and to the bitterness of past defeats. Four years later, in different mood, he gives an alternative explanation.

Well-educated Frenchmen *do not believe that we have beaten them* . . . They hate you because you are stupid, hard to please, and intolerably insolent and air-giving . . . This is why we are hated—for pride . . . Of all European people, which is the nation that has the most haughtiness, the strongest prejudices, the greatest reserve, the greatest dulness? I say an Englishman of the genteel classes . . . Look at him, how he scowls at you on your entering an inn-room; think how you scowl yourself to meet his scowl. [7]

Elsewhere he attacks 'that calm, silent, contemptuous conceit of us young Britons, who think our superiority so well established that it is really not worth arguing upon, and who take upon us to despise thoroughly the whole world through which we pass. We are hated on the Continent, they say, and no wonder.' [8] To say the least, this is engaging candor.

[6] *Caricatures and Lithography in Paris.*
[7] *Ghent:* in *Little Travels and Roadside Sketches,* 1844.
[8] *Fitz-Boodle's Confessions:* 'Miss Löwe,' *Fraser's,* October 1842.

But the other side of Thackeray's view of the French is a combination of amused contempt and open disapproval. Here the evidence is much more concrete and extensive. Their politics amused and irritated him; their theatre offended him; and for the literature of the romantic school flourishing in the 'thirties and 'forties he had little sympathy or liking. He praised Dumas for his humour and eloquence but disliked the emphatic bullying manner of his novels and the absurdity and violence of his plays. After *The Three Musketeers,* however, he found him 'charming,' and he burlesqued him tenderly in *A Legend of the Rhine.* By the time of the *Roundabout Papers* Dumas has become the 'brave, kind, gallant old Alexandre.'

Although he admits that Victor Hugo has a splendid style and a poetic imagery, Thackeray always found him egotistical and bombastic. He liked Sue, although he felt that he ought not to like him. Flaubert's *Madame Bovary* was a 'heartless, cold-blooded study of the downfall and degeneration of a woman.' [9] He liked George Sand's novels, but his low opinion of her as a reformer and social philosopher is stated with pungent forthrightness in the *Paris Sketch Book:* 'Madame Sand and the New Apocalypse' is a review of her *Spiridion.* Thackeray is here very much the British Philistine as he subjects her life to a moral scrutiny; he is on somewhat firmer ground as he pillories her 'muddy French transcendentalism.'

Thackeray is an Englishman and an Englishman of his own generation when, one hand to his nose, he picks up gingerly the current French drama. He is pleased by the decline of the French classical drama, and he has melancholy fun with Racine's sonorous Alexandrines, his 'lugubrious good things,' his 'sparkling undertaker's wit' and 'ghastly epigrams.' Thackeray is offended by the easy and universal adulteries of modern French comedy fathered by Scribe, and is appalled at its cynicism. He holds up hands of horror at the *drame* of Hugo and Dumas— the murders, rapes, adulteries, blasphemies. Today it is the absurdity rather than the immorality of this sort of thing which

9 H. Sutherland Edwards: *Personal Recollections,* London, 1900, p. 36.

impresses us, but Thackeray is here the Victorian Englishman standing respectably, and, be it said, with reasonable dignity, on his inherited prejudices.

When he came to survey the French political scene Thackeray was again incapable of appreciating his neighbours. There was a sensible way of doing these things—the English way—and there was a ridiculous, illogical, claptrap, humbugging way of doing them—the French way. Thackeray not only disapproved of the Revolution of July, which put the 'bourgeois king,' Louis Philippe, into power,[10] but he disapproved of the general French lack of taste in conducting revolutions. He scorned the French habit of mingling poetry and sentiment with politics: 'tawdry stage tricks and braggadocio claptraps uttered, on every occasion, however sacred or solemn.'[11]

A visit to Versailles leads Thackeray not only to meditate mournfully upon the shabbiness of military glory in general and of the *ancien régime* in particular, but also to toss and tear Louis XIV as 'stupid, heartless, short, of doubtful personal courage.'[12] As so often in his abuse of kings, Thackeray is impulsively unfair here, but the chapter is memorable for its caricature of 'Ludovicus Rex,' in which the satire is generic as well as particular. 'Majesty is made out of the wig, the high-heeled shoes, and the cloak, all fleur-de-lis bespangled. Thus do barbers and cobblers make the gods that we worship.'

This is a good example, incidentally, of how Thackeray could approximate, in idea if not in apocalyptic style, the historical virtuosity of Carlyle. He had reviewed *The French Revolution* sympathetically; he was clearly familiar with *Sartor Resartus;* and, much as he disapproved of Carlyle's excommunication of

[10] Thackeray often denounced Louis Philippe scornfully; he felt that the regime was based upon dishonesty: 'a tyranny, that is, under the title and function of a democracy.' [*Caricatures and Lithography in Paris.*] And in 1844 *Punch* was excluded from France for some time because of Thackeray's article 'A Case of Real Distress,' satirizing the parsimonious king. [See Spielmann's *History of Punch*, 1895, p. 191.]

[11] *The Fêtes of July.*

[12] *Meditations at Versailles.*

the greater part of contemporary civilization, he was obviously
impressed by Carlyle's picturesque theory of clothes, of the social
veneers by which men are accustomed to hide their common
humanity. In the *Book of Snobs* Thackeray satirizes the illogi-
cality of an hereditary aristocracy and cries out against hereditary
great-man worship. In the *Second Funeral of Napoleon* he declares:

Ah, my dear, when big and little men come to be measured rightly,
and great and small actions to be weighed properly, and people to
be stripped of their Royal robes, beggar's rags, general's uniforms,
seedy out-at-elbowed coats, and the like—or the contrary say, when
souls come to be stripped of their wicked deceiving bodies, and
turned out stark naked as they were before they were born—what
a strange startling sight we shall see, and what a pretty figure some
of us shall cut . . . Fancy some Angelic Virtue whose white rai-
ment is suddenly whisked over his head, showing us cloven feet
and a tail! . . . Fig-leaves are a very decent becoming wear, and
have been now in fashion for four thousand years. And so, my dear,
History is written on fig-leaves . . . Fools look very solemnly out
of the dusk of the leaves, and we fancy in the gloom that they are
sages.

Thackeray and Carlyle moved in different intellectual orbits,
yet occasionally there was a conjunction of the planets.

Thackeray's most trenchant criticism of the French aptitude
for political self-deception is found in the little book written as
the year 1840 was drawing to a close, and published in a separate
volume.[13] *The Second Funeral of Napoleon* is more than a
piece of reporting; it is Thackeray's best bit of writing to date.
In spite of this it fell almost dead from the press. Thackeray was
wittily lugubrious about its failure. *The Times* gave it a rather
pontifical and patronizing review which Thackeray (writing to
Mrs. Procter) hoped would 'make people curious to get the
book.'[14] But still it did not sell.

---

[13] Incorporating, also, his ballad *The Chronicle of the Drum*.

[14] The review [19 January 1841] blames M. A. Titmarsh with 'twaddling a
little' and says that he is not a first-rate specimen of flippancy. He is, however,
a 'laughing, not a scowling philosopher.' In his article 'On Men and Pictures,'

The Second Funeral is a mixture of close, vigorous observation and pointed comments on that peculiar quality of the French nature which, to Thackeray, helped to render absurd their most ceremonial occasions. It is penetrated with an irony so rich and so fused with a debonair gaiety that the blows kill without hurting. The occasion of the piece was the expedition to bring Napoleon's body from St. Helena to the Hôtel des Invalides. The absurdities which Thackeray punctured were two. First, the ridiculous mock-heroics of young Prince de Joinville, who, when the English had shown every courtesy to the French in giving them Napoleon's body, made ferocious preparations to protect the ship against any English who might want to steal the body away.[15] Second, the tawdriness of the pageantry and display of the funeral procession, which Thackeray witnessed, and of the later ceremonials. To Thackeray it was a funeral of shams and humbuggery which would have betokened a sham respect 'if one had not known that the name of Napoleon is held in real reverence, and observed somewhat of the character of the nation. Real feelings they have, but they distort them by exaggeration: real courage, which they render ludicrous by intolerable braggadocio.' Thackeray is not open in this book to the charge that has mistakenly been brought against him: that he is exercising, in poor taste, an undertaker's wit. Whatever he might think about Napoleon as a man, for the dead hero he has only generous respect. For the figurative plumes on the hearse, however, he felt less than awe.

There is more of Thackeray here than is to be found in the story of the funeral itself. He ranges in typically discursive fashion over a variety of related topics, all of which are given a Thackerayan illumination and point. He is thinking out for

Fraser's, July 1841, Thackeray, always sensitive to criticism, wrote concerning *The Times* review: 'It is very hard that a man may not tell the truth as he fancies it without being accused of conceit: but so the world wags.'

[15] Thackeray took another fall out of Joinville in 1844. The Prince had published a pamphlet pointing out with great relish how easy it would be to attack and pillage English towns. Thackeray, irritated by such jingoism, published in *Punch* an attack, more severe than judicial, on French perfidiousness.

himself the ideas on history, on gentility, on aristocracy and its relation to English society, which are to appear in many places from the *Snob Papers* to the *Roundabouts,* and which are a heavy part of his literary baggage.

He is penetrative, but not cheaply cynical.

You and I, dear Miss Smith, know the exact value of heraldic bearings. We know that though the greatest pleasure of all is to *act* like a gentleman, it is a pleasure, nay, a merit, to *be* one—to come of an old stock, to have an honourable pedigree . . . There *is* a good in gentility; the man who questions it is envious, or a coarse dullard not able to perceive the difference between high breeding and low . . .

If, respected madam, you say that there is something *better* than gentility in this wicked world, and that honesty and personal worth are more valuable than all the politeness and high breeding that ever wore red-heeled pumps, knight's spurs, or Hoby's boots, Titmarsh for one is never going to say you nay. If you ever go so far as to say that the very existence of this super-genteel society among us, from the slavish respect that we pay to it, from the dastardly manner in which we attempt to imitate its airs and ape its vices, goes far to destroy honesty of intercourse, to make us meanly ashamed of our natural affections and honest harmless usages, and so does a great deal more harm than it is possible it can do good by its example,—perhaps, madam, you speak with some sort of reason.

Thus by 1840 the cut of the jib is very distinct. Before he reaches *Vanity Fair* Thackeray has still much to learn about his art, but the composite nature of that Fair is already clearly visible to him. For our part we can see, even before his art fixes itself, the steady evolution of the mind which was to inform it, which brought to the *vanitas vanitatum* a healthy, antiseptic hatred for shabbiness and insincerity of spirit, and a corollary affection for honesty and simplicity. To this native clear-sightedness time and a variety of experiences, some terrible, some tender, were to add a texture of pity and awe. Indeed, by 1840 the most fearful of those experiences had already come from out the darkness.

CHAPTER FOUR

The Great Hoggarty Diamond to Barry Lyndon (1841-44); The Irish Sketch Book and Cornhill to Cairo

IN 1837 Carlyle had written to his brother that the man who had reviewed *The French Revolution* for *The Times* was 'one Thackeray, a half-monstrous Cornish giant, kind of painter, Cambridge man, and Paris newspaper correspondent, who is now writing for his life in London.'[1] In 1840 Thackeray was still writing for his life. 'I am in a ceaseless whirl and whizz from morning to night, now with the book [*The Paris Sketch Book*], now with the drawings, now with the articles for *The Times, Fraser,* here and there,' he wrote to his mother on 30 April. He had enjoyed a certain pseudonymous success as a literary and art critic and as author of the *Yellowplush Papers,* but *Catherine* and the *Paris Sketch Book,* his major efforts to date, were disappointingly unsuccessful. An incurable optimist about newspaper publishing, he was planning to start a weekly paper called *The Whitey-Brown Paper Magazine.* For the most part, however, he was pouring himself into the magazines—stories, sketches, book reviews, art criticisms, burlesques—hard work which brought in little enough money with which to sup-

[1] *Letters of Thomas Carlyle to his Youngest Sister,* ed. C. T. Copeland, London, 1899.

port his growing family. He and his young wife were happy, nevertheless, although their home had been shadowed in 1839 by the death of an infant daughter. Alfred Tennyson used to come to their little house in Coram Street, and the Kembles, and Edward FitzGerald, with whom Thackeray held long talks about books and pictures, smoking, as he said, 'too many cigars.'[2]

The Thackerays' third daughter was born on 28 May 1840.[3] Mrs. Thackeray was slow in recovering, and in August her husband took her to Margate for the sea air. There, writing an article on Fielding for *The Times* and working on *A Shabby Genteel Story,* he became progressively more concerned about his wife's health. Years later he wrote to Mrs. Brookfield that he 'used to walk out three miles to a little bowling green, and write there in an arbour—coming home and wondering what was the melancholy oppressing the poor little woman.' Suddenly, about mid-September, the fearful truth could no longer be evaded— she was losing her mind. There followed weeks of frenzied worry and activity. He took her to visit her parents in Ireland, but the experience had no visible effect upon her mental condition. He took her to Paris and to European watering-places, hoping against hope. But over the mind of the wife and mother remained the cloud of a gentle insanity which was to keep her from her family until her death in 1894, more than thirty years after that of her husband. For Thackeray himself, the terrible worry was succeeded by a settled despair. Sending the children to live with their grandparents in Paris, he placed Mrs. Thackeray in a private asylum near by. Later she was brought to England and put under capable and gentle care. In 1855 Thackeray wrote to his old Cambridge schoolfellow, John Allen:

The poor dear little wife whom you remember is very well and very cheerful thank God, though cut off for 15 years from husband and children. She does not miss them though: and the care of her

[2] Biographical Introduction to *The Great Hoggarty Diamond*, p. xxii.
[3] Harriet Marian, later the first wife of Leslie Stephen.

serves to maintain a very worthy old couple who treat her with the utmost kindness and watchfulness—so that her illness serves for some good.[4]

The simple facts of this tragic episode are such that they need no biographical embroidery here. What went on in Thackeray's mind during the early days of his suffering no one is ever likely to know; FitzGerald burned all the letters he received from him at that time. From then on Thackeray's life was inevitably at loose ends. 'I can't live without the tenderness of some woman,' he wrote to Mrs. Brookfield later, but hungry as he was for affection he was condemned to a life of perpetual bachelorhood, salvaging as much as he could from his domestic tragedy by making, when he could, a home for his daughters. To them he devoted himself thereafter with an absorbing devotion. For some years, however, they lived with their grandparents, while Thackeray, in the intervals of visits to Paris and trips to Ireland and Egypt, lived a bachelor's existence in London lodgings and apartments. Not until 1846, when he took the house at 13 Young Street, were Thackeray and his children able to live together.

All this gives more than a conventional meaning to his picture of himself as the pathetic jester, gloomy behind the comic mask. The clue to Thackeray's personality is his acute nervous sensibility, which not all his bluff heartiness, his love of the ridiculous, his full-throated delight in the commonplaces of living could hide. The collapse of his home seemed to drive him more and more outside himself, into clubdom and its assorted pleasures. As a matter of fact it intensified in him a congenital melancholy which often just avoids shading off into a grim morbidity, but which is saved always by a tenderness and a humour which are just as native to him. Out of it all comes that distinctive Thackerayan atmosphere of gentle retrospective wistfulness, a sort of pervasive world-sorrow for man's pathetic lot, for his puny egotisms, his self-deceptions, his frustrate ambitions and his abortive achievements. What gives poise and depth to this

[4] MS. letter, Trinity College Library.

view of life is the kindness which impregnates it and the humour through which it is sifted. Thackeray in his maturity is never the *spectator ab extra,* the angry satirist lashing universal mankind. He is rueful rather than bitter, always himself taking a share of the blows aimed at the follies of his fellow men, claiming no peculiar exemption, and reading their weakness mercifully in the light of an humble self-knowledge. This deepening can be traced steadily in his work. In his education suffering played no small part.

In the early days of his domestic affliction he felt the feverish necessity to write, for somehow money must be had to meet increasing expenses. He had broken off *A Shabby Genteel Story* abruptly, but on 8 December 1840 he wrote to Fraser asking if he wanted it to be continued and at the same time rebelling somewhat against Fraser's prices. 'I shall probably,' he wrote, 'publish the whole tale which has a very moral ending in a volume with illustrations.'[5] He said that he believed that some four sheets would finish the affair. Fraser evidently was tepid in his enthusiasm, for *A Shabby Genteel Story* had to wait until 1861 for its continuation in *Philip*.

At the same time Thackeray was writing *The History of Samuel Titmarsh and the Great Hoggarty Diamond;* as he told Mrs. Brookfield later, 'at a time of great affliction, when my heart was very soft and humble.'[6] He offered it first to *Blackwood's,* which turned it down—'the best thing I ever wrote.' It began to appear serially in *Fraser's* in September 1841, and ran through December. Thackeray's self-appraisal was just; it really was the best thing he had yet written in narrative. And if the reading public failed to acclaim Michael Angelo Titmarsh's story of his cousin Sam, the discriminating few were well aware of its excellence. 'What is there better in Fielding and Goldsmith? The man is a true genius,' wrote John Sterling.[7]

The atmosphere is again one of shabby gentility, but it is

---

[5] MS. letter in the Huntington Library.
[6] *Brookfield Correspondence,* p. 281.
[7] Carlyle's *Life of Sterling.*

not self-consciously so, and marks a distinct advance in every way over *A Shabby Genteel Story.* The satire is softened; the humour is unobtrusive if no less keen; and the sense of integrated characterization is very clear. Thackeray is shaping his materials here with a firm hand and his chief actors have a three-dimensional tangibility. Sam Titmarsh tells the story in the first person, in a style flexible and smooth and yet somehow completely his own. Thackeray maintains with exactness the outlook of a thirteenth clerk in the West Diddlesex Fire and Life Insurance Company to whom, through the initial gift of a family heirloom, comes rapid advancement in a fabulously corrupt corporation, a brush with high life, marriage, financial collapse and the debtor's prison, and the ultimate salvage of his prospects. Sam is the soul of clerkdom but he has his own blend of shrewdness and *naïveté.* He is an engagingly honest and likable young fellow, without affectation, true to his humble friends, unassumingly courageous.

Mary, the simple girl who in Sam's days of seeming prosperity becomes his wife, is more than just another of Thackeray's sweet females; she has firmness of character and a steady cheerfulness in the face of disaster. The passages telling of the death of their infant were written out of Thackeray's fresh memories of the loss of his own child two years before.

The gallery of minor characters is remarkably vivid. Lady Drum, cousin to all the world, is a 'humour' creation, but amusing and lusty. Aunt Hoggarty of Castle Hoggarty in Ireland, incorrigibly stingy and disagreeable, is one of Thackeray's studies in ancient feminine shrewishness, but there is an authenticity about her, too. Indeed all these people live in a world of graphic and robustious detail through which the story slips easily and convincingly.

Brough, the pious fraud who mouths long hypocritical moral speeches and welcomes into his leaky company, with gently smiling jaws, all the savings of widows and clerks and orphans upon which he can lay his hands, is a good example of Thackeray's increasing firmness of portraiture. Three years earlier he would have been made sinister and savage. Now he is given careful and subtle elaboration. He remains, of course, a swindling oily hypocrite, but credibly so.

The whole story has unity, strength, and the careful documentation of an infinitude of amusing and realistic touches. The most noticeable advance is not in the conscious pathos, which, understandable though it is in the light of Thackeray's personal troubles at the time, skirts closely at some points the shoals of dangerous sentiment; but rather in the close-packed variety of character and situation, and in the understanding sympathy by means of which Thackeray gives his story humanity and charm.

Early in this year Thackeray persuaded Hugh Cunningham to publish in two volumes his *Comic Tales and Sketches,* an attempt to bring under the single Titmarshian signature a collection of the previously published adventures of Yellowplush and Gahagan, together with *The Bedford-Row Conspiracy* and *Stubbs's Calendar.* Thackeray's title-page shows Titmarsh, arm in arm with Yellowplush and the fire-eating Gahagan, about to step blithely and inadvertently over a precipice—'on the very brink of Immortality,' as Thackeray said in the preface. But the inscrutable public which Thackeray was wooing so assiduously stubbornly kept its hand in its pockets. The happy Titmarshian trio had to remain for some time poised on the brink, waiting for their delayed acceptance among the Immortals.

Thackeray was not yet finished, however, with his protean array of *noms de plume.* In June 1842, George Fitz-Boodle burst upon the world through the pages of *Fraser's,* there for more than a year to unburden himself of 'Confessions' and 'Professions,' until he reached his apotheosis as the author of *Barry Lyndon* in 1844.

Fitz-Boodle, as he reveals himself in his papers, is a good-natured, addle-pated sentimentalist, who has a great reputation for smoking and who would like to gamble, were he not so poor. He cultivates a hatred for women, but he has loved madly. The early 'Confessions' are to be distinguished sharply from the later confessions known as 'Men's Wives,' for they are in quite a different manner. The early papers are largely broad burlesque, told merrily in a racy style, with some good-natured satire, some horseplay, and much broad comedy. Thackeray is reverting here, with some modifications, to his gift for extravagant, not-too-intellectual laughter.

The 'Professions' are of irregular quality; most of them don't quite come off. Only the one in which he presents the claims of the profession of 'Dinner-Master' seems worth noting. Here Thackeray—or Fitz-Boodle—discourses drolly on the incapacity of women as epicures. They don't understand and care for what they eat and drink; they have no real appetites and love sugar-tarts, trifles, and such gew-gaws. Nor can they prepare meals in the grand style—they grudge paying for small things magnificently. 'In brief, the mental constitution of lovely woman is such that she cannot give a great dinner. It must be done by a man.'

Thackeray is always good when discoursing on foods. As we know from the elaborate menus that have been preserved, the Victorian age must have been a time of hearty eating and drinking. One wonders how the Victorians had time to build an Empire when they were so busy digesting their too solid dinners. In the novels of the period it fairly snows meat and drink, and although Thackeray's novels have not the gargantuan preoccupation with the dinner table which is one of Dickens's minor glories (where else does one get such a sense of kitchen odors and steaming puddings and jolly self-sacrificial fowl?) he does have a relish for good cooking and a nice discrimination of taste amid such creature comforts. One of his most delightful essays about this time is the *Memorials of Gormandizing,*[8] an enthusiastic eulogy of good food by one who admits 'a genius for victuals.' As he puts it mock-pedantically, he wishes to give 'a picture or table of the development of the human mind under a series of gastronomic experiments, diversified in their nature,

[8] *Fraser's,* June 1841.

and diversified, consequently, in their effects . . . Sir, *respect your dinner;* idolise it, enjoy it properly . . . All a man's senses are worthy of employment, and should be cultivated as a duty. The senses are the arts.'

What a relish there is too in Thackeray's *Barmecide Banquets,* a review of a contemporary cook-book! [9] Here, behind the frolic mask of Fitz-Boodle, he licks genteel chops for sixteen pages. He likes the ceremonies of dining, but is still more interested in dinner. His imagination goes ramping through stupendous menus. He also hymns the pleasures of good eating in *Greenwich-Whitebait,* [10] pointing out its social virtues. 'A man who brags regarding himself,' he says, 'that whatever he swallows is the same to him, and that his coarse palate recognizes no difference between venison and turtle, pudding, or mutton-broth, as his indifferent jaws close over them, brags about a personal defect—the wretch—and not about a virtue.'

Yes, in Thackeray as in Dickens, the digestive juices flow freely.

The series of *Confessions* under the title *Men's Wives* [11] is in a medley of veins ranging from farce to sternest tragedy. The longest of these, *The Ravenswing,* ran through five numbers of *Fraser's* and covers 132 pages in the Biographical Edition of the *Works.* It is just about the same length as the *Hoggarty Diamond* and is one of his major ventures up to this time. It is full of good things, but as a story it is somewhat broken-backed, lacking the unity of tone and the general well-knit integrity that belonged to the adventures of Samuel Titmarsh. The tale as a whole is a rather obvious combination of caricature and sentiment, larded with some excellent social observation. One remembers longest the inimitable small bits like Thackeray's burlesque anatomy of newspaper puffing, and the excellent vignettes of such people as Mrs. Crump and Sir George Thrum, the latter stuffily dull, pious, respectable—not insincere, exactly, but—well,

9 *Fraser's,* November 1845.
10 *Colburn's New Monthly Magazine,* July 1844.
11 *Fraser's,* March-November 1843.

respectability *does* pay! In its entirety, the story languishes—in parts it sparkles. For all its weakness, no one but Thackeray could have written it.

Already he is permitting himself ironic digressions, as for instance in the passage on the superficiality of club friendships, 'the noble feeling of selfishness which they are likely to encourage in the male race.' But that is the beauty of club-institutions.

If it were otherwise—if, forsooth, we were to be sorry when our friends died, or to draw out our purses when our friends were in want, we should be insolvent, and life would be miserable. Be it ours to button up our pockets and our hearts; and to make merry—it is enough to swim down this life-stream for ourselves; if Poverty is clutching hold of our heels, or Friendship would catch an arm, kick them both off. Every man for himself, is the word, and plenty to do too.

This is the sort of irony which, misunderstood by literal-minded contemporaries, brought down upon Thackeray's head the cry of 'cynic.' And as for clubdom, no small part of the joke is that Thackeray himself was of course an inveterate clubman, and as likely as not was writing this very paragraph in a corner of the Garrick.

One other passage here reveals a side of Thackeray's temperament of which we shall see a good deal later. He is speaking of Sir George Thrum, who had written songs which had enjoyed a considerable success in their day but 'are forgotten now, and are as much faded and out of fashion as those old carpets which we have described in the professor's home, and which were, doubtless, very brilliant once. But such is the fate of carpets, of flowers, of music, of men, and of the most admirable novels—even this story will not be alive for many centuries. Well, well, why struggle against Fate?' A few years later Thackeray would not have added that banal conclusion, but the mood is indicative of a fundamental chord in his personality. His imagination is always stimulated to its most perceptive pitch by relics of the past, of decay, and by the tender emotions arising thence—seen through a filter compounded delicately of misty sentiment and tender humour, with that typical cadenced return at the end upon himself and his own writing. Very often he is saved a drop into the dangerously sentimental by the balance of a self-laughter, not mocking, frequently retrospective and a little wistful, but eminently sane. He laughs that he may not weep.

Of the other *Men's Wives,* Thackeray did not reprint (wisely) *The Executioner's Wife,* an extravagant grotesque-romantic tale in the German manner. *Mr. and Mrs. Frank Berry* shows Thackeray hovering about his proper *milieu* of social satire, but except for the famous Slaughter-House fight between Berry and Biggs, the story is little more than a series of character sketches, the best of which is that of Mrs. Berry, an ill-tempered, snobbish, imperious female who makes her husband's life miserable—a kind of woman who seemed to fascinate Thackeray. Such another woman is Mrs. Haggerty in *Dennis Haggerty's Wife.* Dennis himself is an earlier Dobbin—shy, uncouth, but with a warm and faithful heart. His wife had married him only after she had been blinded and disfigured with small-pox. Living in wretched squalor, Dennis cares for her tenderly, mean and selfish and proud as she still is. After he has settled all his property on her, she rewards his devotion by deserting him. 'What myriads of souls there are of this admirable sort,' says Thackeray, 'selfish, stingy, ignorant, passionate, brutal; bad sons, mothers, fathers, never known to do kind actions.' His realism here in describing both the mean surroundings and the hideous face and worse temper of Mrs. Haggerty is unflinching, undiluted by any tenderness. Nevertheless in its very implacability there is a sort of unpleasant power. It does not represent the main stream of Thackeray's development, yet the mordant skill he shows here in biting corrosively into mean and paltry souls was always a part of his mature genius. And occasionally, even here, a more felicitous lightness of touch shows through, which is none the less withering because propelled by wit—as, for example, in the case of the Reverend Samuel Whey in *Mr. and*

Mrs. Frank Berry: 'full of the milk-and-water of human kindness.'

Thackeray's most important undertaking for 1842 was his tour of Ireland and his subsequent report of it in the *Irish Sketch Book,* published by Chapman and Hall in the spring of the next year. He had planned to call the book *A Cockney in Ireland,* but his publishers insisted upon the less provocative title.[12] However, the pot of Irish politics, always simmering, was beginning to bubble even more dangerously during those days, and it was thought that a candid Titmarshian appraisal of the country and its people might be successful. Thackeray reached Dublin in the early days of July.

As might be expected, the *Irish Sketch Book* is above all else an honest travel-book. If it is more monotonous than the later *Cornhill to Cairo,* it is perhaps through the repetition of much the same kind of scene in the various towns and counties. Although Thackeray is as quick as ever to catch the humorous and the picturesque in both scenery and people, his tone is somewhat constrained. His disappointment in much of the scenery, as, for example, the Giant's Causeway, is patent. He often refers to himself as the Cockney in Ireland and tries to refrain from unseemly comparisons with England. He labours to be fair and is openly appreciative of much in the Irish character. Nevertheless one feels that he is straining to be judicial, and his manner lends some stiffness to his account in spite of its frequent bright and whimsical manner. At this distance, his account is not likely to be read by many. For us here, it is important in so far as it reveals Thackeray labouring with and not quite overcoming his prejudices. He is revolted by much that he sees, yet

[12] Lady Ritchie published for the first time in the *Cornhill Magazine,* July 1911, a paper of Thackeray's dealing with his travels through western England and Wales on his way to Ireland. This he had called 'Cockney Travels' and had perhaps planned originally to publish it separately in *Fraser's.* Here, as in the *Irish Sketch Book,* he is informally discursive, with a nice eye for scenery (barring a general disapproval of mountains and mountain-climbing), but more interested in the people than in the countryside.

he is sympathetic in his desire to understand it. Thus, for instance, he lingers over the poverty that he finds in Cork—its dirty, raw, hideous humanity and its shabby buildings. At the same time he praises the literary taste and talent of Cork gentlemen, the wit and vivacity of their conversation.

In general he succeeds in giving an impression of dreariness and dirt, particularly in his descriptions of Dublin and southern Ireland. With an open pity for the hungry, starving people, he yet recurs frequently to the idea that people need not be dirty 'if they are ever so idle. If they are ever so poor, pigs and men need not live together.' Thackeray is oppressed by the uneasy feeling that there are so many beggars because the poor had rather stare, swagger, and be idle in the streets than work. The obvious misery and wretchedness depresses him, however, and enters much into the book; as it would have had to enter, one supposes, into any accurate description. Yet Thackeray carefully balances praise and blame: the inns are slovenly, but the Irish women are graceful and vivacious; the Irish fawn upon titles and the relics of a decrepit nobility, but, in contrast to the English, they make the stranger feel at home; the people are given to monstrous howling about English tyranny, but in such schools as Templemoyle they have set an educational standard which puts to shame the useless and brutal traditions of the English public schools.

On the Catholic problem Thackeray was the victim of a prejudice which clung to him all his life. He blames the Catholic Church, openly and by implication, for not elevating the people to a higher level of industry and cleanliness. In his visit to a convent he is reverent but most naïvely nervous. He tries to be liberal but is so instinctively and parochially Protestant that he can't understand why the nuns seem to be so happy, and wonders if their obvious contentment is not assumed for visitors. He cries out violently against the Catholic system of 'immuring girls behind nunnery walls . . . what has God's world done to *her,* that she should run from it . . . I declare

I think for my part that we have as much right to permit Sutteeism in India as to allow women in the United Kingdom to take these wicked vows, or Catholic bishops to receive them.' This is one place where Thackeray's native tolerance seems unable to function. Such a deficiency in temper helps us to understand some of his sudden literary prejudices. His warm-blooded sympathies and dislikes could make him treacherously uncritical, just as the same qualities could give reach to his better thinking.

Thackeray enjoyed many aspects of his trip, particularly his visit with Charles Lever, where, according to the account of another guest, he convulsed the company with laughter by his description of a ridiculous French ballet, in the course of which he rose from his seat and pirouetted—all six-feet-three-inches of him—most admirably about the room.[13] But Thackeray was living at this time under the shadow of his recent affliction, which drove him from mood to mood. 'Solitude creates a muzziness and incoherency in me,' he wrote to his mother at this time, 'and I must get back to the little ones, that is clear. I am never thinking of what I am writing about. All the time I was writing . . . there was something else in my thoughts, and so on. Oh, I am glad the end of my trip is at hand. I have been heart-weary for months past, that's the truth.'

Always fond of Lever, Thackeray dedicated the *Irish Sketch Book* to him, somewhat to Lever's embarrassment, for as Thackeray said about the book shortly after its publication: 'The Irish are in a rage about it.' Nevertheless, Lever reviewed the book favourably, if a little mournfully, in the *Dublin University Magazine,* of which he was editor.[14] There he regretfully admits the truth of much that Thackeray delineates: 'In nearly all he says, he has our hearty concurrence.'

The fact of the matter is that Thackeray never really made

[13] The account of one Major Dwyer, who wrote a most impenetrably solemn description of Thackeray on this visit, found in W. J. Fitzpatrick's *Life of Charles Lever,* 2 vols., 1879, ii, 410.

[14] June 1843.

up his mind about the Irish. He liked their wit and good humour and friendliness (he married an Irish girl); his quick sympathy went out to them in their hunger and wretchedness.[15] Yet in the *Irish Sketch Book* he demonstrates his belief that a large part of their poverty was due to shiftlessness and laziness, and many times later he displayed his impatience with the fiery threats of Feargus O'Connor and the Young Ireland party. He had sympathy with their cause, but the fierce unreasonableness of their leaders wearied him. The Irishmen in his stories are not very flattering to the nation, even if they are highly amusing. His Gahagans and Shandons and Costigans and Mulligans are likely to be improvident, blustering braggarts, full of windy discourse about old Irish kings. Thackeray disliked the truculent nationalism of the Irishman, who was always 'insisting that you are determined to insult and trample upon his beautiful country, whether you are thinking about it or no.'[16] He was more kindly to them than many Englishmen were, but like most Englishmen he could neither thoroughly understand nor approve them.

Although Thackeray's trip to the East was not made until the autumn of 1844, two years after the Irish journey, and the resultant book, *Notes of a Journey from Cornhill to Grand Cairo, by way of Lisbon, Athens, Constantinople, and Jerusalem* was not published until early in 1846, it is convenient to look at the book here, and so conclude our observation of Titmarsh's publications as a traveller. *Cornhill to Cairo* was much more favourably received than the *Irish Sketch Book* and went into a second edition within seven months. Thackeray's sensitiveness to criticism, however, was shown by his reaction to a review (probably by his friend, Ainsworth) in the *New Monthly Magazine*. Ainsworth wrote to Horace Smith:

[15] Witness his picture and verses published in Charles Gavan Duffy's *Nation*, 13 May 1843, called 'Daddy, I'm Hungry,' and representing the starving family of an Irish coachmaker.
[16] *Sketches and Travels in London.*

Titmarsh was out of humour because he was reviewed and attacked as he thinks, in the last *New Monthly.* The paper on the contrary was very friendly . . . He threatened retorts, and I told him if he did he should have rejoinders . . . He went home with me to the Albion and kept me up till one o'clock, drinking brandy and soda, and abusing Byron in a ludicrously absurd and Cockney fashion . . .[17]

As a matter of fact the review mixes a very temperate praise with patronizing censure. But by the time Thackeray wrote the Postscript to the second edition he had quieted down:

. . . another [critic]—but this was a private friend, and I can conceive the pain it cost his amiable heart—was obliged to give judgement against the coarseness, heartlessness, flippancy, and personality of the present performance. It becomes writers to bear praise and blame alike meekly; and I think the truth is that most of us get more of the former, and less of the latter, than we merit.

Thackeray was pricked into one other answer to a criticism of this trip, a puling criticism, yet at the same time a good example of the kind of thing that always stirred him to a rather unnecessary wrath. *Tait's Edinburgh Magazine* had published a review of *Cornhill to Cairo* which implied that the P. and O. Company had carried Thackeray cost free for a reason, and that his book was mere publicity for the company. Thackeray was compared with the blind fiddler who, on a Scotch boat, 'sends round his hat.'[18] Thackeray replied in *Punch*[19] under the title: 'Titmarsh vs. Tait.' He showed the absurdity of the charge, taking a few swinging blows at the Scotch and at professional critics who befoul their own nest.

Cornhill to Cairo still holds a worthy place among travel books —by the supreme felicity of its style, often lighted by flashes of

[17] Goodyear Sales Catalogue, 1927, item No. 167.

[18] Carlyle had said much the same thing about Thackeray. In conversation with Charles Gavan Duffy [*Conversations with Carlyle*] he had compared the transaction with the practice of a blind fiddler going to and fro on a penny ferry-boat in Scotland.

[19] 14 March 1846.

amusement, for Thackeray could catch the grotesque and the ridiculous as well as the picturesque; by its lively and shrewdly observant descriptions, catching in its net a wide variety of manners and people and scenery; and by its complete honesty. It is admirably good humoured from the very beginning, where he pays sly tribute to English national pride on the Channel crossing: ' "There's none but Britons to rule the waves!" and we gave ourselves piratical airs, and went down presently and were sick in our little buggy berths.'

The book is that refreshing thing among travel-books: completely a record of its author's own reactions. Thackeray is no whit disturbed that it reveals his limitations as well as his ability to appreciate keenly. When Thackeray travels, he is an Englishman, and an honest Englishman. There is nothing brash about him; he is modest and humble, and apologetic over his shortcomings, but he will not disguise them. Knowing that such a rapid observation of peoples and places must of necessity be superficial, he does not pretend to profundity of interpretation. Above all (and this is always true of Thackeray) he is afraid of exaggerated enthusiasm, the bane of sentimental travel-books. He prefers to fall into the error of under-writing rather than of over-writing, and thus he lays himself open to the charge of affecting a pose. Such is not the case, however; he is simply frank, and frankness has not always been too common a commodity with those who make trips in order to write about them.

His prejudices Thackeray reveals candidly as such. In Athens, for instance, he thinks he recognizes the beauty of the Temple of Jupiter, and can admire 'the astonishing grace, severity, elegance, completeness of the Parthenon.' The very excess of his modesty, however, puts him out of sympathy with the gaping squires who think it proper to be enthusiastic about a country of which they know nothing. As for himself—he had been overcharged at the inn, had secured little rest, was bitten all over by bugs, found Greek women distinctly unbeautiful (he takes a side-swipe at Byron here) and discovers, in short, 'that Athens is a disappointment; and I am angry that it should be so.' He admits that he approaches Greece under a handicap; it reminds him of his classical education, that 'banishment of infernal misery.'

He tries hard to be impressed by the Pyramids, for they *are* old, majestic, mystical—but breakfast intervenes, 'a rush was made at the coffee and cold pies, and the sentiment of awe was lost in the scramble for victuals.' He is ashamed that the view should awaken no respect in him; at the same time, however, he notices that his fellow travellers are not seriously moved, either. 'I confess, for my part, that the Pyramids are very big.' Then comes a very characteristic and revealing paragraph, the humour of which cannot hide a fundamental bit of self-revelation:

—And is this all you have to tell about the Pyramids? Oh! for shame! Not a compliment to their age and size? Not a big phrase,— not a rapture? . . . Try, man, and build up a monument of words as lofty as they are . . . No: be that work for great geniuses, great painters, great poets! This quill was never made to take such flights; it comes from the wing of an humble domestic bird, who walks a common; who talks a great deal (and hisses sometimes); who can't fly far or high, and drops always very quickly . . .

Jerusalem, too, is spoiled for him by the religious frauds he finds there. He does express, however, with a sort of breathless awe (his typical religious attitude) his feelings in the face of the historical, religious significance of the spot. Smyrna he likes because it is sufficiently odd and picturesque and Arabian-Night-ish. Thackeray had always an innate timidity when approaching the sublime; he is fearful lest it shade off into the sham-sublime. Here he likes instead the bazaars, the children, the wild swarthy Arabs, and he gives us rich and twinkling descriptions of the scene. He has found the East, at last, as he dreamed of it in his youth, and is content with camels, melons, figs, coffee-houses, bubbling marble fountains, bedaggered and bepistoled Turks. Constantinople he likes intensely too, for it is the complete realization of Stanfield's diorama that he saw at Drury

Lane in his childhood. The scene is 'perhaps not sublime, but charming, magnificent, and cheerful beyond any I have ever seen.' When Thackeray does get around to it he can like nicely, and for each misfire there are a dozen good things. We should not willingly lose the pages about his experience in a Turkish bath, nor his description of the cook 'who used (with a touching affection) to send us locks of hair in the soup.'

On his eastern trip Thackeray, in addition to writing the 'Fat Contributor' sketches for *Punch,* was working on *Barry Lyndon.* At the end of the trip, while lying in quarantine at Malta, he wrote in his diary: 'Nov. 3—Finished "Barry" after great throes last night.' The novel had been running in monthly instalments in *Fraser's* since January. Few of Thackeray's works seem to have more vitality and energy than this book, and it is illuminating to find through his diary a trail of entries indicating that the composition had been difficult. Thackeray was weary with writing. 'Jan. 20—In these days got through the fag-end of chap. iv. of "Barry Lyndon" with a great deal of dulness, unwillingness, and labour. Aug. 14—At home all day dawdling and dawdling, with "B.L." lying like a nightmare on my mind. Nov. 1.—Wrote "Barry," but slowly and with great difficulty.' He always wrote in travail of spirit; it was his occupational disease. No signs of fatigue enter into *Barry Lyndon* itself, however. It has all the verve and the rounded perfection of style that one expects of Thackeray at his best. With *Barry Lyndon* he leaves his apprenticeship behind.

Yet the book somehow failed to catch the public taste. Its unflattering portrait of an Irish adventurer enraged the Irish—that was to be expected—but except from the observing few who saw the marks of genius, the story failed to receive much acclaim. Although it was of novel's length, Thackeray did not reprint it until the *Miscellanies* of 1856.[20]

[20] It did, to be sure, reach a separate (and of course pirated) American edition in 1853. In the 1856 edition Thackeray made certain omissions from the *Fraser* text which are worth studying. He leaves out some long Thackerayan but un-

Barry Lyndon is the consummation of that revolt against the sentimental treatment of crime in popular fiction which we have noted in Thackeray's literary reviews and in his *Catherine*. Here, however, he forgets to be didactic and becomes fertilely creative. Barry is no lay figure but a creature of flesh and blood, and his career is turned into absorbing narrative. He has, to be sure, good literary antecedents. He is a picaro of the first water and his adventures have their roots back in the eighteenth century with Defoe and Fielding. Thackeray's relation to Fielding will require a fuller discussion; be it noted here, however, that Thackeray does not attempt the double-edged satire of *Jonathan Wild,* where Fielding's concern is to show that the great men of all ages have succeeded through the exercise of the same qualities of greatness as Wild's: that is, cruelty and fraud. Thackeray attempts and achieves something subtler and more artistic—the damning of a rogue out of his own mouth. Barry tells his own story.

In the earlier portions of the story the picaresque element is strong, and Barry, though a scapegrace, has a certain youthful animal charm. As he progresses into crime and becomes an artist in debauchery his narrative becomes the record of a heartless and depraved rascal who insists, nevertheless, that he has been mistreated by Fate and who defends his most atrocious rascalities with the bland air of one who simply does not know right from wrong. He complains when others treat him as he would have treated them, but he is buttressed by an astounding egotism which enables him to tell with a straight face and with no sense of shame the record of a misspent life. In the latter chapters particularly, which deal with his cruelty to his wife and stepson, he becomes malevolently evil. All this appears in his own narrative—a sustained piece of consummate irony. Thackeray was to find broader and more engaging themes, but never was his control of his materials firmer, his artistic intui-

Barrian digressions (particularly one on love) and a number of 'editor's' notes serving as guide-posts to Barry's depravity. By 1856 he must have realized that such a lily needed no gilding.

tion keener, than in this story of the slow decay of a bragging scoundrel.

In spite of its subject, *Barry Lyndon* is not depressing and never tedious. The completely ironic point of view makes Barry's exposure infinitely amusing. Thus, for example, he defends the unsavoury tricks to which he fears some 'rigid moralist' might object: 'What is life good for but for honour? And that is so indispensable, that we should obtain it anyhow.' His mock-heroic defense of gambling is a piece of genius. And the epitome of the book is contained in one superb sentence of self-vindication: 'For the first three years I never struck my wife but when I was in liquor.' For his gentle and abused wife, whom he bullied into marrying him by spreading compromising lies about her, he has only contempt, and a sort of savage glee in contemplating her affection for him. There is good irony, too, in the passages in which Barry tells of the violence, impudence, and brutality of his stepson, Bullingdon, who, even on the face of Barry's own telling, is a sturdy honest lad. All Barry's praise of his own son by Lady Lyndon does not hide the fact that under his father's tutelage the boy had developed into a gross, cruel creature who delights in inflicting pain, sings bawdy songs his father taught him, gets drunk, and obviously even in his tender years is turning into a rake-hell. This debauching of a son by a father who blubbers sentimentally over his darling boy is perhaps the most sinister aspect of a story which does not flinch at ugliness of soul, yet which makes the recital bearable (and here is the art) by an antiseptic irony.

There is a sort of wild justice at the end: Barry dies, imbecilic, in Fleet Prison during an attack of *delirium tremens*. But Thackeray, in the original conclusion to the story, is careful to point out that, as the world wags, poetical justice is a novelist's illusion.

Justice, forsooth! Does human life exhibit justice after this fashion? Is it the good always who ride in gold coaches, and the wicked who go to the workhouse? Is a humbug never preferred before a capable man? Does the world always reward merit, never worship cant, never

raise mediocrity to distinction? never crowd to hear a donkey bray-
ing from a pulpit, nor ever buy the tenth edition of a fool's book?
Sometimes the contrary occurs, so that fools and wise, bad men and
good, are more or less lucky in their turn, and honesty is 'the best
policy,' or not, as the case may be.

Here, then, is Thackeray's first unqualified artistic success in
the art of the novel. There is enough fused intellect in it for half
a dozen stories; never before or after did he give more deftly
the very anatomy of baseness. And yet by the persuasiveness of
his style and the brilliance of his sustained point of view, this
seeming *tour de force* becomes narrative art of a high order.

There is one unimportant story of Thackeray's written about
this time which is nevertheless interesting because it is typical
of his humorous approach and because it is connected with
something he started to do later. *Bluebeard's Ghost* appeared in
Fraser's in October 1843. The story of Bluebeard always stirred
Thackeray's comic spirit,[21] and he liked to turn it inside out,
reversing the normal emphasis for humorous effect. Here, Bluebeard is dead, killed by Mrs. Bluebeard's brothers to save her
life, but Mrs. Bluebeard is in mourning for 'the best of men.'
She refuses to believe that Bluebeard had killed his former wives.
Nevertheless she does fall in love again, and the chief interest
in the story is the contrast between Mrs. Bluebeard's seeming
grief for her departed husband and her new growth of affection for one Blackbeard. A genial and unmomentous tale.

Thackeray returned to the Bluebeard theme some seven years
later, in 1850. He wrote to Mrs. Brookfield from Paris: 'I have
been advancing in Blue Beard, but must give it up, it is too
dreadfully cynical and wicked. It is in blank verse and all a diabolical sneer . . .'[22] This fragment has never been published,[23]
and is worthy of resurrection here not because it is either 'cyn-

---

[21] He drew a series of Bluebeard initial-letters for *Punch.*
[22] *A Collection of Letters,* 1847-55, p. 147.
[23] My thanks are due to Dr. A. S. W. Rosenbach, who very graciously gave
me access to the manuscript.

ical' or 'diabolical,' for it is neither, or because of its blank verse, for that is wretched, but because it shows Thackeray's trick of building up a comic situation—this time by making Bluebeard an abused, discouraged husband, and Mrs. Bluebeard (who does not appear in this fragment of dialogue) a shrewish wife not incapable of looking over the matrimonial fence into greener pastures.

The scene is Bluebeard Castle. Bluebeard is at the breakfast table reading, anachronistically, *The Times,* and talking gloomily to his old friend Butts. Lady Bluebeard will not come down to breakfast, is eating in her room. Bluebeard speaks of her wearily—she sits up late of nights reading French novels and playing duets with her sister, Ann.

'With Sister Ann!' says Butts. 'Yes and with Captain Jones.'

BLUEBEARD.   The captain is a fine musician, Butts,
                      You have no ear for music.

Bluebeard goes on to speak in a placid, resigned, melancholy tone of his early schooldays, wistfully looking back to his lost youth and the days when he was happy. He refers to the dozen wives whom he has loved and lost.

When any one of 'em came to know me well
And love me, she was always sure to die.

He is pathetically curious to learn what Butts and the rest of the world think about the successive deaths of all his wives. Butts, however, shies off from the dangerous subject.

BLUEBEARD.   We all remember youth, my Butts. I do.
                      The beardless time, before my chin was blue
                      Bluebeard!

BUTTS.   It aint so *very* blue. Pooh Pooh.

The talk turns to the burning of Troy.

BLUEBEARD.   Pious Aneas was a hero Butts
                      "   "   "   " humbug Butts
                      He knew the eyes of all the world were on him

> And he did this to figure in a song
> And go down hexametrically to fame.

Bluebeard has been making half-hearted attempts to convince Butts of Lady Bluebeard's worthiness, but gradually the bitterness in his soul creeps out.

> . . . we take the best we can in life
> And leave the rest behind—we make the best on't
> When cold in bed, we creep into the corner
> Where the most clothes are—when we dine we drink
> What wine's before us be it strong or small
> And when we cannot get the mutton hot
> We eat it cold with the best grace we may.

* * *

> . . . Hearken to me
> THERE IS COLD MUTTON, BUTTS, IN EVERY HOUSE.

BUTTS.　　Great heavens! my good lord Bluebeard, what d'you mean?

BLUEBEARD.　There are short commons and short comings Butts
> Sometimes your lovely wife's at difference with you
> And gives you the cold shoulder, doesn't she?

* * *

> You want for quiet sometimes and she scolds you
> And sometimes when you look for sympathy
> Yawns in your face. You make a joke sometimes
> And she doesn't laugh.

BUTTS.　　　　　　　Dammy, I never try her.

But Bluebeard is inconsolable. He enjoys wit and gaiety and sympathy, and is cheated of it. So he has to be content to see his lady dress and dance while he pays the music and the milliner. 'Rich men are made for this.' The situation is typically Thackeray's—a sort of burlesque in reverse. It is easy to see why he never finished it, for it could not have come to much; once the theme is stated and the mood set the fun is about finished. Yet the fragment is a not uninteresting addition to the Thackeray bibliography.

CHAPTER FIVE

Punch: The Prize Novelists; The Book of Snobs. The Christmas Books

NOT THE LEAST of the ironies of Thackeray's literary career was that during the mid-'forties the author who was about to write *Vanity Fair* was known almost entirely as a *'Punch* man.' The Titmarsh who had laboured for recognition in *Fraser's* with *The Great Hoggarty Diamond* and with *Barry Lyndon* was to make his first really notable success as an anonymous contributor to a comic magazine. He had published his books of travel; his stories and reviews for *Fraser's* were still literally meat and drink for him; but after 1844 more and more of his energy was thrown into his work for *Punch,* until by the time he withdrew from the magazine he had contributed to it well over four hundred bits of writing and something under four hundred drawings.

His *Punch* papers vary a great deal in quality and effectiveness. One can trace in his major efforts an advance in literary power and the strengthening of tendencies which were to become still more apparent in the novels, but in the mass of his miscellaneous contributions there seems to be no discernible line of growth. Typically they are burlesque, with occasional broad shots of satire. Almost always they depend for their effect upon extravagant exaggeration. Some seem slight today because of their topical subject matter; others are slight because they never could have been anything else. If there are dull stretches and if Thackeray too frequently forces the fun, it must be remembered that he was writing for a living, and had to be funny on schedule. What is more surprising is the vast amount of good stuff. To name no others, the Jeames de la Pluche letters, the letters of Mr. Brown to his nephew, the inimitable *Novels by Eminent Hands,* and the *Snob Papers* were all brought to bed by *Punch.*

From its inception in 1841 under the guidance of Mark Lemon, Henry Mayhew, Douglas Jerrold, and Gilbert à Beckett, the *London Charivari* was of course more than just a comic magazine. It took its humour very seriously, fancying itself as an arbiter of taste and manners, surveying the social scene with a sense of responsibility towards conduct as well as towards laughter. *Punch* is the proper guide for those who would understand the average intelligent middle-class point of view in the mid-century, with all its impeccable insularity, its deep mistrust of foreigners, its strong moral tone, its generous enthusiasms and its blind prejudices, its hatred of shams and of social injustice, and its genial assumption that, although many a head wanted knocking, the heart of old England was sound, et cetera. The magazine was as English as beef-pie, with much of the same honest solidity. If that dish sometimes lies a little heavy on the stomach, still it is eminently wholesome, and above all it pretends to be nothing it is not. Thackeray hit exactly the right note when he said in his *Concluding Observations on Snobs* that it was Mr. Punch's business to laugh at mean affectations, but 'May he laugh honestly, hit no foul blow, and tell the truth when at his very broadest grin—never forgetting that if Fun is good, Truth is still better and Love best of all.'

Punch frequently toned its muscles with a lively crusade of some kind, and to list its campaigns would be to give an idea both of its delightful rightness and of its inevitable limitations. It always took the side of the oppressed poor, and cried out violently against the Corn Laws, discriminatory legislation, and the miserable conditions of factory workers. It favoured the ballot. It was severe upon Louis Philippe and upon French nationalism. It tried to be fair to Ireland but was perpetually irritated by the violent demands of the Irish. It never liked Jews. It grew shrill over the Catholic question and the Papal Brief. (Thackeray, in spite of his prejudices, was very temperate here.) At the time of the Crimean War it turned violent patriot. Always, even when wrong-headed, it was warm-hearted.

Thackeray too had his favourite objects of pursuit. He poured out the vials of his wrath upon the rigid moralists who kept the museums closed on Sundays; he decried the flogging of soldies; with a recurring and disproportionate anger he heaped contempt upon the snobberies of the Court Circular. A survey, then, of his more miscellaneous *Punch* articles reveals a keen interest in current affairs as well as a sensible analysis of the minor grotesqueries of Victorian civilization.[1]

Thackeray began to write for *Punch* in 1842, but he contributed little until after Christmas 1843, at which time he joined the staff as successor to Albert Smith. From then on he was of the inner circle, indefatigably pouring forth stories, parodies, jokes, travel sketches, burlesques of history, political satires, verses, and whimsical drawings. Then as his novels began to absorb his attention and energy, the *Punch* duties became something of an incubus. After 1851 he severed his formal connection with the magazine and wrote little more for it. The immediate cause of his resignation from the staff was his increasing

[1] One of his lighter comments on the active campaign being waged against the abominably unsanitary condition of the Serpentine and the Thames is worth a note, for it carries to a logical humorous conclusion the species of warfare against adulterated foods of which we hear (justifiably, no doubt) so much today. Thackeray purports to be a man driven almost to suicide by the terror inspired by the reports that almost everything he eats, and even the air he breathes, is full of poison. He can buy, in a certain place, coffee that is guaranteed non-poisonous, but 'if my milk is poisoned, my tea poisoned, my bread ditto, the air which I breathe poisoned . . . if my Thames is a regular Lethe, in which every eel is a mortal writhing serpent, and every white bait a small dose of death, what is the odds of taking a little more or less pyroligenous acid in my coffee?' (xv, 127, 1848.)

irritation at *Punch's* slashing attacks upon Prince Albert and the Crystal Palace, and even more specifically its abuse of Lord Palmerston and of Louis Napoleon. A hitherto unpublished letter written to Lady Stanley 28 December 1851 gives his reasons for the resignation.

I was so disgusted [he wrote] with that caricature [2] which appeared in Punch of the Nobleholder that I remonstrated with all my force at the indecency and injustice of attacking the only man who was bottleholding the liberal cause in Europe and received an answer promising better behaviour and in which the Editor of the paper said that they intended to be good-natured in the article not wicked, and as no bones were broken, that matter was left to drop. But on coming to London the first thing I see is that iniquitous cut against Louis Napoleon which enraged me so that I went in and resigned at once saying that I couldn't and wouldn't pull any longer in a boat where there was such a crew and such a steersman. So you see that political events influence small men as well as big and I have gone out of office too in my small way.[3]

He still remained on good terms, however, with his old colleagues, and as late as 1854 wrote a few pieces for the magazine.

The first extended series of papers that Thackeray wrote for *Punch* fell cold upon its readers. *Miss Tickletoby's Lectures on English History* ran through eleven issues [4] and was broken off at the request of the editors. Later commentators have almost always followed contemporary opinion by dismissing the *Lectures* with a brief and blanketing condemnation. I must enter the confession, however, of having found them amusing in places. The induction is admittedly dull and long-winded; there are some atrocious puns; the first half of the papers is better than the latter half. But Miss Tickletoby is a lively figure and her opinion full of ironic juice.

The first lecture begins:

[2] Louis Napoleon, bloody sword in hand, riding over the brink of a cliff marked 'To Glory.'

[3] MS. letter in the Huntington Library.

[4] July-October 1842.

My Loves—With regard to the early history of our beloved country, before King Alfred ascended the throne, I have very little indeed to say; in the first place, because the story itself is none of the most moral—consisting of accounts of murders agreeably varied by invasions; and secondly, dears, because, to tell you the truth, I have always found those first chapters so abominably stupid, that I have made a point to pass them over . . . Well, then, about the abominable, odious Danes and Saxons, the Picts and the Scots, I know very little, and must say have passed through life pretty comfortably in spite of my ignorance. Not that this should be an excuse to *you*— no, no, darlings; learn for learning's sake; if not, I have something hanging up in the cupboard, and you know my name is Tickletoby. [*Great sensation.*] . . .

About the year 450, the Romans, having quite enough to do at home, quitted Britain for good, when the Scots, who were hungry then, and have been hungry ever since, rushed in among the poor unprotected Britoners, who were forced to call the Saxons to their aid.

Without labouring a minor point, I submit that this is not as dull as the failure of the *Lectures* would make it seem. If for nothing more than the drollery of the 'Song of King Canute' in mock Anglo-Saxon measures, their publication would have been vindicated. And in all probability they gave the suggestion to Gilbert à Beckett and Leech for their later *Comic Histories* of England and of Rome.[5]

Another series of papers, *The Wanderings of Our Fat Contributor,* are for the most part a burlesque pendant to the more literal account of Thackeray's travels as recorded in *Cornhill to Cairo*. There is in these papers from first to last a great deal of animal spirits and some highly inventive description. The Fat Contributor reveals himself as of dour and bilious disposition, flying into mock rages at bad wine and poor food, grumbling at passport officials, making acid comments on his fellow travellers, bored by historical relics, full of mock-heroics and mock-ecstatics, pasting, at last, the great placard of *Punch* on the Pyramid of Cheops. It is all somewhat forced and lacks the

[5] M. H. Spielmann: *History of Punch*, 1895, p. 309.

grand sweep of the inspired burlesque of *Gahagan.* To use an expression of which he himself would have been capable, the humour of the Fat Contributor wears a little thin.

It is a curious and not always heartening journey, this tracing of a great novelist among the ephemera of his professionally comic publications. But while Thackeray was writing for *Punch* he was also publishing *Barry Lyndon* and *Vanity Fair* and *Pendennis,* and there is a parallel substantiality about some of the better *Punch* work that shows Thackeray perfecting not only the wit and satire always native to him but also the gentler, more discursive vein of reflective contemplation. The satire is seen sharpening itself in such articles as *Lady L's Journal of a Visit to Foreign Courts* and the later *Lion Huntress of Belgravia.* The former plays excellent havoc with the affected, insolent, journal-publishing aristocrat.[6] The Lion Huntress, a collector of shop-worn lions, is revealed in her smug saying: 'People may not be in society—and yet, I dare say, mean very well.'

With *Punch's Prize Novelists,* later to be published as *Novels by Eminent Hands,* Thackeray joins the select number of those who have done a difficult thing supremely well. As a form of literary criticism, parody is doubtless a treacherous implement, its very essence being that it is transparently unfair, or at least unjudicial. But to those who can away with such pedantries there is no more deft or satisfying means for puncturing pomposity, for letting the air gracefully out of wind-bags. Thackeray, with his acute eye for sponginess of thought and flatulency of style, was the predestined scourge of literary meretriciousness. Working in a form which any one can try but in which excellence is reserved for the very few, he distilled the very spirit of parody from the pages of Bulwer, Disraeli, Lever, and others. The victims writhed, and retaliated—not in kind, for no one has ever successfully parodied Thackeray—but the

[6] Says Lord St. Paul's: 'I don't think that ladies, of however exalted rank, are quite justified in shuddering at being brought in contact with their fellow-creatures.' The Duke: 'Fellow-creatures! No, no. For Heaven's sake moderate your expressions! My Lord, this is dangerous levelling doctrine.'

extent of their squirming was the measure of Thackeray's success. In his early literary reviews Thackeray had raised the knife against romantic absurdities in fiction; in the *Prize Novelists*[7] he ties off the arteries and neatly completes the operation.

Bulwer, to whom Thackeray had devoted much tender attention in the past, was led first to the sacrifice. As early as 27 January Thackeray had written to Albany Fonblanque explaining an honourable reluctance to meet Bulwer at a dinner:

A great qualm has just come over me about our conversation this morning. I am going to do a series of novels by the most popular authors for *Punch,* and Bulwer's is actually done, the blocks designed, and the story in progress. It is George Barnwell. He will quote Plato, speak in Big Phrases, and let out his Nunky's old, etc. Numbers of others are to follow—Cooper, James, Dickens, Lever, etc., but they will all be good-natured, and I can't afford to give up my plan. It is my bread, indeed, for next year.

I am bound to tell you this (how the deuce did I forget it in our talk this morning?), lest you should be putting your hospitable intentions into execution, and after having had my legs *sub iisdem trabibus* with Bulwer, should seem to betray him. I can't leave him out of the caricature; all that I promise is to be friendly and meek in spirit.[8]

George De Barnwell, 'by Sir E.L. B.L. BB. LL. BBB. LLL.' is a superb job. Into the mouth of the uncle-murderer Barnwell is put all the vaporous philosophizing, the pseudo-mystical apostrophizing of the Good, the True, the Beautiful, that is so typical of Bulwer's drivelling early heroes. Crime is idealized, and though Barnwell is executed, he melts his mistress and his jailor into tears with his oratorical declarations that he has performed a Service to Humanity. Barnwell is a complete paragon of windy, melancholy moralizing. All this is thrown against an anachronistic eighteenth-century background introducing Dr. Johnson, Swift, Pope, Steele, and Bolingbroke, most of whom

[7] April to October 1847.

[8] Copied from the original in the Huntington Library. It is almost identically the same as given in Malcolm Elwin's *Thackeray: A Personality,* 1932, p. 176.

George instructs in their particular fields. The turgid, self-consciously learned style of Bulwer is parodied in sweet perfection.

I tell thee a tale—not of Kings—but of Men—not of Thrones, but of Love, and Grief, and Crime. Listen, and but once more. 'Tis for the last time (probably) these fingers shall sweep the strings . . . 'Twas noonday in Chepe . . . the dauntless street urchins, as they gaily threaded the Labyrinth of Life, enjoyed the perplexities and quarrels of the scene, and exacerbated the already furious combatants by their poignant infantile satire . . . O Youth, Youth! Happy and Beautiful! . . .

It may be repeated that Thackeray had no personal animus against Bulwer. As he wrote to Lady Blessington in 1848:

I have no sort of personal dislike (not that it matters whether I have or not) to Sir. E.L.B.L., on the contrary the only time I met him, at the immortal Ainsworth's years ago, I thought him very pleasant, and I know from his conduct to my dear little Blanchard that he can be a most generous and delicate-minded friend. BUT there air [sic] sentiments in his writings which always anger me, big words which make me furious, and a premeditated fine writing against which I can't help rebelling.

Five years afterward, recognizing perhaps that Bulwer (Bulwer-Lytton by that time) had atoned for the sins of his youth by his later and more sincere work, Thackeray wrote him a letter crying 'Peccavi,' in which he quoted from the 1853 preface to the American edition of his minor works:

There are two performances especially (among the critical and biographical works of the erudite Mr. Yellowplush) which I am sorry to see reproduced, and I ask pardon of the author of 'The Caxtons' for a lampoon, which I know he himself has forgiven and which I wish I could recall. I had never seen that eminent writer but once in public when this satire was penned, and wonder at the recklessness of the young man who could fancy such personality was harmless jocularity, and never calculated that it might give pain.

Thus did Thackeray regret, as he grew older and more temperate, the personalities of *Mr. Yellowplush's Ajew* and *Epistles to the Literati. George De Barnwell* contained no personal references to Bulwer, but it is all the more cleanly destructive because of that.

The next victim was Disraeli, in *Codlingsby,* 'by D. Shrewsberry, Esq.' Stylistically this is subtler than the parody of Bulwer, for Disraeli was himself a better writer. Thackeray catches almost the very cadences of the style of *Coningsby.* The situations and the characters of that novel are magnified into burlesque grotesqueness, as are the racial consciousness and the love of rich, exotic description. The parody does more, however, than make fun of Disraeli's oriental splendour and magnificence; it catches his real narrative manner and blows it up, of course, to exaggerated proportions. Thus: 'Where the idols are fed with incense by the streams of Ching-wang-foo; where the minarets soar sparkling above the cypresses, their reflections quivering in the lucid waters of the Golden Horn; where the yellow Tiber flows under broken bridges and over imperial glories,' et cetera.

The place of central prominence is given to Rafael Mendoza, the friend of Lord Codlingsby. Mendoza is a Jewish superman, rich as the Rothschilds but fond of hiding behind an old-clothes business. He lives in elaborate apartments behind his shop, visited there by royalty arranging for loans and asking his advice in politics. The parody is audacious but brilliant. Disraeli waited thirty-three years for his revenge, and then took it by writing Thackeray into *Endymion* as 'St. Barbe.'

Thackeray was on familiar ground when he turned to the fustian of the fashionable novel as written by Mrs. Gore, in his *Lords and Liveries,* 'By the Authoress of "Dukes and Déjeuners," "Hearts and Diamonds," "Marchionesses and Milliners," etc., etc.' From the very beginning Thackeray had been sharp against the affectations of the silver-fork school. By this time his hand is sure and the edge of his satire keen.

The breeziness of Thackeray's laughter ventilated the looped and windowed raggedness of a literary absurdity. *Lords and Liv-*

eries is full of the foreign tags which were the hall-mark of elegance in the fashionable novel. 'Everybody stared,' runs one passage, 'at such an exclamation of enthusiasm from the lips of the young Earl of Bagnigge, who was never heard to admire anything except a *coulis de dindonneau à la Ste. Ménéhould,* or a *suprême de cochon en torticolis à la Piffarde;* such as Champollion, the *chef* of the Travellers, only knows how to dress; or the bouquet of a flask of *Médoc,* of Carbonell's best quality; or a *goutte* of Marasquin, from the cellars of Briggs and Hobson.' The hero, at twenty-three, was a cynic and an epicure who had 'drained the cup of pleasure till it had palled in his unnerved hand.' And nowhere is Thackeray's relish for the ridiculous more vigorous than it is here in the complete and devastating inanity of the affected conversation, a grotesque brew of stupid chatter and polite whinnying.

Lords and Liveries, however, is as much generic satire as it is a specific criticism of Mrs. Gore, who, unlike some of her sisters of the fashionable sorority, viewed with a certain level-headed common sense the shallowness of her characters. Bulwer said of her that 'she preceded Thackeray, and as she knew good society infinitely better than he did, her satire makes his look like caricature.' In view of its background, this criticism may perhaps be somewhat discounted. Nevertheless, two years later, upon receipt of her novel *The Hamiltons,* Thackeray wrote Mrs. Gore a characteristically friendly letter containing a very interesting if rather tempered apology for his earlier burlesques.[9] He had been pleased and amused by the novel, 'and that is a great thing,' he says, 'for a professional man to own.' He continues:

I liked the part of the death of George IV and the babby very much—the touch of kindness gave a sort of chance and hope for the poor old departing reprobate, and gives him a drop of water in that warm place between which and Abraham's bosom there is a great gulph fixed. What an awful radical you are Ma'am or you was!—

[9] Hitherto unpublished, as nearly as I can discover. Now in the manuscript collection of the Huntington Library.

There's tremendous revolutionary sentiments in the Hamiltons. Su-san is a party after my own sort—mild and sweet cheering but not inebriating[.] I should like to have such a woman to bully—she would like it so too.

And I think some critics who carped at some writers for talking too much about fine company ought to hold their tongues. If you live with great folks, why should you not describe their manners? There is nothing in the least strained in these descriptions as I now think—and believe it was only a secret envy and black malignity of disposition which made me say in former times this author is talk-ing too much about grand people, this author is of the silver fork school, this author uses too much French, etc. There's none in this book to speak, perhaps that's why you send it to me you malicious woman, and the only point I object to is perhaps a too frequent use of the note of hadmiration! After all one must object to something.

In spite of Thackeray's graceful acknowledgment here, it is difficult to discover behind *Lords and Liveries* any 'secret envy and black malignity.' Thackeray's standards of literary excel-lence did not soften as he grew older—as he applied them to himself they became more and more exacting—but the letter to Mrs. Gore does dovetail with other evidence to show that as his own position in the world of letters became more secure he tended to become more tolerant. Without losing the sharp edge of his observation, Thackeray was growing into benignity. Fortunately for us, however, he was still unregenerate in 1847.

Barbazure, 'by G.P.R. Jeames, Esq.,' is a sparkling travesty of James's historical novels with their luxuriance of romantic description, their solitary horsemen riding against the sky (who thenceforth disappeared from James's books), and their melo-dramatic situations. Thackeray had a sneaking sort of likeness of this sort of story and himself wanted to write a medieval his-torical novel. He therefore enjoys himself thoroughly romping about amid an aroma of antique dialogue and romantic oaths. There is great vivacity here and no ill will.

Charles Lever, with whom Thackeray's relations had been most cordial, chilled though they were for a time by the *Irish*

Sketch Book, was angered by *Phil Fogarty—a Tale of the Fighting Onety-Oneth,* 'by Harry Rollicker.' This was a parody of his *Harry Lorrequer* type of military high jinks, and is a curious mingling of the horseplay, fighting, and adventures in high life that were the staple of Lever's episodic novels. There is much brogue, exuberant Irish spirit, and many cheap jokes which (in the text) always receive hearty laughter Phil has the impudence and the bravado of his prototype. His adventures take him to France; at a court ball he meets Talleyrand, who joins him in a double hornpipe with Pauline Bonaparte and Madame de Staël. There is nothing malicious in the satire, but it is acutely apropos, so much so that Lever changed the style of his later novels. In his turn he caricatured Thackeray as 'Elias Howle' in *Roland Cashel.* Later, however, he forgot his hostility and came to be on very good terms with Thackeray.

Crinoline is the only one of the *Prize Novels* which is not aimed at a particular author. This, in the curious orthography of 'Je-mes Pl-sh, Esq.' (and his last literary appearance), is an unfinished satire on the brazen impudence of French authors who generalize about English life on the basis of an extremely narrow knowledge. 'Munseer Jools de Chacabac,' a French journalist, has read *The Vicar of Wakefield* in the original and therefore assumes his competency to write about the English. He comes to London, lives in a cheap hotel in a shabby part of the city, and believes that the foreigners he meets there are typical specimens of the English *élite.* His French readers learn, therefore, that all the English drink half-and-half, although gin-and-water is the national beverage—and other social information of equal accuracy.[10] In this, as in Jeames's other documents,

[10] It is worth remembering that Thackeray refused to write a book about America on the basis of his brief visits there, although there has been good British precedent (before and since) for such a book. 'What could Dickens mean by writing that book of American Notes?' he wrote to Albany Fonblanque during his first tour. 'No man should write about the country under 5 years of experience, and as many of previous reading.'

the humour of misspelling has its limitations, but as a whole the piece is deftly turned.

The last of the *Prize Novels,* a burlesque of Fenimore Cooper (whose novels Thackeray admired greatly) is the slightest of the lot. *The Stars and Stripes,* 'by the Author of "The Last of the Mulligans," "Pilot," etc.' pokes genteel fun at the self-complacent American feeling of superiority to the rest of the world. It has little merit, however, as a parody of Cooper.

Thackeray originally planned to include among the *Prize Novelists* parodies of both Dickens and himself. *Punch* timorously vetoed the idea of a burlesque of Dickens and so Thackeray wrote neither of the contemplated chapters. Dickens wrote to Thackeray deprecating the fact that he had been left out, yet at the same time reproving him gently.

I will tell you now candidly that I did not admire the design and I think it a great pity [he wrote] that we take advantage of the means our calling gives us with such accursed readiness of at all depreciating or vulgarising each other, that this seems to me to be one of the main reasons why we are more generally divided among ourselves than artists who have not those means at their command . . . I thought your power thrown away on that series, however happily executed.[11]

This would seem to turn neatly against Thackeray his own protests about the necessity of maintaining the dignity and integrity of the literary profession. This accusation of 'vulgarising,' however, hardly holds water. No one had a deeper sense than Thackeray of the desirability of amicable relations among authors. It is true that in his salad days he wrote things which stung some notoriously sensitive skins and that he showed frequently a mild surprise that others should be hurt by a criticism which, had it been directed against him, he would have felt keenly. His own acute sensibility should have told him that the arrows which he meant not unkindly could quiver angrily in the flesh of a peculiarly susceptible brotherhood. This incon-

11 Biographical introduction to *Punch,* 1, xxviii.

sistency is a curious blind spot in Thackeray. The distinction needs to be made, however, that Thackeray's own complaints usually came when he felt that he had been attacked personally; he had an honest artistic modesty. On the other hand, he saw no literary treason in parodying the palpable absurdities of his fellow writers as he did in the *Prize Novelists*. And indeed behind the truculence of those authors fearful of parody there is seen something of the stuffed shirt which is not exclusively a Victorian heritage. Not all could exclaim with Walter Scott, who, when he saw himself parodied in *Rejected Addresses,* declared, 'Why, I must have written that myself.'

One other of Thackeray's most characteristic pieces must be mentioned here. The year after the *Prize Novelists,* he wrote for *Punch* 'A Little Dinner at Timmins's.' [12] It embodies a familiar Thackerayan moral—the absurdity of living beyond your means in order to make a social impression; but the vital spirit of the piece lies rather in the facile characterization and in the series of entirely natural but amusing complications attending the sending of the invitations, the preparations for the dinner, and the dinner-party itself. The humour arises naturally out of the cumulative small aggravations, disappointments, and worries of those concerned. Young Mrs. Timmins *will* go in for tuft-hunting; the honoured guests—M.P.'s and bankers—accept the invitation with open eagerness but private wrath. Because certain people are not invited there is an aftermath of misery and dissension. The dinner is awkward and stiff—the table too crowded, the conversation dull, the Timminses nervous and constrained when not dismally facetious; Timmins goes into debt for a dinner he could not afford to give. The humour here is unforced and the observation amiably acute.

In tracing the growth of Thackeray as a literary craftsman, *Punch* serves as a sort of transition. At one end are Tickletoby and Yellowplush and the Fat Contributor, pointing back to the earlier Yellowplush, to Gahagan, and to the Fitz-Boodle of

[12] May-July 1848.

the *Confessions*. At the other end, falling within the years 1847-50, are the 'Spec' of *Travels in London,* Mr. Brown of the *Letters to a Young Man about Town,* and Solomon Pacifico of the *Proser,* pointing forward just as clearly to the Thackeray who was to be the genial fireside philosopher of the later *Roundabout Papers*. When we remember that the years of Mr. Brown and the Proser were the years of *Pendennis* as well, we realize that these essays, which often incorporate little narratives, and *Pendennis,* which is itself full of little essays, are not so far apart. The later *Punch* papers represent a mellowing of Thackeray's personality and the exercise of that faculty of quiet contemplation which so impregnates the novels. They lead us towards *Vanity Fair* and *Pendennis*. Spec., Mr. Brown, Dr. Solomon Pacifico are all the Thackeray who was later to shake his mop of white hair, look benignly over his spectacles, and settle down in his arm-chair to discuss with sympathetic chuckles the whimsical weaknesses and the amazing humanity of men. The blue eyes behind the spectacles were, to be sure, very sharp, and could twinkle mischievously as well as become clouded with tender sentiment. In these *Punch* papers there is somewhat more of the imp and less of the wistful philosopher. Yet even here, amid the glint of satire and the sparkle of humorous description, Thackeray has assumed the role of the old man mildly evaluating the social scene, lashing out against cruelty and snobbery but commending, where he finds it, honour, tenderness, and magnanimity.

The *Travels in London,*[18] which are the earliest of these in point of time, show Thackeray both as humanitarian and humorist. In *The Curate's Walk* Thackeray accompanies the Reverend Frank Whitestock on his visits to his poverty-stricken parishioners. Thackeray meets ragged little children and gives them sixpence, sees wretchedness and suffering and courage-in-suffering, and without being in the slightest degree either maudlin or patronizing conveys, by his controlled objectivity, an im-

---

[18] November 1847-March 1848.

pression of great-hearted sympathy. That Thackeray does not pause here to ask why such poverty should be does not mean that he shared the bland assumption of those who believed that God had so ordered the estate of the rich and poor, or that somehow poverty was evidence of sin. In a later paper, *Waiting at the Station*,[14] he enters into a discussion of poverty which is so revealing that it is worth quoting.

But what I note, what I marvel at, what I acknowledge, what I am ashamed of, what is contrary to Christian morals, manly modesty and honesty, and to the national well-being, is that there should be that immense social distinction between the well-dressed classes (as, if you will permit me, we will call ourselves), and our brethren and sisters in the fustian jackets and pattens. If you deny it for your part, I say that you are mistaken, and deceive yourself woefully. I say that you have been educated to it through Gothic ages, and have had it handed down to you from your fathers (not that they were anybody in particular, but respectable well-dressed progenitors, let us say for a generation or two)—from your well-dressed fathers before you. How long ago is it that our preachers were teaching the poor 'to know their station'? that it was the peculiar boast of Englishmen, that any man, the humblest among us, could, by talent, industry, and good luck, hope to take his place in the aristocracy of his country, and that we pointed with pride to Lord This, who was the grandson of a barber; and to Earl That, whose father was an apothecary? What a multitude of most respectable folks pride themselves on these things still! The gulf is not impassable, because one man in a million swims over it, and we hail him for his strength and success. He has landed on the happy island. He is one of the aristocracy. Let us clap hands and applaud. There's no country like ours for rational freedom.

* * *

You are not unkind; not ungenerous. But of such wondrous and complicated misery as this you confess you had no idea. No. How should you?—you and I—we are of the upper classes; we have had hitherto no community with the poor. We never speak a word to the servant who waits on us for twenty years; we condescend to employ a tradesman, keeping him at a proper distance, mind, of

[14] *Punch,* 9 March 1850.

course, at a proper distance—we laugh at his young men, if they dance, jig, and amuse themselves like their betters, and call them counter-jumpers, snobs, and what not; of his workmen we know nothing, how pitilessly they are ground down, how they live and die, here close by us at the backs of our houses—until some poet like Hood wakes and sings that dreadful 'Song of the Shirt'; some prophet like Carlyle rises up and denounces woe; some clear-sighted energetic man like the writer of the *Chronicle* travels into the poor man's country for us, and comes back with his tale of terror and wonder.

Thackeray's literary orbit took him more frequently into Belgravia than into the slums, and he wisely knew the path of his genius. But behind the satirist there lay the humanitarian, and he who would understand the first must know the second.

More miscellaneous in their comments are *Mr. Brown's Letters to His Nephew*.[15] Here Thackeray is genially sententious, amiable and benevolent, but critically evaluating, too. He advises the young man about women, for one thing, admitting that some are vulgar and ill humoured, rancorous and narrow-minded, slaves of fashion and hypocrites—'but I do respect, admire, and almost worship good women; and I think there is a very fair number of such to be found in this world.' He gives a wry analysis of club life, exposing the bores, the parasites, the drunkards, the spongers, et cetera. An inveterate diner-out, he praises English society for being a dinner-giving society. 'I hardly remember in my life,' he says in a burst of philanthropy, 'to have had a bad dinner.'

Later in *The Proser*,[16] Thackeray in expansive mood takes the whole world to his bosom. He discourses on 'gentility' as the destroyer of social happiness amongst the middle classes in England. It kills naturalness, he says, and kindly sympathies. 'The object of life, as I take it, is to be friendly with everybody . . . as there is, if one would or could but discover it, something notable, something worthy of observation, of sympathy, of wonder and amusement, in every fellow mortal.'

15 *Punch*, March-August 1849.
16 *Punch*, April-August 1850.

This, then, is the stage which Thackeray has reached midway in his career. The thing which impresses one in his letters and in the anecdotes about him is this vast fund of tenderness and the sensitive warmth of his affection. These lie closely upon his novels, too, and give balance and depth to his pointed comments upon contemporary society. Nevertheless, the value of those comments depends just as much upon his complementary instinct for inexorably and with an appalling pertinence stripping the hide from vulgarity and selfishness. From that point of view the most important as well as the most extensive of his *Punch* papers are those the discussion of which has been reserved until now. *The Book of Snobs* is a muted overture for the full symphony of *Vanity Fair*.

For the critic of manners like Thackeray the contemporary scene offered an impressive amount of material. Snobbishness will no doubt continue to exist as long as social inequalities remain, but Victorian society presented peculiar possibilities to the anatomist of snobs. In spite of the fact that the Victorians were prone to declare their age the best of all ages and the Victorian Englishman God's most satisfying special creation, it was in many ways an uncertain society, throwing up bulwarks of optimism against a secret quivering doubt and uncertainty. The social order which had seemed so stable in the eighteenth century was now fluid and shifting, caught in the backwaters of the Industrial Revolution. The old aristocracy, though still socially dominant, had watched the balance of power swing from the land to the new industrial cities and had seen the emergence of a new plutocracy. As yet this moneyed middle class, bearing the stigma of its bourgeois origin, was crude and uneasy. It had no tradition, no social inheritance, and so it yearned and panted after the marks of gentility of which the landed aristocracy had been in exclusive possession. In a shifting society anything might happen; the gates of the elect might open even to the Merchant Prince and his wife. Not infrequently they did open, and if titles were not actually purchased, at least convenient alliances were made between the sons of birth and the daughters of wealth. Many of those who could get only the narrowest foothold on the social ladder strove valiantly to acquire the veneer of gentility. There is something a trifle pathetic, as well as something hard and unlovely, about this scramble towards the social appurtenances of Success, this admission of inferiority and the desperate effort to draw somehow a cloth of gold about Respectability. But its chief by-product, if we can believe the voices on every side, was to make snobbery for a time an endemic national disease. For such a disease, Thackeray carried just the proper purgative.

Thackeray was not the first to isolate the virus or the last to treat it. Bulwer had pointed it out with surprising lucidity as early as his *England and the English* in 1833. Disraeli saw it. It is found in the pages of Dickens and Trollope. *Punch* continued to hunt it out long after Thackeray had dropped the chase. It was Thackeray, however, who first traced the thing in its various manifestations and who became the proper historian of the particular forms of servility and arrogance and pride that infested his time.

With *The Snobs of England,* 'by One of Themselves,' which ran through fifty-three consecutive numbers of *Punch,* from 28 February 1846 to 27 February 1847, Thackeray tasted for the first time really unmitigated success. The circulation of the magazine boomed with their publication, and Thackeray, having caught a good thing by the tail, was unable to let it go until it had carried him out of Snobdom proper into a twilight land where disagreeable people of whatever kind, not snobs even in the loosest sense of the word, had to qualify for admission to the fraternity. When Thackeray reprinted the papers later he omitted seven of the chapters, having found them, he said, 'so stupid, so personal, so snobbish—in a word—that I have withdrawn them from this collection.' But in 1846 he swung the lash vigorously, and all sorts of egotistical dullards had to run for shelter. He is consciously using broad strokes in the *Snob Papers,* and his honest indignation fumes and splutters at times. Yet the satire is sharp enough to constitute a kind of preliminary cartoon for the subtler analyses of *Vanity Fair.* The papers are full of inimitable phrases, trenchant, but luminous too with that easy grace which Thackeray brought even to his most occasional satire.

In view of the breadth of his categories Thackeray was wise in saying that it is impossible to define a snob accurately. His tentative definition, 'one who meanly admires mean things,' though it is of course central, is not all-inclusive. There are two broad aspects of snobbishness: that in which those at the foot of the ladder cringe and fawn upon those who are a few rungs above them; and that in which those perched at the top trample with supercilious arrogance the fingers of the aspirants beneath. Thackeray paid most attention to the former class, as being both ubiquitous and more offensive.

He begins playfully enough but soon swings his heavy guns into action against the 'Snob Royal' (a savage attack upon George IV) and continues with a denunciation of the influence of the aristocracy on snobs. With a Carlylean fervour he attacks Peerage-worship and the absurdity of hereditary aristocracy—'base Man-and-Mammon worship, instituted by command of law:—Snobbishness, in a word, perpetuated.' It is among the respectable that snobbishness flourishes, he says, on Baker Street and on Wimpole Street, which is 'as cheerful as the Catacombs—a dingy Mausoleum of the genteel.' Their sacred Bible is the *Peerage,* a 'foolish lying book' to which Thackeray's automatic and somewhat extravagant literary reaction was always a gnashing of teeth.

So he runs down the list of his elect: the banker Muggins, whose son becomes Alured Mogyns Smith de Mogyns, with the crest 'a tomtit rampant regardant,' and the great city snob with a mania for aristocratic marriages; 'I like to see such,' says Thackeray, 'I like to see these two humbugs which, dividing, as they do, the social empire of this kingdom between them, hate each other naturally, making truce and uniting, for the sordid interests of either.' Military snobs, who will last as long as commissions are bought and sold. University snobs. Dinner-giving snobs (the 'character' later to be elaborated into *A Little Dinner at Timmins's*). English travelling snobs. And in a beautifully ironic chapter, 'Literary Snobs.' There are, he says solemnly, no snobs in the literary profession. One literary man may abuse his brother, but not in the least out of malice or envy—merely from a sense of truth and public duty. He praises the *Quarterly* and *Blackwood's* for just the wrong quality—their temperate justice—and concludes, 'It is because we know and respect each other, that the world respects us so much; that we hold such a good position in society, and demean ourselves so irreproachably when there.'

Thus Thackeray rings the changes. He devotes eight loving papers to 'Club Snobs,' but his central idea was becoming progressively more and more attenuated, and 'club snobs' are often merely 'club bores.' Nevertheless, the 'endless greasy simper' of old Fawney is unforgettable, as is the description of the Sarcophagus Club. Thackeray was boring from within here; the story runs that in search of material he gained access to the complaint-books of several clubs. Certainly there is a lively verisimilitude. The eight chapters, too, of 'Country Snobs' are among the most amusing in the book. Mr. Snob's visit at Major Ponto's establishment—the Major, dull and lazy but pretending vigour and learning; his wife, eager for fashionable gossip—is described with a wealth of high satiric detail and reminds one of a *Spectator* paper turned acid.

Within the limitations of his restricted theme Thackeray accomplished a great deal. Certainly insolence, conceit, and crawling flattery have never been more carefully dissected. Yet through all the hard hitting and behind the distortion that came from riding a fruitful but limited subject a little too extensively, one can see the Thackeray who wishes no ill to any honest soul—the champion of 'love and simplicity and natural kindness.' Thackeray knew of course that one who hunted snobs so vigorously would himself be accused of snobbery. He attempted to disarm criticism by including himself with his victims; of such calm moralists as himself 'is there one, I wonder, whose heart would not throb with pleasure if he could be seen walking arm-in-arm with a couple of dukes down Pall Mall?' His severest blows were aimed at the condition of society which made snob-bishness so easy. Nevertheless, some of the pitch clung to his own fingers, and he has been written down snob by not a few hostile critics.[17]

The drift of the attack seems to be that because Thackeray later told Motley that he did not like the *Book of Snobs,* and because he was, in the days of his success, wooed successfully by aristocratic circles, he was therefore a snob and a hypocrite. Now Thackeray delighted in being thought well of. He was by nature fond of society and though he saw through its foibles he nevertheless had a reasonably good time in it. He enjoyed the company of intelligent and cultured people and hunted them out wherever he could find them. Nevertheless it is impossible, without ignoring the weight of all reliable testimony, to show that he was ever supercilious or affected on the one hand or servile on the other. He sometimes turned upon bores or upon those who grated upon his excessive sensitiveness, but one gets a very distinct impression of a man completely unpretentious and modest, so much so that he could rub shoulders with titles without endangering at all his love for the simpler world to which he belonged. It is to be remembered also that his friends among the aristocracy were not of the *genre* whose failings it was a part of his life's work to pillory. Parenthetically, the visitor with whom he shared most frequently the hospitality of Lord and Lady Ashburton at 'The Grange' was that other old snob, Thomas Carlyle!

As we approach the great novels in narrowing circles there remains to be discussed one significant phase of Thackeray's

[17] The most bitter attack in recent years upon Thackeray as a man is that of Michael Sadleir in *Bulwer—A Panorama: Edward and Rosina* 1803-36, London, 1931. In his zeal for his hero Mr. Sadleir forgets to check the accuracy of his charges against Thackeray, and those charges are vulnerable throughout. One may or may not like Thackeray, who is patently open to criticism—but it must be more discriminating than this. For a partial answer to Sadleir's abuse see Simon Nowell Smith: 'In Defense of Thackeray,' *Nineteenth Century,* July 1933.

minor literary activity. The first of his Christmas Books was published one month before the initial number of *Vanity Fair*. Each year from then on through 1850, and again in 1855, he presented in December for the Christmas trade one of these little volumes. They were 'small beer,' as Thackeray admitted. They pretended to be nothing else, and were warmly received from the first, in spite of the fact that such satirical sketches of English society were hardly as seasonable as the hearty, chirping, plum-pudding-and-turkey stories with which Dickens was accustomed to warm the English heart at Christmas time. The first one, *Mrs. Perkins's Ball,* appearing in December 1846,[18] caught the public fancy. '*Mrs. Perkins* is a great success—the greatest I have had,' Thackeray wrote to his mother. The next year *Our Street* sold even more copies. Although the chronology of the Christmas Books takes us well beyond *The Newcomes,* it is convenient to discuss them together here, along with that Titmarshian tale which might well have been a Christmas Book but was not: *A Legend of the Rhine.* Taken together, they are the chief minor work (aside from the *Punch* articles) which Thackeray wrote during the years of *Vanity Fair, Pendennis,* and *The Newcomes;* and they illustrate, at their best, the ripening of the literary burlesque of which Thackeray had become a complete master.

Both *Mrs. Perkins's Ball* (1847) and *Our Street* (1848) are little more than galleries of portraits both pen and pencil, the letter-press serving only as a text for Thackeray's illustrations. The characterizations, satirical but jovial too, impress one as being a novelist's trial flights—a story-teller stretching his descriptive wings. Thus in the former book we get a very vivid picture of the ball; of the young Perkinses, stealing macaroons and drinking negus on the sly; of Miss Bunion, the ugly fashionable authoress; and particularly of the egregious Mulligan, the improvident Irishman who tags along with Titmarsh to the

---

18 But dated 1847. The first four of the Christmas Books, appearing in December, bore the date of the next year. *The Kickleburys* and *The Rose and the Ring* carried the dates of the years in which they actually appeared.

ball and ends by staying, after the other guests have departed, to insult his host. *Our Street* is very much the same sort of thing, with sketches of families as well as of individuals. In the history of Thackeray's literary development neither book needs much discussion.

Dr. Birch and His Young Friends (1849) is not much more significant. The narrative here is a little more coherent: Titmarsh, as assistant master in a boys' school, falls in love with a beauteous governess; he catches, too, the sour old spinster Miss Birch surreptitiously eating raspberry jam from a boy's cupboard—such is the very thin thread of narrative. Small beer again.

With *Rebecca and Rowena* (1850) Thackeray reaches an entirely different literary level. And akin to this, but earlier, was *A Legend of the Rhine,* which was written for George Cruikshank's *Table Book* in 1845 and which therefore should be looked at first. Both of these have as much of Thackeray's literary mark upon them as anything he ever wrote. Both are literary burlesques of his own unique and engaging kind.

In *A Legend of the Rhine* he takes a story of Dumas', *Othon l'Archer,* looks at it with twinkling eyes, and turns to burlesque what had been romantic. Romance, as refracted through Thackeray's spectacles, always looked a little ridiculous, not because the romantic heroes and heroines failed to be Victorian but because so often they were not quite credible. Just as Thackeray was always a little afraid of the sublime lest it turn suddenly into the sham-sublime, so he mistrusted the heroic lest it prove to be mock-heroic. Driven by a desire to see life steadily, he was suspicious of any appeal which might distort that level realism, and his effort is always to reach beyond the peripheries of romance to whatever appearance of truth might be there. This impatience with romantic trappings carries him at times into a studied realism.

A case in point:

They are passed away:—those old knights and ladies: their golden hair first changed to silver, and then the silver dropped off and disappeared for ever; their elegant legs, so slim and active in the dance, became swollen and gouty, and then, from being swollen and gouty, dwindled down to bare bone-shanks; the roses left their cheeks, and then their cheeks disappeared, and left their skulls, and then their skulls powdered into dust, and all sign of them was gone. And as it was with them, so shall it be with us. Ho, seneschal! fill me a cup with liquor! put sugar in it, good fellow—yea, and a little hot water; a very little, for my soul is sad, as I think of those days and knights of old.

The mood here is so completely Thackeray's! First the determined fixing upon rather gruesome details; then the alas! poor Yorick! tenderness for the past combined with a wilful inability to see the past too romantically; and finally the informal humorous twist at the end which fixes the mood of comfortable sadness. For here is the point: there is much of Cervantes in Thackeray. *A Legend of the Rhine* is burlesque, but a tender burlesque. Even as Thackeray makes fun of Dumas' extravagances he shows his affection for the kind of thing Dumas did. He likes to catch glimpses of the knights as they walk in the grey limbo of romance, 'shining faintly in their coats of steel, wandering by the side of long-haired ladies, with long-tailed gowns that little pages carry.' Loving them, he can afford to make merry with them, and hence the rich apparatus of anachronisms: armoured knights on horseback carrying little umbrellas in the rain, references to a notary-public, crowds of English coming to an archery tournament armed with Murray's guide-book. He revels too in all the paraphernalia of pseudo-antique expressions and in the flavour of old oaths. Thus Sir Ludwig kneels before a saint's image to recite 'a censer, an ave, and a couple of acolytes.'

Rebecca and Rowena is in the same vein, but is a better piece of work. Three years earlier in *Fraser's,* M. A. Titmarsh had presented his *Proposals for a Continuation of Ivanhoe.* In a prefatory letter to Dumas he had lamented the flood of fashionable novels and the dearth of historical romances. He proposed that when Dumas had exhausted most of his heroes at their ripe old age he should take up other people's heroes and give a continuation of *their* lives. And of all romantic novels that of which the conclusion gives the greatest dissatisfaction to Thackeray is dear old *Ivanhoe.*

I have quite too great a love for the disinherited knight, whose blood has been fired by the suns of Palestine, and whose heart has been warmed in the company of the tender and beautiful Rebecca, to suppose that he could sit down contented for life by the side of such a frigid piece of propriety as that icy, faultless, prim, niminy-piminy Rowena.

It was this story which, grown to twice its original length, made *Rebecca and Rowena.* The difference in the two versions is not merely that of length. The later version takes over ver-batim certain pages of the earlier one, develops some of the earlier hints and omits others, but there is a subtle difference in tone. Thackeray's skill has matured in the intervening three years. The atmosphere of the *Proposals* is that of broad and exaggerated comedy. Into *Rebecca and Rowena,* without losing any of the fun, Thackeray manages to insinuate a richer quality.

The story itself, as is natural with an ironic continuation, a post-marriage sequel, makes great capital of reversal. At the same time it develops hints of character implicit in Scott. To all those (and they must be legion) who feel that Scott was unfair to Rebecca, Thackeray offers a pious, stern, consumingly jealous Rowena who never forgave Rebecca her beauty, with whom Ivanhoe leads a dull and dreary life, and who, when Ivanhoe is reported dead, complacently marries the impossible Athelstane. Wamba is scourged at Rowena's order when he tries to crack a joke. Robin Hood, now earl of Huntingdon, is never known to miss church and is the strictest game proprietor in all the Riding. The Reverend Mr. Tuck is now 'as prim as a lady in his dress' and has forgotten what a quarter-staff is. The twilight of the gods has come. But finally, as promised, Rowena dies, and to the satisfaction of all happy lovers Ivanhoe hunts out Rebecca and marries her.

Here again, amid the genial digs at Scott and at heroic romance in general, is burlesque written by one as fond of the old romance of knighthood as he is eager to right the injustice done to Rebecca. As Thackeray burlesques the battles and the aspirations of the age of chivalry and points out its dullness and its cruelties, revealing as it were the reverse side of romance, he shows at the same time his love for old unhappy far-off things.

Thackeray's real attachment to historical romance is shown in his desire to write a novel about the times of Henry V. 'It would be a most magnificent performance,' he told Motley, 'and no one would read it.' The fragment that he did write, printed by his daughter as *The Knights of Borsellen,* is a most instructive study. Here is Thackeray grappling seriously with the past, with kings and knights in armour, with culverins and ribaldequins and all the romantic machinery which he elsewhere burlesqued. We know that he read widely for his background material; the story shows a careful and authentic assembling of details. And the fragment written is pathetically stiff and ineffective. This kind of story demands a sweep and gesture which Thackeray seemed unable to give it—except in burlesque. He could work comfortably in the form only when he made gentle fun of that of which he was so fond. Thus was the ironist his own greatest irony.

The Kickleburys on the Rhine, the Christmas offering for 1850, was the occasion of a stuffy sneering review in *The Times* which Thackeray, stung by its unfairness, answered in a preface, 'Thunder and Small Beer,' to the almost immediate second edition of the book. He might just as well have held silence, but he is justified in taking exception to the tone of the reviewer, who 'compares me to a scavenger who leaves a copy of verses at his door and begs for a Christmas-box,' and who damned the book as 'the rinsings of a void brain after the more important concoctions of the expired year.' The old charge of cynicism was also dragged forth and aired by the reviewer. Thackeray puts his defence upon a sound basis: he admits that his Christmas books are small beer, meant to amuse at Christmas time. And the truth is that only such an explanation goes very far towards explaining *Mrs. Perkins's Ball, Our Street,* and *Dr. Birch.* They were frankly trivia, acceptable because they did not pretend to be anything more. *Rebecca and Rowena* was quite another matter, as was *The Kickleburys* in a different fashion.

This last was a combination travel-book (this element is slight) and a not too flattering record of the manners of Englishmen abroad. They are proud and haughty, like Lady Kicklebury, or wastrels like her son, or weak sprigs of nobility like Mr. Milliken, or swaggerers like Captain Hicks. The exceptions are the lovely but innocuous Fanny Kicklebury and the shadowy Countess of Knightsbridge, whose calmness and courtesy are played off against the pride and imperiousness of the others. It is a story full of high spirits, however, and of satire sufficiently close to reality to escape caricature. The scene is crowded with life in the bustling humorous manner which Thackeray could command so dexterously.

The most pointed comment is that which enfolds Lady Kicklebury. 'If our matrons are virtuous, as they are, and it is Britain's boast,' Thackeray observed, 'permit me to say that they certainly know it.' And when Lady Kicklebury is pulling the wires to snare young Lord Talboys for her daughter Fanny, Thackeray explodes:

And you don't suppose that Lady Kicklebury fancies that she is doing anything mean, or anything wrong? Heaven bless you! she never did anything wrong in her life. She has no idea but that everything she says, and thinks, and does is right. And no doubt she never did rob a church: and was a faithful wife to Sir Thomas, and pays her tradesmen. Confound her virtue! It is that which makes her so wonderful—that brass armour in which she walks impenetrable—not knowing what pity is, or charity; crying sometimes when she is vexed, or thwarted, but laughing never; cringing, and domineering by the same natural instinct—never doubting about herself above all.

Thus the gallery of snobdom receives one more vigorous portrait.

The last of the Christmas books was *The Rose and the Ring* (1855), begun at Rome as a Twelfth Night book for his two daughters, at the time ill with scarlatina. Thackeray is never more pleasing than when he is doing something for children, who always touched his heart deeply and whom he never mentions without a flood of kindness and affection. Children loved him, too, as well they might. This 'fireside pantomime for great and small children' is in a sense beyond criticism, for it is a fairy tale perfect of its kind—a fairy tale woven with a sparkling humour. The Princes Giglio and Bulbo and the Princesses Angelica and Rosalba—to say nothing of the unforgettable Countess Gruffanuff, most delightful of villainesses, and that most impressionable of usurping kings, Valoroso XXIV—are real enough and yet not too real. Over such characters the satire slides without hurting. Thackeray's illustrations, too, are exactly right for the sort of Gilbertian world which these people inhabit.

There are few novelists of equal rank with Thackeray the survey of whose preliminary and collateral work would have taken us down as many avenues as we have surveyed thus far.[19] Yet almost all of those avenues give upon the broad highway of *Vanity Fair,* and with few novelists are we able to trace so distinctly the steps by which genius refined and cleared itself. There is little in the later novels which is not implicit by 1847. From the very first he had lingered among the booths of the Fair, lifting the curtains and surveying the occupants with a quizzical eye. Now he is ready to give them his very special attention.

[19] Fielding's career, of course, is a case in point. He was thirty-five when he wrote *Joseph Andrews* and forty-two when *Tom Jones* appeared. But with Fielding and Thackeray we shall have more to do later.

CHAPTER SIX

Vanity Fair

MOST LONDONERS who awoke on 1 January 1847 were pardonably more interested in the birth of the new year than in the birth of a new novel called *Vanity Fair*. The 'W. M. Thackeray' whose name appeared on the yellow cover of the first monthly part had published under his own name, in a literary career of over a dozen years, only two very slight pieces.[1] To be sure, the information on the title-page that W. M. Thackeray was also 'Author of "The Irish Sketch Book;" "Journey from Cornhill to Grand Cairo;" of "Jeames's Diary" and the "Snob Papers" in "Punch"' would perhaps catch the eye of his hitherto very scattered public. But the clear fact was that Thackeray, still embroiled in miscellaneous journalism for the magazines, had still to win his way as a novelist. As late as 1845 Macvey Napier, editor of the *Edinburgh Review,* had written to Abraham Hayward:

Will you tell me—confidently [sic], of course—whether you know anything of a Mr. Thackeray, about whom Longman has written me, thinking he would be a good hand for light articles? He says (Longman) that this Mr. Thackeray is one of the best writers in

---

[1] 'Captain Rook and Mr. Pigeon' and 'The Fashionable Authoress,' in Kenny Meadows's *Heads of the People* (1840). He had also given the initials 'W. M. T.' to the *Fraser's* article 'Going to See a Man Hanged.'

Punch. One requires to be very much on one's guard in engaging with mere strangers.

Thackeray needed a popular success and needed it badly. Gradually *Vanity Fair* took hold, aided not inconsiderably by an appreciative review by Hayward in the *Edinburgh Review.* Soon Jane Carlyle was writing to her husband that *Vanity Fair* was 'very good indeed, beats Dickens out of the world.' Although Thackeray told FitzGerald that the book 'does everything but pay,' both he and his publishers professed themselves satisfied with the venture. As the monthly parts continued to appear they attracted increasing attention, and long before the final number was published in July 1848 Thackeray was riding eagerly a wave of social and literary popularity. Early in 1848 Charlotte Brontë dedicated the second edition of *Jane Eyre* to the author of *Vanity Fair,* who 'comes before the great ones of society—much as the son of Imlah comes before the throned Kings of Judah and Israel.' Later she was to meet Thackeray and to discover a distressing levity in this Hebrew prophet come to puncture universal pretension. At the time, however, she saw him as 'the first social regenerator of the day.'

Thus Thackeray turned the corner. Having lingered long on the threshold of success, he began to hear himself mentioned in the same breath with Dickens and even, among the discriminating few, preferred to the latter. Popularity he found quite tolerable; indeed he never pretended that it was anything else. Characteristically, however, he wrote to his mother of his hope that he might not feel too much elation from the praise he was getting.

Much of the typical Thackerayan quality of *Vanity Fair* had been foreshadowed, as we have seen, in the earlier miscellaneous work. Thackeray had not come with one leap into artistic maturity; he was Titmarsh still. Many of the characters who crowd the pages of the novels have family resemblances to earlier creations. The view of life is essentially the same, too: clear, cool, astringent, eyeing the grotesqueries and hypocrisies and inanities of life's battles with a shrewd appraising glance. Yet Thackeray combines with the acidulous an infiltration of love and pity. Something has been added, too, since *A Shabby Genteel Story* and *The Great Hoggarty Diamond*. To discover what that is, it is necessary to examine the scope and concept of *Vanity Fair,* the technique by which he achieves his effects, and his own conception of the novelist's task. Such a survey reveals as much about Thackeray himself as it does about his work. In few instances does the study of the art teach one as much about the artist. The paradoxes and the brilliant achievements of *Vanity Fair* are the paradoxes and the brilliance of the man.

The scope of the novel grew under Thackeray's hands, and before long it broke through the frame of reference in which it had originally been conceived. It is clear, from the initial chapters, that it was planned as a series of connected comic sketches in fulfilment of the promise in the sub-title: 'Pen and Pencil Sketches of English Society.' He even, at one place, offers samples of variant methods by which he might have written the story of Jos and Becky: in the genteel, the facetious, or the romantic manner. But as Thackeray so often testified, once he had created two or three characters and had started them out on their adventures they seemed to assume an independent life and to dictate to his pen. 'I know the sound of their voices,' he said. Becky Sharp and the others refused to be confined to the range of a series of 'sketches of English society.' So the sketches grew into a novel, and by Becky, one might say, Thackeray was betrayed into felicity.

What is it that gives one, as he lays down *Vanity Fair,* such a sense of life lived? What is the special quality of Thackeray's creative imagination and how does it work itself out into character? If we can answer these questions we shall be close to his secret.

It is probable that this sense of life comes partly from the very conditions under which *Vanity Fair* was written, even from the seeming formlessness which offends critics to whom the novel is an art-form whose rules of structure are as precise as those of a symphony. Writing for publication in monthly instalments over a period of a year and a half, writing frequently against a deadline, getting his characters into situations with small idea how he was going to extricate them the next month but one—inevitably this tempted Thackeray into the quagmires of diffuseness and repetition which sometimes closed over him. It is true, however, that the novel as Thackeray wrote it was of the kind least likely to be hampered by formlessness. Thackeray was in the main line of the English novel of character. He was unlike Dickens, who felt the restriction of a plot and the necessity of ending each instalment with a climactic scene. Dickens sprayed his stories with melodramatics and mystery. Yet he is artistically best when he is working in the realm of pure humour, making almost tangibly credible the most incredible people, lavishing his best effort, for the most part, upon secondary characters, for whom the plot most happily stops while the train of fun goes by. With Thackeray the characters *are* the plot, or at least the plot springs easily and unostentatiously from the relationships in which the characters stand to one another. This casualness and steady avoidance of manipulated drama yields that lack of scenic tension which is basic to Thackeray's method.

Part of this method stems from his own awareness of his limitations as well as his instinctive recognition that 'big scenes' are the more powerful if they are few. Thus he evades the description of Jos's reunion with his father and sister after his return from India: 'For, you see, we have adroitly shut the door upon the meeting between Jos and the old father, and the poor little gentle sister inside.' On the other hand, he cannot avoid describing the scene in which Rawdon Crawley discovers Becky and Lord Steyne alone together, for it is the climax of a long episode and the turning point in Becky's fortunes. He dismisses it in two pages, however, and seems glad when it is over. For the most part he feared dropping into melodrama and preferred understatement.

There are no death-bed scenes in *Vanity Fair*. Instead, with a controlled, precise objectivity he lets a cadenced sentence carry a heavy weight of implication. The death of George Osborne is the best-known example. 'No more firing was heard at Brussels—the pursuit rolled far away. Darkness came down on the field and city: and Amelia was praying for George, who was lying on his face, dead, with a bullet through his heart.' English prose can do no better than that. Later in the story he has to describe the passing of Mr. Sedley, and once more he deals quietly with the great mystery. 'So there came one morning and sunrise, when all the world got up and set about its various works and pleasures, with the exception of old John Sedley, who was not to fight with fortune, or to hope or scheme any more: but to go and take up a quiet and utterly unknown residence in a church-yard at Brompton by the side of his old wife.' Thackeray, with the death of Little Nell ringing in his ears, was too sensitive an artist to fall into that particular kind of mawkishness. He had his own faults of sensibility, but they were not Dickens's.

In like manner, by an effective indirection and selection of significant details, he could make catastrophe serve his ironic purpose. Sir Pitt Crawley has been mortally stricken in the night but we learn of it obliquely. There is a great hurry and bustle in the house. Lights go about from window to window in the lonely desolate old Hall. A boy on a pony goes galloping off to Mudbury, to the Doctor's house there. In another hour the Reverend and Mrs. Bute Crawley, Sir Pitt's neighbours and hopeful relatives, enter the mansion by the open hall door, pass on into Sir Pitt's study, and there find Miss Horrocks, Sir Pitt's housekeeper of doubtful reputation, wildly trying the escritoires with a bunch of keys. That is all, but that is all we need.

Out of Thackeray's panoramic method, then, comes an effect which is expanding and cumulative. We seem to catch the very ebb and flow of life, which is itself, for the most part, un-dramatic. Two families, the Osbornes and the Sedleys, live in Russell Square. Becky marries Rawdon, Amelia marries George; they win some success and suffer some failure; they drift to-gether at Brussels before the battle of Waterloo; George is killed and Amelia lives on in a sort of self-conscious desperation;

Becky and Rawdon live excitingly over the gulf of financial disaster; Lord Steyne comes into the scene and precipitates a domestic cataclysm; Dobbin, the faithful lover, finally wins Amelia by virtue of an almost incredible devotion; Becky, on the outer edge of society, salvages Jos Sedley from the ruins, and when he dies lives on in pious hypocrisy—and lo, the twentieth monthly instalment is out and it is time to end the story. Novels like this live by something else than plot and their action has no need of final resolution or dénouement. They stop, but their life goes on; and when Becky is mentioned again in *The Newcomes,* it seems a perfectly proper extension into time and space of a character whom the six hundred-odd pages of *Vanity Fair* could never quite contain. It is this sense of expansion beyond the limits of the story itself which gives an impression of deep reality to Thackeray's best work.

In this respect one of his greatest triumphs is his treatment of the episode in Brussels at the time of Waterloo. Here again he shows his tact for exactly the right emphasis. We hear the steady rumble of guns in the distance, and the streams of wounded come back from the battle which means so much in the lives and the fortunes of the people we know. Of the troops and the battle itself we see nothing. Only a series of quick vignettes in Brussels which set the tempo of excitement. Jos Sedley shaving his military-style mustachios against the reported coming of the French. Jos's valet already anticipating the loot from his master's wardrobe. Mrs. Major O'Dowd preparing her warrior-husband for battle. Amelia reproaching Becky for alienating George's affections. The frenzied search for horses. Lady Bareacres, sitting in lonely aristocratic splendour in her horseless carriage under the *porte-cochère.* Through a technique almost that of the modern cinema we get an impression of excited suspense. Thackeray is of course profoundly right in his emphasis here; his people, and not Waterloo, are important for us. Against the background of battle he brings out the hopes and fears and cowardice and bravery and tenderness and primitive selfishness of the little group whose story the novel tells. Those critics who complain that Thackeray misses the chance to capitalize on the Duchess of Richmond's ball and the affair at Quatre-Bras are blind to the delicacy of an art which gives him superbly the effect he wanted, and exactly the right effect.

Collateral to Thackeray's structural plan is the whole implied breadth of what he calls Vanity Fair. It is a picture of society, a social order, in which families rather than individuals become the units. This gives a tremendous extension to the scene. Instead of concentrating on a few characters, the story traces the pattern of a whole social *milieu*. If the effect of a novel like *Wuthering Heights* is centripetal in its dramatic intensity, *Vanity Fair* is centrifugal. It tends constantly to throw off parts of itself which in turn become planets in related stellar systems.

Thackeray makes no attempt to see life whole, of course, however steadily he sees that part of it within the range of his vision. Entire social areas of Victorian London never enter the scene. But it does not get us far in criticism to say, as has been said, that he deals only in 'the Vanities of Victorian Mayfair,' or that he is merely the 'historian of the fashionable manners of the early nineteenth century.' For *Vanity Fair,* like any great work of literary art, is written simultaneously on two levels. It is in time, and for all time. It is the book to which one turns to catch the flavour of upper-middle-class London in the days just before Victoria, and the snobbishness peculiar to that particular society. But behind the hypocrisy, selfishness, and cruelty of Thackeray's scene we get an uneasy sense of social iniquities which are not unknown in modern dress. The Victorians had their own kind of snobbishness. But who would say that snobbishness has disappeared with the twentieth century?

It is of great value, in attempting to understand Thackeray, to place over against his actual achievement his own theories of the art of his own work. He had definite views concerning the function of art. 'The effect of the artist, as I take it,' he writes, 'ought to be to produce upon his hearer's mind, by his art, an effect something similar to that produced on his own by the sight of the natural object. Only music, and the best poetry, can do this.' Nevertheless this is not a bad statement of what Thackeray himself tried to do in the novel. He laboured to keep his grip on reality, but reality as it turns up in *Vanity Fair,* for instance, is reality filtered through the cool mind and warm sensibilities of W.M.T., bearing the strong imprint of that personality. One takes with a grain of salt Thackeray's contention that his characters controlled him. He liked to stand off from them, praising them or blaming them, and pretending that they led independent lives. But in the selection of just the right, significant detail, the hand of the showman is always behind the puppet.

Thackeray thought of himself as a satirist but liked to think too that 'under the mask satirical there walks about a sentimental gentleman who means not unkindly to any mortal person.'[2] Many times he gives his creed as a craftsman: 'To tell truth, hit no foul blow, give no servile puffery . . .'[3] Always he wanted to get as near the truth as he could.

I cannot help telling the truth as I view it, and describing what I see. To describe it otherwise than it seems to me would be falsehood in that calling in which it has pleased Heaven to place me; treason to that conscience which says that men are weak; that truth must be told; that faults must be owned; that pardon must be prayed for; and that love reigns supreme over all.[4]

In an important letter to Masson he holds that

The Art of Novels *is* to represent Nature: to convey as strongly as possible the sentiment of reality—in a tragedy or a poem or a lofty drama you aim at producing different emotions; the figures moving, and their words sounding, heroically: but in a drawingroom drama a coat is a coat and a poker a poker; and must be nothing else according to my ethics, not an embroidered tunic, nor a great red-hot instrument like the Pantomime weapon.

[2] Letter to Dr. John Brown, 11 May 1848. See Brown's 'Thackeray,' *North British Review,* February 1864.
[3] 'A Brother of the Press on . . . the Chances of the Literary Profession,' *Fraser's,* March 1846.
[4] Lecture: *Charity and Humour.*

Here he also took issue with Dickens who, he said, 'has in many things quite a divine genius.' But 'I quarrel with his Art in many respects: which I don't think represents Nature duly; for instance Micawber appears to me an exaggeration of a man, as his name is of a name. It is delightful and makes me laugh: but it is no more a real man than my friend Punch is: and in so far I protest against him . . .' [5]

This, then, is his concept of realism. Some of his contemporaries, although impressed by the power of *Vanity Fair,* the 'novel without a hero,' had yet a restless feeling that Thackeray 'hated excellence.' Not a few reviewers carped at the absence of 'noble' characters in the novel.[6] In spite of his reading of Victorian fiction in which pluperfect heroes walked through shoals of very decorous temptation and tribulation to reach a safe matrimonial harbour in the last chapter, Thackeray held stubbornly to the conviction that most men are not heroic and that it is the novelist's task to show men as they are. One of his critics has called him 'the apostle of mediocrity,' a charge to which Thackeray had humorously pleaded guilty as early as *The Paris Sketch Book:* 'Let us thank Heaven, my dear sir, for according to us the power to taste and appreciate the pleasures of mediocrity. I have never heard that we were great geniuses. Earthy we are, and of the earth.' Elsewhere he speaks angrily against 'success-story fiction': 'Why should we keep all our admiration for those who win in this world, as we do, sycophants that we are? When we write a novel, our great stupid imaginations can go no further than to marry the hero to a fortune at the end, and to find out that he is a lord by right. O blundering lick-spittle morality!' [7]

Thackeray, like all great humorists from Cervantes to Fielding, saw that most men are an inscrutable mixture of the heroic and

[5] *Cornhill Magazine,* June 1911, p. 797.

[6] The wheel has come full circle, and today the critics are as likely to be severe on Thackeray's 'sentimentalism' as his contemporaries were on his 'cynicism.'

[7] *Cornhill to Cairo.*

the ridiculous, the noble and the ignoble; human nature is an infinitely complex thing, and its complexity needs to be underlined and accented rather than simplified for the sentimental reader. Possessing a strong vein of scepticism, Thackeray looked about him and saw that poetic justice, outside a popular novel, is a rare commodity. He felt keenly the affectations and hypocrisies of the world about him, and saw into the cosmic irony that injustice is as likely to be victorious as justice.

But Thackeray himself was as complex as any of his non-heroes. His scepticism, born of a native melancholy and a quivering sensitiveness which are basic in his personality, was crossed not merely by a love of the ludicrous but also by a strong vein of tenderness and humanity. This is seen in his expressed theories about humour. A sentimentalist who shrank from heavily larded sentiment, he was at the same time a satirist who, as he said, 'hated Juvenal' and disapproved of Swift. His lecture on 'Charity and Humour,' delivered first in New York in 1853, is a revealing document. There he develops the idea that our humorous writers are 'gay and kind week-day preachers' who have done much in the cause of the poor, the weak, and the unhappy, besides contributing to 'our scorn for falsehood and pretension, to our righteous hatred of hypocrisy, to our education in the perception of truth, our love of honesty, our knowledge of life, and shrewd guidance through the world.' 'A literary man of a humoristic turn,' he goes on to say, and he might almost be speaking of himself, 'is pretty sure to be of a philanthropic nature, to have a great sensibility, to be easily moved to pain or pleasure, keenly to appreciate the varieties of temper of people round about him, and sympathize in their laughter, love, amusement, tears.' Then comes the return upon himself which is so characteristically his: 'I would arrogate no particular merit to literary men for the possession of this faculty of doing good which some of them enjoy. It costs a gentleman no sacrifice to be benevolent on paper; and the luxury of indulging in the most beautiful and brilliant sentiments never makes any man a penny the poorer . . .'

Humour, he concludes, is wit and love, and 'the best humour is that which contains most humanity, that which is flavoured throughout with tenderness and kindness.' Thackeray's comic spirit led him not infrequently into a wistful contemplation of the *lacrimæ rerum*. 'The best of your poems,' he wrote to Horace Smith, 'instead of making me laugh, has had the other effect . . . Do you consider this an insult? All the best comic stuff so affects me—Sancho, Falstaff, even Fielding in "Amelia."' [8]

It is clear where a literary philosophy like this is likely to emerge. Join an antiseptic hatred for cruelty and insincerity to a corollary affection for gentleness and honesty; add to that a quality of subtle observation and a nice sense for just the right amount of artistic distortion, and you have the ironist of *Vanity Fair*. Some critics, misled by Thackeray's 'I have no head above my eyes. I describe what I see,' have brought heavy guns to bear on what they call his lack of a philosophy or even of an adequate equipment of ideas. It is true that Thackeray had small talent for abstract thinking; and his generalizations are not infrequently comfortably conventional. Nevertheless he did bring the scenes of the Fair within the framework of a conception of life which had point and penetration and which conveyed a moral concept of human nature, in its large sense. His thinking is fused thought, concrete, objectified in action and speech, but to the careful reader unmistakable. It is always expressed through character and exists, in the great novels, on several planes of realism, from near-caricature to the subtlest and most acute revelation of personality.

The clue to Thackeray's art in the novels, then, is not its occasional devastating satire, or its wit, or its amiable moralizing digressions, or its occasional bursts of sentiment controlled and tempered by a quizzical humour (and nothing is more distinctive in Thackeray than his checking himself in the midst of sentiment, turning its edge back against himself). The clue to his art is the complete and covering irony through which his

[8] Centenary Biographical Edition of the *Works*, ed. Lady Ritchie, 26 vols., London, 1910-11, IX, xxviii.

view of life is filtered. It is an irony softened by a sad and wistful humanity, sharpened at times by an indignation against cant and affectation, but warmed also by the gentle melancholy that comes with the ironist's perception of the gap between man's aspiration and achievement.

Of the irony which lies in the twist of a phrase Thackeray makes judicious use in *Vanity Fair*. Thus Figs, in the Swishtail Seminary, writes a letter to his mother, 'who was fond of him, although she was a grocer's wife.' Pitt Crawley, at college, 'failed somehow, in spite of a mediocrity which ought to have insured any man a success.' After Becky, already secretly married to Rawdon Crawley, has listened to the offers of Sir Pitt Crawley, Thackeray asks, 'What well-bred young person is there in all Vanity Fair, who will not feel for a hard-working, ingenious, meritorious girl, who gets such an honorable, advantageous, provoking offer, just at the very moment when it is out of her power to accept it? I am sure our friend Becky's disappointment deserves and will command every sympathy.' And one final passage of extended ironic comment in Thackeray's best manner:

I protest it is quite shameful in the world to abuse a simple creature, as people of her time abuse Becky, and I warn the public against believing one-tenth of the stories against her. If every person is to be banished from society who runs into debt and cannot pay—if we are to be peering into everybody's private life, speculating upon their income, and cutting them if we don't approve of their expenditure— why, what a howling wilderness and intolerable dwelling Vanity Fair would be! Every man's hand would be against his neighbour in this case, my dear sir, and the benefits of civilisation would be done away with. We should be quarrelling, abusing, avoiding one another. Our houses would become caverns: and we should go in rags because we cared for nobody. Rents would go down. Parties wouldn't be given any more. All the tradesmen of the town would be bankrupt. Wine, wax-lights, comestibles, rouge, crinoline-petticoats, diamonds, wigs, Louis-Quatorze gimcracks, and old china, park hacks, and splendid high-stepping carriage horses—all the delights of life, I say—would go to the deuce, if people did but act upon their silly principles, and avoid those whom they dislike and abuse. Whereas, by a little charity and mutual forbearance, things are made to go on pleasantly enough; we may abuse a man as much as we like, and call him the greatest rascal unhanged—but do we wish to hang him therefore? No. We shake hands when we meet. If his cook is good we forgive him, and go and dine with him; and we expect he will do the same by us. Thus trade flourishes—civilisation advances: peace is kept; new dresses are wanted for new assemblies every week; and the last year's vintage of Lafitte will remunerate the honest proprietor who reared it.

With this sort of thing *Vanity Fair* is liberally and saltily sprinkled. It does not, however, bite as deeply as the less tangible but more pervasive ironic tone which marks Thackeray's whole view of the Fair and its inhabitants—a philosophic irony, a sense of the irony of things, of the contrast between the real and the apparent: that the best love is often expended upon unworthy objects; that rascals flourish while innocence suffers; that virtue is frequently dull and rascality lively; that old age and disappointment are as likely to sour character as to sweeten it. All this is explored relentlessly—never sneeringly but with consummate skill.

It is worth noting that Thackeray never expands a comic scene just for the sake of the comedy, as Dickens does. His laughter is seldom gusty and free. Comedy is refracted through the lenses of his critical spectacles and becomes a humorous commentary on life. Perhaps this was one reason that Thackeray was never as popular as Dickens. Satire the Victorians knew and liked; humorous exaggeration they delighted in; tears were a benediction to them. But irony left them uneasy. The reader never knew when his superior laughter might be stifled by a sudden sense of self-recognition. Give us blacks and whites; confound these greys! The only hope for the reader is that in the puzzling blend of light and shadow which makes up his world Thackeray may make us recognize—not ourselves, of course—but our neighbours!

Connected with this large ironic treatment is the point of view from which Thackeray tells the story. It is not as easy to identify and fix here as it is in the later novels. Sometimes he seems to be the omniscient novelist, sharing the inmost thoughts and feelings of his characters; sometimes the spectator *ab extra,* pretending to be unable to know the minds of his people, even going out of his way to validate their independent existence. These inconsistencies, however, distress the critic more than the reader. For all practical purposes, with one exception to be noted later, we know sufficiently well at any given point in the story where Thackeray stands. Moreover, he seized upon the one method which could give coherence to his sprawling, panoramic materials, and which at the same time would allow him to stand in very close personal relation to the story.

This method is of course the seemingly casual, chatty soliloquizing of a man sitting in his arm-chair by the fireside and telling a story. It is of all narrative manners the most flexible, but also the one most likely to lead into windy digression. Thackeray keeps the digressions under reasonably good control in *Vanity Fair,* although his approach allows for a variety of moods and comments. Typically it permits him to pluck the reader by the sleeve and draw him off into a corner, there to comment familiarly upon the passing scene. Thus the reader 'will please to remember that this history has "Vanity Fair" for a title, and that Vanity Fair is a very vain, wicked, foolish place, full of all sorts of humbugs and falsenesses and pretensions. And while the moralist, who is holding forth on the cover (an accurate portrait of your humble servant), professes to wear neither gown nor bands, but only the very same long-eared livery in which his congregation is arrayed: yet, look you, one is bound to speak the truth as far as one knows it, whether one mounts a cap and bells or a shovel-hat; and a deal of disagreeable matter must come out in the course of such an undertaking.' He makes clear, too, that he reserves the right, as master of the puppet-show, to come down into the crowd to look at his own creations.

And, as we bring our characters forward, I will ask leave, as a man and a brother, not only to introduce them, but occasionally to step down from the platform, and talk about them: if they are good and kindly, to love them and shake them by the hand: if they are silly, to laugh at them confidentially in the reader's sleeve: if they are wicked and heartless, to abuse them in the strongest terms which politeness admits of . . Some there are, and very successful too, mere quacks and fools: and it was to combat and expose such as those, no doubt, that Laughter was made.

Thackeray's comments usually take the form of an amused, whimsical aside, often with an ironic twist. For instance, he tells about the griefs of those in high station:

And let us, my brethren, who have not our names in the Red Book, console ourselves by thinking comfortably how miserable our betters may be, and that Damocles, who sits on satin cushions, and is served on gold plate, has an awful sword hanging over his head in the shape of a bailiff, or an hereditary disease, or a family secret, which peeps out every now and then from the embroidered arras in a ghastly manner, and will be sure to drop one day or the other in the right place.

Thackeray has come in for a good deal of abuse because of this habit. The test ought to be: does it help the story or get in the way? Does it make it seem more or less real? Does it add to or detract from our enjoyment? Thackeray's literary affinities were with the eighteenth century, and it was Fielding who introduced him to such a personal embroidery of the text. Fielding, however, usually held his comments to specific sections and Thackeray sticks them into the interstices of his story.

It seems to me that Thackeray's interpolations add, in the long run, to the illusion of reality, certainly to our enjoyment of the story. In the dramatic novel they would be quite out of place, but in the discursive novel of manners they indicate the mood of the story and intensify the mellow, introspective manner which is the very tissue of a Thackeray novel. The answer to the question hinges largely upon the quality of the mind which makes the comments. When it is Thackeray, we can usually afford to pause with him briefly. One distinction needs to be made, however. When he is adding an ironic or a whimsical note to the margin of the action he can be completely felicitous. Yet occasionally the moralist defeats the artist and upon the characters are poured the vials of Thackeray's ethical indignation. Still worse are the places where, in a fervour of sentimental adoration, Thackeray releases a flood of sensibility about some character who, on his own showing, is not worth the emotion.

Usually his comments are only parenthetical observations on the passing show, often ruefully humorous, in a vein of tempered melancholy. Thus in describing Miss Crawley's illness he admits that

Sick-bed homilies and pious reflections are, to be sure, out of place in mere story-books, and we are not going (after the fashion of some novelists of the present day) to cajole the public into a sermon, when it is only a comedy that the reader pays his money to witness. But, without preaching, the truth may surely be borne in mind, that the bustle, and triumph, and laughter, and gaiety which Vanity Fair exhibits in public, do not always pursue the performer into private life, and that the most dreary depression of spirits and dismal repentances sometimes overcome him . . . O brother wearers of motley! Are there not moments when one grows sick of grinning and tumbling, and the jingling of cap and bells? This, dear friends and companions, is my amiable object—to walk with you through the Fair, to examine the shops and the shows there; and that we should all come home after the flare, and the noise, and the gaiety, and be perfectly miserable in private.

There is much of Thackeray in that passage, not merely the self-inclusion in the parade of vanities, but also the wistful recognition of the gulf that stretches between man's outward mirth and the lonely places of his soul.

When one turns, in a consideration of *Vanity Fair,* to the characters themselves, the full richness of Thackeray's fictional world is immediately apparent. The first impression is one of great variety within a narrowly controlled range. It is not, to be sure, Dickens's variety. Thackeray lacked the fecundity and vigour which made Dickens able to crowd his pages with fan-

tastic and spectacular figures who could never have lived elsewhere but who do live there with an incredible vitality. Thackeray's world is the world of upper-middle-class London, focused
in Russell Square, with occasional excursions to Gaunt House
and the seamier side of the titular aristocracy. His fashionable
world is often that which careens constantly on the rim of social
and moral bankruptcy, where people live precariously on nothing
a year. The story moves to Brussels and Pumpernickel and
Queen's Crawley, but the sky which covers it is really that of
the particular London which Thackeray knew. As in his earlier
stories of shabby vulgarity, we meet with an uncommon number
of rogues and dupes. Behind the glitter of fashionable life and
the greedy dullness of Baker Street is fought the primal battle
between the varieties of selfishness which infest the Fair and
the humility and kindness which, in Thackeray's view, redeem
the human race from complete barbarism. There is an advance
over the early tables, however, in the broad conception here of
the intricacies of character. The worldlings are occasionally deceived by their better instincts into temporary benignity; the
innocents, patient and loving, are also sometimes self-deceived
into indulgent vanities.

At one end of the scale is that gallery of minor figures who
give to the novel such a sense of crowded, bustling life—servants,
housekeepers, landladies, tradesmen, sponging-house keepers,
decayed countesses, adventurers, ambitious mothers, military
men, clergymen. Sometimes they are merely sketched in broadly,
as types, and are given burlesque names: Lady Jane Sheepshanks,
daughter of Lord Southdown; Doctor von Glauber; Lady Bareacres; Captain Swankey; the Reverend Mr. Felix Rabbits, father
of fourteen girls; Sir Huddleston Fuddleston, the country squire;
Lord Heehaw; and the *Chargé d'Affaires* at Pumpernickel, Tape-
worm. Not infrequently, however, these background figures have
their own breezy individuality, live their little day for half a
page, and pass on.

More carefully delineated are the members of the family
groups whose interaction makes the story of *Vanity Fair:* the

Sedleys, the Osbornes, and the assorted Crawleys. Old Miss Crawley is one of Thackeray's best studies of worldly old women. Intelligent and humorous, much given to the delights of eating and drinking, she 'read Voltaire and had Rousseau by heart, and talked very lightly about divorce, and most energetically about the rights of women.' She is flattered and pampered by her predatory relatives, who show great affection—for her £70,000.

It is lamentable but true that evil is not infrequently more interesting than virtue: witness *Paradise Lost*. The hardest and cruelest of Thackeray's disreputable characters have a tenacious energy about them. Sir Pitt Crawley, for instance, is ignorant, crude, stingy, dirty, litigious, cunning, truculent, and depraved. Likewise Lord Steyne,[9] less broadly done than Sir Pitt, is a monument of cold-blooded wickedness. But he is one of Thackeray's greatest successes, a perfectly convincing combination of keen intellect and calculating profligacy. There is a sort of contemptuous sublimity about him.

Equally selfish but less in the grand style are George Osborne and Rawdon Crawley. The former is a conceited young buck, spoiled by his father, without love or loyalty. He marries Amelia Sedley in a moment of sentimental weakness. Six weeks later he is making love to Becky. He was a hero, as Thackeray says, 'among third-rate men.' Rawdon is also a rake and a dandy, given to sports and dueling. He comes under Becky's spell, marries her, loses his inheritance thereby, and gives himself over to Becky and the art of living on nothing a year. Yet there is something likable about this stupid young officer, and something pathetic in his devotion to Becky. Thackeray gives him one big moment, in the crucial encounter with Lord Steyne.

It has been said that Thackeray's men and women are static characters, that they do not develop or deteriorate in the course of the book, and that what we get is a progressive revelation or

[9] The third Marquis of Hertford was Steyne's original. Thackeray stated, however, that Sir Pitt Crawley was 'almost the only exact portrait in the whole book.' He is identified with the eccentric Lord Roble of Devonshire.

unfolding of people whose dominant tendencies are fixed when they first appear. Within certain limits this is true, as indeed it must be in the character novel of broad range, where the interest comes not so much from the inner growth or decay of the individual as from the interplay between individuals and groups. Nevertheless the sense of time lies heavy upon *Vanity Fair*. It is not merely that the action covers almost two decades, but rather that time, under Thackeray's hand, becomes a thing almost palpable. He evokes, through his retrospective, brooding manner and the wide slow movement of his narrative, a sense of hours and years slipping past. His characters, therefore, live in time as well as in space, and the mutation of character as it goes through the furnace of the years approximates, if it does not actually constitute, development. This is seen clearly in the careers of the older Osborne and of the older Sedleys. As the story opens both Sedley and Osborne are rich, proud, and successful; Sedley somewhat the more genial, Osborne harder and more ambitious. George Osborne is killed at Waterloo after his father had disinherited him and had blotted his name from the family Bible: the ungrateful boy had insisted upon marrying the dowerless Amelia, against old Osborne's express command. The word of George's death crushes Osborne, but he will not relent towards his son's wife or child. Finally he does adopt the child, only to spoil the lad as he had spoiled the father before him. Thackeray penetrates deeply into the stubborn pride of this man whose better instincts, his grief and his love for his dead son, were imprisoned by a hard selfish bitterness. Thackeray's clairvoyance into character is seen in his description of Osborne after George's death. The old man is heavily stricken. He had been waiting for George to give in and ask forgiveness, and there is no hope now. 'He strove to think that a judgment was on the boy for his disobedience,' writes Thackeray. 'And it is hard to say which pang it was that tore the proud father's heart most keenly—that his son should have gone out of the reach of his forgiveness, or that the apology which his own pride expected should have escaped him.' Thackeray continues:

Old Osborne did not speculate much on the mingled nature of his feelings, and how his instinct and his selfishness were combatting together. He firmly believed that everything he did was right . . . He was proud of his hatred as of everything else. Always to be right, always to trample forward, and never to doubt, are not these the great qualities with which dullness takes the lead in the world?

Even more strongly marked is the decline of Sedley and his wife after their bankruptcy. Old Sedley dwindles into a petty speculator, living a wretched, poverty-stricken existence while boasting pathetically of his former prestige. Thackeray is concerned here (though he leaves the implications to the reader) with showing that trouble does not always sanctify and bless. Mrs. Sedley, who in the days of her success was a cheerful, affectionate wife and mother, decays gradually into a querulous old woman, jealous of her daughter Amelia, irritatingly obtrusive in dosing Amelia's child with medicine, indulging to the end of her life in petty recriminations. The tragedy of Vanity Fair is not always sin in the grand manner, but selfish vices and meannesses, souring the temper and rotting the soul.

More of a comic creation, though distinctly a denizen of the Fair, is Jos Sedley, the Collector of Boggley Wollah. He is lazy, conceited, peevish, fat, bashful, gluttonous. His 'life of dignified otiosity,' his cowardice and his flight from Brussels, his steady decline after Becky Sharp has decided to use him as a means of rehabilitating her reputation and her fortune—these are sketched in by Thackeray with a firm, unrelenting hand.

In all this hardened crew of self-seekers there are a few for whom we feel sorry at odd moments, but none whom we respect. Thackeray needed someone who might serve as a norm of decent reference, who might engage our sympathies. So he created Dobbin and Amelia.

Dobbin, like so many people in the novel, is self-deceived, in this case by the excess of his own good qualities. He is bumbling, awkward, large-eared, with more heart than head. He is deceived initially into a raw-boned admiration of the more spectacular George, and later, by his own sentimental idealization, into a love for a woman who came to count on his fidelity as her prerogative. Amelia, in her turn, lived in the vanity of her enshrined sentimental memory of a dead husband whose coarseness and faithlessness she would not allow herself to remember. Thackeray clearly loved Dobbin, as did his readers, but he did not blink the fact that the amiable Captain has a mental as well as a physical awkwardness. In spite of this, Dobbin is clearly too good for Amelia. Although Thackeray early set the scene which pointed towards an ultimate union between Dobbin and Amelia, there is a story to the effect that he meant *not* to marry them to each other, and was urged into it by solicitous friends. That may be true, but Thackeray barbed that conventional happy ending with some of the sharpest ironic darts in his bag of tricks. He spared no pains to show that Dobbin, devoted as he had been, came to see Amelia as she really was before he married her. He had quivered over her sufferings for fifteen years, and when he finally won her he did not find her much worth the winning. Thackeray ends the novel on this ultimate irony. 'Ah! *Vanitas Vanitatum!*' Which of us is happy in the world? Which of us has his desire? or, having it, is satisfied?'

The case of Amelia is of great critical importance, for it carries us into the heart of the contradiction which sometimes disturbed the balance of Thackeray's art. She came near being the technical heroine of the novel without a hero. Nevertheless from the very first Thackeray meant her to be at least an obbligato to the other symphonic vanities.

You are quite right [he told his mother] about 'Vanity Fair' and Amelia being selfish. It is mentioned in this very number. My object is not to make a perfect character, or anything like it. Don't you see how odious all the people are in the book (with the exception of Dobbin), behind all of which there is a dark moral, I hope.

What I want is to make a set of people living without God in the world (only that is a cant phrase), greedy, pompous men, perfectly self-satisfied for the most part, and at ease about their superior virtue. Dobbin and poor Briggs are the only two people with real humility as yet. Amelia's is to come when her scoundrel of a husband is well dead with a ball in his odious bowels, when she has had sufferings, a child, and a religion. But she has at present a quality above most people, whizz—Love—by which she shall be saved . . .[10]

But as it worked out, her particular variety of love was not enough to save her; for her love-in-grief itself deceived her. In much the same mood Thackeray declares his purpose in *Vanity Fair* in a letter written 3 September 1848 to Robert Bell, who had reviewed the novel intelligently in *Fraser's*.

If I had put in more fresh air as you call it my object would have been defeated— It is to indicate, in cheerful terms, that we are for the most part an abominably foolish and selfish people, 'desperately wicked' and all eager after vanities. Everybody is you see in that book, —for instance if I had made Amelia a higher order of woman there would have been no vanity in Dobbin's falling in love with her, whereas the impression at present is that he has married a silly little thing and in fact has found out his error rather a sweet and tender one however, *quia multum amavit*. I want to leave everybody dissatisfied and unhappy at the end of the story—we ought all to be with our own and all other stories. Good God don't I see (in that may-be cracked and warped looking glass in which I am always looking) my own weaknesses wickednesses lusts follies shortcomings? In company let us hope with better qualities about which we will pretermit discourse. We must lift up our voices about these and howl to a congregation of fools: so much at least has been my endeavour . . .[11]

It is a strange person who could read 'cynic' into such an outburst. Here was a man of excessive sensitiveness, hungering after love and dismayed, not by the thing itself, but by its manifest imperfections in this world.

A later passage in the same letter shows, curiously enough, that Thackeray considered his novel a 'humorous' work.

Pathos I hold should be very occasional indeed in humorous works and indicated rather than expressed, or expressed very rarely. In the passage where Amelia is represented as trying to separate herself

---

[10] *Works,* I, xliv.   [11] *The Times,* 17 July 1911.

from the boy— She goes upstairs and leaves him with his aunt 'as that poor Lady Jane Grey tried the axe that was to separate her slender life'— I say that is a fine image whoever wrote it (& I came on it quite by surprize in a review the other day) that is greatly pathetic I think: it leaves you to make your own sad pictures— We shouldn't do much more than that I think in comic books— In a story written in the pathetic key it would be different & then the comedy perhaps should be occasional . . .

Amelia, then, both in Thackeray's original conception of her character and in her actions throughout the novel, is something less than the ideal of femininity which some hasty persons assume all Victorians believed in. Just here, however, comes the paradox. It was Taine who first pointed out the discrepancy between what Amelia does and what Thackeray says about her in the novel. Thackeray's pity for her was as strong as his recognition of her weakness and vanity. Thus he will follow the description of some selfishly sentimental act of Amelia's (he admits freely that she inevitably has 'recourse to the waterworks') with an almost maudlin release of tenderness, hovering and fluttering over 'our poor little creature and harmless lost wanderer,' 'our tender little parasite,' apostrophizing her as 'thou poor panting soul.'

The conflict in Thackeray seems to have been between a deeply set worship of womanhood as an ideal, and a critical inability to see things except as they are. All things gentle and soft and honourable appealed to him; yet he knew that lovely woman can stoop to the most banal follies. And so he defends Amelia against herself and writes in the margin comments with which to soften the stern reality of his reporting. Amelia is patently not worth the sentiment he lavishes on her. This inconsistency, a conflict of head and heart, extends, as we shall see, into the other novels; it emerges, too, from his letters. He wrote to his mother that candid evaluation of Amelia's selfishness—but in a letter to Mrs. Brookfield he says that Amelia is a composite of his mother, Mrs. Brookfield, and his 'poor wife.' Elsewhere he declares that he likes clever women (in spite of the fact that the heroines of Shakespeare [!] and Scott are 'humble, flattering, and wheedling'); that the world has made a set against clever women, and they haven't had fair play.[12] But again he writes to Mrs. Brookfield: 'I am afraid I don't respect your sex enough, though. Yes I do, when they are occupied with loving and sentiment rather than with other business of life.' 'What do men know,' he laments in *Vanity Fair,* 'about women's martyrdoms? We should go mad had we to endure the hundredth part of those daily pains which are meekly borne by many women. Ceaseless slavery meeting with no reward; constant gentleness and kindness met by cruelty as constant,' etc., etc.

One need not disbelieve in feminine worth to say that Thackeray does not do the sex justice when he falls into this vein. There were at least three women of his day, too, who disagreed with him. Charlotte Brontë said that he was quite unjust to women. Mrs. Jameson declared: 'No woman resents his Rebecca . . . but every woman resents the selfish inane Amelia.' And Mrs. Brookfield herself wrote to Harry Hallam in 1847:

I wish he had made Amelia more exciting especially as the remark is he has thought of me in her character . . . You know he told William that though Amelia was not a copy of me he should not have conceived the character if he had not known me—and though she has the right amount of antiphlegm and affectionateness she is really an uncommonly dull and selfish character . . .[13]

The interesting point is not merely that there was a conflict within Thackeray between an innate scepticism and a strong tendency to idealize a certain kind of womanhood, or that such a conflict sometimes weakened his grasp of characterization. The interesting point is that, however ecstatic the commentary may be, tempering the wind to the shorn lamb, the sinews of the narrative itself are unflinchingly firm.

Becky Sharp is a female of quite another colour and one of

---

[12] *Sketches and Travels in London:* 'A Word About Dinners.'
[13] Charles and Frances Brookfield: *Mrs. Brookfield and her Circle,* London, 1908 ed., pp. 247-8.

Thackeray's unequivocal triumphs. From the time she throws the copy of Johnson's Dictionary out of the carriage in the direction of Miss Pinkerton, she fixes the reader with her glittering green eye, and he remains under her spell. Not that he is unable to see that she is unprincipled, selfish, cunning, and cynical. She is all of that; but those are not esoteric qualities in Vanity Fair. Other women there, equally cunning and selfish, are also malicious and savagely envious. The mark of Becky's cool intellectuality and her common sense is that she can afford to be good-natured and charitable when there is nothing to lose. We admire her poise, her buoyancy, her tact. What in other people would seem a cold self-seeking appears in her a sort of inverted wisdom, selfishness apotheosized. Were it not that she employs her wits against people even less admirable than herself we might be shocked by our absence of moral qualms concerning her. As it is, there is a kind of wild justice in her breezy assault upon the citadels of the stupid and the mighty. There is something in her reminiscent of the heroine of a Restoration comedy: the same quick intellect, the same amused tolerance, the same brisk amorality, the same conquest of wit over dullness. Quite simply and literally she walks away with the story.

For Thackeray she became, whether he would or no, the dominating character of the book, giving a unity to its heterogeneous action and pulling into one framework its several families. More than that, she acts as a catalytic agent upon the others. Jos, Sir Pitt, George, Rawdon, Steyne—all capitulate, in their various ways, to her charm. She releases in them qualities which are not always pleasant but which are very revealing, and so she becomes the touchstone for their characters. Thackeray himself became fond of her. Occasionally he would lash himself into a brief rage and reveal the seamier side of her egoism; he could even at the end, most incredibly, hint that she murdered Jos. Such is the implication of his 'Becky's second appearance in the character of Clytemnestra' plate; he never dared to accuse her in the text of the story. Usually he displays her to the dry light of a satisfying objectivity. She was not malicious. When Mr. Wagg was led on by the ladies to bait her, she 'lighted up in an instant, parried and reposted with a home thrust, which made Wagg's face tingle with shame; then she returned to her soup with the most perfect calm and a quiet smile on her face.' Afterwards 'Becky was always good to him, always amused, never angry.' In the more successful period of her career she patronized Amelia, but when she saw how the good Dobbin (whom she respected, by the way) was being held off by the young widow's sentimental idolization of the worthless dead husband, she sent Amelia to his arms by telling her, at last, of George's treachery at Brussels. Becky was without rancour, just as she was incapable of deep affection for any one but herself.

If there is an agent of poetic justice in *Vanity Fair* it is this same shrewd little governess. We feel it when she laughs in the face of Lady Bareacres, who is waiting for the carriage horses that do not come; and when she extorts from Jos a huge sum of money for her own horses. We like her sense of amiable superiority to her husband: 'If he had but a little more brains,' she thought to herself, 'I might make something of him.' But she never let him perceive the opinion she had of him. She 'listened with indefatigable complacency to his stories of the table and the mess, laughed at all his jokes.' When he leaves for Waterloo she compares him with George Osborne: ' "My poor good Rawdon is worth two of this creature." And then she fell to thinking what she should do if—if anything happened to poor good Rawdon, and what a great piece of luck it was that he had left his horses behind.' When she had said good-bye to him she had 'wisely determined not to give way to unavailing sentimentality.' It is quite typical of this heroine that her point of greatest admiration for her husband should come when, having discovered her alone with Lord Steyne, he is striking the Peer in the face. It meant the collapse of Becky's fortunes, but she had a detached power of viewing life judicially as it swept by her.

The audacity and wit of Thackeray's 'hardened little reprobate' are no less sparkling in her decline than in her success. She is as quick-witted and self-possessed in her little room under the roof of the Elephant Hotel when she is telling her melodramatic tale of woe to the frightened Jos as she had been when she was receiving the flattery of titled admirers in the house of Curzon Street. She is indomitable to the very end.

Thackeray points up the last irony on the Fair in his account of her twilight career, when she 'hangs about Bath and Cheltenham, where a very strong party of excellent people consider her to be a most injured woman. She has her enemies. Who has not? Her life is her answer to them. She busies herself in works of piety. She goes to church, and never without a footman. Her name is in all the Charity Lists. The destitute Orange-girl, the Neglected Washerwoman; the Distressed Muffin-man, find in her a fast and generous friend.'

Becky an angel of light! Somehow, one feels, she will at last rehabilitate herself and go on to further conquests in a subsequent edition. Certainly a person of her incontestable vitality is hard to hold within the yellow covers of one Victorian novel.

Becky's downward career raises the question of Thackeray's treatment of those shadow-line problems of sexual morality which the nineteenth-century novel could not entirely face and which it could not entirely avoid.

There has been a tremendous amount of tub-thumping by modern Emancipators of Literature on the prudery of the Victorians. Some of the complaints against the evasions and the respectable hypocrisies of our great-grandfathers are justifiable, to be sure, on artistic grounds. The Victorians did avert their gaze from part of human life, and if their fictional characters seem sometimes two-dimensional it is because they are occasionally placed in situations calling for a display of passions which their creators deny them. Hence the occasional frustrate ghostliness of men and women obviously created with arms and legs like other people, over whose spiritual and emotional crises the author draws the seemly veil of silence, or worse, of misstatement. In this respect Thackeray, who was of no mind to be a martyr on the altar of Victorian Respectability, conformed to the contemporary *mores*. One wonders if, except in a few important instances, the fault was as debilitating to his art as some critics would have it.

Nevertheless Thackeray, nurtured though he was on eighteenth-century gusto and the fresh vulgar breezes of *Tom Jones,* did conform, sometimes with obvious sincerity, sometimes with grim reluctance. It is significant that his eulogies of contemporary literary decorum come when he is praising the piety of others, like Dickens or Mr. Punch, and his annoyance at restriction when he is deep in the shaping of one of his own creations. No more than his fellow novelists did he build the moral atmosphere in which they all lived and wrote, but like his fellows he was shaped by it and responsible to it. He felt deeply the novelist's obligation to the public in an age which tested its literature first by its fitness to be read aloud in the home circle. When Dickens chose 'Household Words' as the title of his weekly periodical he was nailing aloft the banner of respectability which was the cardinal creed of the Victorian middle classes. And the middle classes, incidentally, were buying the books.

Thackeray was by no means a Victorian unawares. He was a Victorian with roots in the eighteenth century, flowering in an age which seemed often to wish, with Sir Thomas Browne, that men could propagate like trees. That he flowered gracefully, yet with as little intellectual compromise as possible, is to the credit of both his honesty and his good sense. Yet of Thackeray, as of no other of his contemporaries, one can say that he was born out of his time. His impulse was always to drive behind the peripheries of the social scene. He loved Pepys and Montaigne and Fielding and what he called the 'wonderful atrocious vulgarity' of *Peregrine Pickle.* He laments 'the refinements of society which will not allow us to call things by their right names.' [14] Again he says, 'Fielding's men and Hogarth's are

14 Review of *Jack Sheppard, Fraser's,* February 1840.

Dickens's and Cruikshank's, drawn with 10 times more skill and force, only the latter humorists dare not talk of what the elder discussed honestly.' [15]

Yet in spite of his recognition that contemporary restrictions hampered art, Thackeray suffered here from another of his self-contradictions—or perhaps a wilful effort to set his own artistic conscience at peace. In the same review in which he laments the novelist's lack of freedom he gives a half-hearted approval of Victorian squeamishness and wryly admits that perhaps it is good 'to pretend to the virtue of chastity even though we do not possess it,' for 'the very restraint which the hypocrisy lays on a man is not unapt, in some instances, to profit him.'

One does not feel, however, as in the case of some Victorian writers, that Thackeray suffers an automatic anesthesia when confronted with a sex situation. There is not much question about Becky's guilt in the Steyne affair, or about her promiscuous adventuring when she was wandering over the Continent, living by her wits. Here Thackeray, writing within the *convenances* of his time, had to slide round this portion of her history. But he makes very clear what the drift of that story would have been.

We must pass over a part of Mrs. Rebecca Crawley's biography with that lightness and delicacy which the world demands—the moral world, that has, perhaps, no particular objection to vice, but an insuperable repugnance to hearing vice called by its proper name. There are things we do and know perfectly well in Vanity Fair, though we never speak of them: as the Ahrimanians worship the devil, but don't mention him: and a polite public will no more bear to read an authentic description of vice than a truly-refined English or American female will permit the word breeches to be pronounced in her chaste hearing. And yet, Madam, both are walking the world before our faces every day, without much shocking us. If you were to blush every time they went by, what complexions you would have! It is only when their naughty names are called out that your modesty has any occasion to show alarm or sense of outrage, and

[15] Review of Fielding's *Works, The Times,* 2 September 1840.

it has been the wish of the present writer, all through this story, deferentially to submit to the fashion at present prevailing, and only to hint at the existence of wickedness in a light, easy, and agreeable manner, so that nobody's fine feelings may be offended. I defy anyone to say that our Becky, who has certainly some vices, has not been presented to the public in a perfectly genteel and inoffensive manner. In describing this siren, singing and smiling, coaxing and cajoling, the author, with modest pride, asks his readers all round, has he once forgotten the laws of politeness, and showed the monster's hideous tail above water? No! . . . And so, when Becky is out of the way, be sure that she is not particularly well employed, and that the less that is said about her doings is in fact the better.

If we were to give a full account of her proceedings during a couple of years that followed after the Curzon Street catastrophe, there might be some reason for people to say this book was improper . . . And I am inclined to think that there was a period in Mrs. Becky's life, when she was seized, not by remorse, but by a kind of despair, and absolutely neglected her person, and did not even care for her reputation.

This may not be quite plain dealing by present-day standards, but it was pretty good for 1848, and it is almost all we need to go by.

With *Vanity Fair* Thackeray came into the full maturity of his creative power. Certain riper qualities will be apparent in the later novels, but none more brilliant. *Vanity Fair* is one of the great landmarks in the broad stream of the English novel.

CHAPTER SEVEN

Pendennis

ALMOST as soon as the last monthly part of *Vanity Fair* was in the hands of the booksellers Thackeray began work on his new novel, writing the first pages during the course of a short vacation-trip down the Rhine. *Vanity Fair* had brought him such recognition and acclaim that he was now by way of being a social lion. His real humility did not keep him from relishing the tributes he received, and he wrote to Lady Blessington that he had 'reeled from dinner party to dinner party, wallowed in turtle, and swum in claret and champagne.' Thackeray was always gregarious. He loved the dinner-table candle-light of his friends, the bustling club life which he knew so well, the whole hum of the busy London world. Few people have combined so comfortably a liking for the social life and a devastating ability to see the essential shallowness of much which passes for social refinement. Indeed his dominant critical trait as a novelist is his ability to stand outside the social scene and view it with a calm objectivity, quite without rancour, maintaining a delicate poise which permitted an infiltration of pity and an analgesic humour.

Nevertheless those were melancholy days for him. Since his wife's insanity Thackeray had been much at sea emotionally. It is not improbable that clubdom became a sort of anodyne for him during those years when his children were much of the time with their grandmother in Paris and he was living in lodgings, writing desperately that he might leave a competency for the daughters whom he loved with a deep devotion. That he was restless; that he would work feverishly for short spells, after which he would endure a period of miserable exhaustion; that his novels should show clear traces of the sadness which was his daily companion—all this is understandable in Thackeray, whose vein of remote melancholy was just as native to him as were his other moods of buoyant high spirits. He was thankful for friends and for success, but he needed love and home and family. He had felt calamity and grief, and his sensitive spirit was driven back upon itself. He lived in society, and he knew loneliness. In his letters that loneliness marches side by side with the more dominant gusto, affection, and humour. It gets into the novels in the wistful comments and asides, spoken frequently through the humorous mask.

How lonely we are in the world, [he says in *Pendennis*] how selfish and secret, everybody! You and your wife have pressed the same pillow for forty years and fancy yourselves united.—Psha, does she cry out when you have the gout, or do you lie awake when she has the toothache? . . . and, as for your wife—O philosophic reader, answer and say,—Do you tell *her* all? Ah, sir—a distinct universe walks about under your hat and under mine—all things in nature are different to each—the woman we look at has not the same features, the dish we eat from has not the same taste to the one and the other—you and I are but a pair of infinite isolations, with some fellow islands a little more or less near to us.

No honest interpretation of Thackeray's literary career can ignore another influence which meant more to Thackeray during these years than any other one thing, giving him courage and at the same time disturbing him with a haunting disquiet. It is no longer a literary secret that Thackeray fell in love with the wife of his best friend, William Brookfield, and she with him. It was common gossip in London after Thackeray's death, and in the absence of specific information about the affair gossip drew, as gossip always does, the worst implications: that

Jane Brookfield was Thackeray's mistress. It is unfortunate that until now the letters which vindicate Thackeray's integrity in this affair have not been published.[1] They are the immediate record of an exalting and a shattering experience—the words of a man lonely and hungry for affection, in turn angry at Brookfield's lack of understanding of his wife and remorseful for his own seeming treachery to his best friend. He is alternately blessed by the benediction of a strangely idealized passion and plunged into despair by the realization of the only terms upon which such a hopeless affair could end. The letters show Thackeray's weakness as well as his strength, but they help to bring his personality into focus as nothing else can. Thackeray seemed to need, even more than most men, feminine sympathy. As he put it later: 'I can't live without the tenderness of some woman.'

In 1841 William Henry Brookfield, his old friend of Cambridge days, married Jane Octavia Elton, daughter of Charles Elton of Clevedon Court, and brought her to London. A short time later Brookfield, obviously the new and untutored husband, brought Thackeray home unexpectedly to dinner. Thackeray, beaming and jovial, quickly put the embarrassed bride at ease. Thus began the friendship which was to continue with increasing intimacy for ten years.

Brookfield had made a brilliant record at Cambridge and was becoming a fashionable London preacher. He was witty and engaging in manner, knew everybody worth knowing; and the Brookfields soon became part of a circle in which Thackeray also moved—that of Hallam (Henry Hallam, the historian, was Mrs. Brookfield's uncle), Tennyson, Lady Ashburton, the Carlyles, Spedding, and Kinglake. Brookfield liked to think of himself as something of a Bohemian; Kinglake said of him: 'Ever generous, indulgent, large-minded, Brookfield was never in the least demoralised by taking Holy Orders.' If at this distance Brookfield seems something of a flyweight it is perhaps by contrast to his beautiful and intelligent wife, whom he de-

[1] Certain letters of Thackeray's to Mrs. Brookfield, and a series to his friends Kate Perry and Mrs. Elliot.

lighted in displaying to his friends and to whose charm Thackeray was not the only one to pay tribute. She was ten years younger than Thackeray, sweet and feminine, but with a good wit and a keen understanding of people and events. She met the lonely author with just the blend of sympathy, understanding, and common-sense criticism necessary to captivate him completely. He in turn discovered depths in her nature to which her brisk and possessive husband was blind.

Not until about 1847, when the Brookfields were established in Jermyn Street, did Thackeray become a constant visitor at the house. By that time he had acquired for Jane the feeling of an elder brother. He was always dropping in to see her, bringing portions of his current novel as he finished them, and when away from her, writing long letters about his friends and books and travels, letters packed with humour and gentleness, the unpretentious and spontaneous expression of his own rich personality. There is much of the stuff of everyday living in these letters, but the later ones are shot through with an obbligato of vibrant devotion, as if Thackeray were maintaining at some cost the rather delicate poise of his ecstasy and were fearful lest the dream should be broken.

And broken it was, when, in September 1851, the most amiable of husbands at last became impatient at Thackeray's claim upon his wife's time and attention. Thackeray's fierce distress, his discovery in the crisis that his feelings had gone further than even he himself had surmised, and the final choice of the only path possible for people of their integrity are recorded in the series of letters to Kate Perry and Mrs. Elliot, both of whom were friends of the Brookfields as well as of Thackeray. Brookfield was angry; Thackeray was wretched. Finally came a sort of conciliation, after which he and the Brookfields met again, but never on terms of intimacy. He did write Mrs. Brookfield a few chatty letters from the States during his first lecture tour there in 1852-3, but again it was to Kate Perry that he revealed the melancholy which was haunting him in the midst of his successful tour. Gradually the bitterness of his grief wore away.

During his second trip to America he wrote to Kate Perry on St. Valentine's Day, 1855:

As I go this journey, I remember other thoughts scattered along the journey 3 years ago: and griefs which used to make me wild and fierce, and which are now sweet and bearable. We get out of the stormy region of longing passion unfulfilled—we don't love any the less—please God— Let the young folks step in and play the game of tears and hearts. We have played our game: and we have lost. And at 45 we smoke our pipes and clear the drawing room for the sports of the young ones.

But during the months that he was writing *Pendennis,* Jane Brookfield was his encouragement and his inspiration. In May 1849, he wrote to her: 'I have written such a stupid number of *Pendennis* in consequence of not seeing you, that I shall be ruined if you are to stay away much longer.'

The first number of *Pendennis* appeared in November 1848, and the last in December 1850.[2] Publication was interrupted for three months during the latter part of 1849 when Thackeray suffered an illness which threatened for a time to bring the adventures of *Pendennis* to a sudden and irrevocable end. His friends had been increasingly worried about his health, and his letters to Mrs. Brookfield had been sprinkled with despondent speculations. In July 1849 he had written:

I don't see that living is such a benefit, and could find it in my heart pretty readily to have an end of it,— After wasting a good deal of opportunities and time and desires in vanitarianism. What makes one so blasé and tired I wonder at 38? Is it pain or pleasure? Present solitude or too much company before? both very likely. You see I am here as yesterday, gloomy again, and thrumming on the old egotistical string.

When the fever struck him in September he composed himself quietly for what seemed to him the probable end, his only worry being that of leaving his children unprotected. Gradually, however, he grew better. A year later he dedicated the first edition

[2] A double number, consisting of Parts 23 and 24.

of *Pendennis* to his physician, Dr. John Elliotson, to whose skill
he attributed his recovery.

In December Thackeray's old friend Edward FitzGerald, who
at first had liked *Pendennis* greatly, wrote: 'I saw poor old
Thackeray in London: getting very slowly better of a bilious
fever that had almost killed him . . . People in general thought
Pendennis got dull as it went on; and I confess I thought so
too: he would do well to take the opportunity of his illness to
discontinue it altogether. He told me last June he himself was
tired of it: must not his readers naturally tire too?' Thackeray
himself was not too happy about the story; as late as the summer of 1850 he wrote to Mrs. Brookfield that No. 19 was 'stupid,
rickety, and of feeble intellect, I fear.' But he always created
in travail, and the monthly numbers continued to appear. In
November he wrote to his mother: 'Having completed my
story this day and wrote *Finis,* I am very tired, weary, and sol-
emn-minded.'

Early in 1850 an event occurred which is of interest both for
the light it throws on Thackeray and for its implications concerning the attitude of the mid-nineteenth-century literary world
towards itself. Those engaged in the art of letters were a peculiarly self-conscious family. For one thing, they were likely to
think of themselves as Moral Forces, as Custodians of the Ideal.
Dickens became aware of himself as a sort of national institu-
tion; and Thackeray spoke frequently of the novelist's solemn
responsibility to the public. Along with this ran, in many instances, a curious uncertainty about the social status of the literary man in a shifting society. Literature no longer lived on
patronage, yet writers were still on the defensive, or felt that
they should be, concerning the dignity of their profession. Thackeray kept repeating that literary men ought not to be in the least
querulous about their position any more, that the social esti-
mation of the man of letters was as good as it deserved to be.
Yet if he dared to parody any of his fellow novelists or if, as
in *Pendennis,* he showed that some publishers were not very
elegant rivals and that some novelists and editors were improvi-

dent and parasitical, he was accused of fouling his own nest and vilifying his profession. He shows Captain Shandon editing the *Pall Mall Gazette* from Fleet Prison—kind, sweet-tempered, witty, learned, but weak and dissipated. For this the *Morning Chronicle* and the *Examiner* (in an article by John Forster, later Dickens's biographer) accused Thackeray of 'fostering a baneful prejudice' against literary men, for 'stooping to flatter' this prejudice in the public mind, and 'condescending to caricature (as is too often his habit) his literary fellow-labourers in order to pay court to the non-literary class.' In a letter to the *Chronicle*[3] called 'The Dignity of Literature,' Thackeray defended himself against the charge, and his defense is also a clear statement of his belief in literary candor.

That I have a prejudice against running into debt [he wrote], and drunkenness and disorderly life, and against quackery and falsehood in my profession, I own; and that I like to have a laugh at those pretenders in it who write confidential news about fashion and politics for provincial *gobemouches;* but I am not aware of feeling any malice in describing this weakness, or of doing anything wrong in exposing the former vices . . . The only moral that I, as a writer, wished to hint in the descriptions against which you protest, was, that it was the duty of a literary man, as well as any other, to practise regularity and sobriety, to love his family, and to pay his tradesmen . . . If it be a caricature, it is the result of a natural perversity of vision, not of an artful desire to mislead; but my attempt was to tell the truth, and I meant to tell it not unkindly. I have seen the bookseller whom Bludyer robbed of his books; I have carried money, and from a noble brother man-of-letters, to some one not unlike Shandon in prison, and have watched the beautiful devotion of his wife in that dreary place. Why are these things not to be described, if they illustrate, as they appear to me to do, that strange and awful struggle of good and wrong which takes place in our hearts and in the world? . . . And, instead of accusing the public of persecuting and disparaging us as a class, it seems to me that men of letters had best silently assume that they are as good as any other gentlemen; nor raise piteous controversies upon a question which

[3] Published in the *Chronicle,* 12 January 1850.

all people of sense must take as settled . . . If I begin straightway with a protest of 'Sir, I am a literary man, but I would have you to know that I am as good as you,' which of us is it that questions the dignity of the literary profession—my neighbour, who would like to eat his soup in quiet, or the man of letters who commences the argument? . . . And if every character in a story is to represent a class, not an individual—if every bad figure is to have its obliged contrast of a good one, and a balance of vice and virtue is to be struck—novels, I think, would become impossible, as they would be intolerably stupid and unnatural; and there would be a lamentable end of writers and readers of such compositions.

The episode is a slight one in Thackeray's career. It illuminates, however, his strong common sense as well as the trap which awaited the satiric author who disturbed the equilibrium of a professional class hungry for honours yet strangely unsure of its social position.

Pendennis, though not Thackeray's best novel, is in some ways his most intimate revelation of himself. It, rather than *Vanity Fair,* reads like a first novel, for it is confessedly autobiographical. Like all such stories it furnishes fruitful but dangerous material for the biographer, for Arthur Pendennis is both more and less than Thackeray; no one can be sure just where the fictional and the creative is superimposed upon the reminiscent. Nevertheless the career of young Pen does parallel in its broad outlines the career of the young Thackeray. 'Fairoaks' is clearly Larkbeare, the house of Thackeray's mother and stepfather; 'Clavering St. Mary' is the near-by small town of Ottery St. Mary; 'Chatteris' is Exeter. Pen in school at Grey Friars under the Doctor who delights in telling him that 'your idleness is incorrigible, and your stupidity beyond example. You are a disgrace to the school, and to your family, and I have no doubt will prove so in after life to your country,' is Thackeray under the Doctor Russell who made his life miserable at Charterhouse. It is not improbable that Thackeray, like Pen when he met the actress Fotheringay, knew the fever of first love and like

Pen 'created the divinity which he loved.' Pen at Oxbridge is Thackeray at Cambridge, and Thackeray, like Pen, had announced to his mother that he proposed to bury himself in Greek and Roman literature—with about the same result in each instance. Both were somewhat wasteful and given to idleness; both had unfortunate gambling experiences; both published verses in the rural newspapers; both entered Inns of Court and read briefly for the bar; both deserted jurisprudence for journalism, writing witty, slashing reviews. Pen's easy-going, convivial life in London amid all sorts of places and men must have paralleled Thackeray's own early career. Both wrote fiction. As *Pendennis* progresses, the careers of author and hero grow farther apart, but some of Thackeray's acquaintances continue to appear under other names. Captain Shandon was William Maginn, the first editor of *Fraser's Magazine*. Foker was Andrew Archdeckne, a member of the Garrick Club who used to greet the author with 'Hello, Thack my boy!' And Thackeray's own mother was the prototype of Helen Pendennis.[4] Certainly Mrs. Carmichael-Smyth was, in her later days especially, as deeply devout and pious as was Helen; one wonders, however, if she would have been greatly pleased by the portrait.

Even more autobiographically important than the specific parallels in the lives of Pendennis and Thackeray is the general retrospective tone which creates the atmosphere of the story. Thackeray says in the preface that he began with a very precise and 'exciting' plan full of escapes, battles, and murders, which he laid aside because he found he lacked experience of his subject. Moreover: 'To describe a real rascal, you must make him so horrible that he would be too hideous to show; and unless the painter paints him fairly, I hold he has no right to show him at all.' Certainly nothing could be more unlike his original Eugène Sue plan than this leisurely, expansive, loosely woven history of the 'fortunes and misfortunes' of an average sensual

[4] So Thackeray once told an American friend. See Maunsell B. Field: *Memories of Many Men*, New York, 1874. Also J. G. Wilson: *Thackeray in the United States*. 2 vols., New York, 1904, I, 229.

young Englishman whose greatest enemy, as the title-page implies and as Thackeray makes clear, was himself. As the novel continues, the plot does rear its head more noticeably. The relation to the other characters of the pseudo-mysterious Colonel Altamont, for example, who turns out to be Lady Clavering's supposedly dead first husband, has the material if not the treatment of melodrama. From the reader's point of view, however, the mystery is never taken very seriously, and for the most part the story is exactly what the title-page calls it, a 'history' in the eighteenth-century understanding of the word—a biography, until marriage in this case, of a young man. Hence *Pendennis,* diverse and episodic as its materials are, has its own sufficient unity. All of the main figures on its broad canvas impinge upon the career of Pendennis himself. Its easy chronological flow made it possible for Thackeray to plan it without artistic danger from month to month, introducing new characters and inventing new situations from such incidental materials as might crop up in the life of any one. Thackeray did not always avoid the dangers of diffuseness and redundancy; *Pendennis* could have been shortened to its artistic improvement. Yet the redundancies are the redundancies of life itself, and here again Thackeray gains that cumulative effect which informs his best novels. Although the story bores us at times, at the end we come away with the feeling that we have lived with these people and that we know them as we know our own friends. Thackeray keeps firm hold of the one thread which could lead him successfully through such a labyrinth of a thousand pages: the sustained projection of character.

The warm imaginative fusion of fiction and personal reminiscence in *Pendennis* is helped by Thackeray's chatty, confidential manner of telling the story, by his bending the narrative into the curves of his own moods. That he knew what he was trying to do he makes clear in the preface.

If this kind of composition, of which the two years' product is now laid before the public, fail in art, as it constantly does and must, it at least has the advantage of a certain truth and honesty, which a work more elaborate might lose . . . It is a sort of confidential talk between writer and reader, which must often be dull, must often flag. In the course of his volubility, the perpetual speaker must of necessity lay bare his own weaknesses, vanities, peculiarities. And as we judge of a man's character, after long frequenting his society, not by one speech, or by one mood or opinion, or by one day's talk, but by the tenor of his general bearing and conversation; so of a writer, who delivers himself up to you perforce unreservedly, you say, Is he honest? Does he tell the truth in the main? Does he seem actuated by a desire to find out and speak it? Is he a quack, who shams sentiment, or mouths for effect? Does he seek popularity by claptraps or other arts? . . . I ask you to believe that this person writing strives to tell the truth. If there is not that, there is nothing.

To get at this truth in *Pendennis* Thackeray winds himself back into his own past. As he wrote the pages—at the Garrick Club, at Brighton, at Paris, at Dieppe, at Southampton, wherever the paths of his restlessness took him—he mused upon the happy days of youth, when love was fresh if sometimes gently ridiculous. Memories of wasted opportunities, of frustrations, of great joys and tender sorrows rose before him; and out of that tissue of memory he wove the pages of his fiction. The mood, when not ironic or tender, is often of a sad serenity. His immense capacity for enjoyment is sometimes checked by the feeling that for our own sake we should not value too highly that which must in the order of things pass away. Beautiful things change and decay; the wisest of us do not know what our own motives are, and the actions 'of which we are the very proudest' may surprise us 'when we trace them, as we shall one day, to their source.' Youth passes into the sadness of maturity: 'that which is snow-white now was glossy black once; that which is sluggish obesity today was boisterous rosy health a few years back; that calm weariness, benevolent, resigned, and disappointed, was ambition, fierce and violent, but a few years since, and has only settled into submissive repose after many a battle and defeat.' And in the midst of change you are the same *you*, 'alone on the hopeless spar, drowning out of sight; alone in the midst of the crowd applauding you.'

All this, to be sure, is background music. As in Cervantes it helps to create the mood, but it is by no means the whole symphony. A gentle disillusion, however serene, could not give the sense of crowded life which fills *Pendennis*. Side by side with this philosophic sense of the irony of things runs a huge relish for the drolleries and lovable preposterous absurdities of human nature, and a gigantic visualizing power which catches every nuance of character and finds unity even in seeming contradiction.

Arthur Pendennis, then, is Thackeray, or at least one side of Thackeray. Perhaps that is the reason Thackeray is so hard on him. He wrote to Mrs. Brookfield concerning Pen: 'I fancy we resemble each other in many points.' He told friends in America as he picked up a copy of the novel: 'Pendennis is very like me.' 'Surely not,' was the objection, 'for Pendennis was so weak.' 'Ah, well, Mrs. Baxter,' (with a shrug of his great shoulders and a comical look) 'your humble servant is not very strong.'[5] In the last two lines of the book he gives Pen, with all his faults and shortcomings, the hand of charity, for Pen 'does not claim to be a hero, but only a man and a brother.' Like all of Thackeray's men and women he is subject to complex passions; he is intricately human. But Thackeray goes out of his way to underline his vagaries, and the reader remains in a state of more or less continuous irritation with this high-spirited youth who insists upon acting for so much of the time like a spoiled brat. He has been spoiled by living too much with his mother and his foster-sister. That was Major Pendennis's view of it, when Pen was displaying a high-minded virtuous attachment for an actress ('the d—d, romantic notions boys get from being brought up by women,' says the Major). That was George Warrington's view of it: 'You have been brought up a mollycoddle, Pen, and spoilt by women.' It was even 'dear Laura's' view of it, for she tells Pen to his face that his mother spoiled him by worshipping

5 *Thackeray's Letters to an American Family*, New York, 1904, p. 6.

him. Moreover, it was Thackeray's view, for he says so in several places!

Pen does not show up too badly in the flush of his first romantic love for Emily Costigan, 'the Fotheringay,' which Thackeray treats in the vein of high if sympathetic comedy. The young man has a keen sense of honour and is too high-minded for a vulgar intrigue. He adores the beautiful, bovine-tempered Emily, a not unkindly girl, but prudent, 'who always kept her fine eyes on the main chance.' Under the skilful direction of her father, Captain Costigan, a grandiose Irishman with a boozy shrewdness, she calmly lets Pen woo her at first and just as calmly jilts him when she is told to. From this episode Pen recovers; no hearts break for love in a Thackeray novel. He writes despairing poems, but 'when a gentleman is cudgelling his brain to find any rhyme for sorrow, besides borrow and tomorrow, his woes are nearer at an end than he thinks for.'

Pen's manner, says Thackeray, is frank and brave (when it is not sulky), and under his waywardness and selfishness there was a kind and generous heart. Then he comes under the influence of his uncle the Major, who encourages his worldly ways. 'Having a lively imagination,' Pen 'mistook himself for a person of importance very easily.' He becomes dandified in dress and manner and cultivates a faded sneer. He is egotistic and supercilious and imperious, very vain as well as very frank. By contrast to the ineffable Blanche Amory, he appears not unfavourably in that early abortive romance—much more so than in its later revival, when he decides to sell himself to Blanche for a fortune and a seat in Parliament. In this he is at least honest, frankly practical, without raptures. Later he feels a generous remorse for this attitude and tells the Major, who had coddled the affair along, that it has been wicked, sordid, and worldly. He declares that if he must marry Blanche he will take her for herself, without the fortune or the seat in Parliament, and he writes her what presumably he thinks is a generous letter, pointing out the poor life they will have to lead together and saying that if she wants such a career he will try to do his duty to her! It must be admitted that Blanche deserved no better, but the point here is the revelation it makes of Pen's character. The situation is at last saved by the fact that the fickle Blanche has succeeded in hooking Pen's ingenuous friend Harry Foker and his fortune. She can afford now to dismiss Pen. The decks are being cleared in these last chapters for the ultimate reunion of Pen and Laura, concerning the poetic justice of which there may be several opinions.

In the Fanny Bolton affair Pen does not come off too well either. Apparently the episode was invented to show Pen successfully resisting temptation—for Fanny is one of those beautiful unconscious flirts whose real innocence and tremulous fluttering sensibility are calculated to get them into difficulty even with less excitable youths than Pen. Nevertheless she gets rather shabby treatment from Pen and, particularly, from his mother, though Thackeray turns the edge of the tragedy by bestowing Fanny upon the egregious young Mr. Huxter. The whole episode is not very edifying, however much it serves to bring out into the clear a number of characterizations such as those of Helen, the Major, and little Bows the musician. To the latter, frustration had become something of a career. He had selflessly devoted his life first to Emily Costigan and then to Fanny, and in each case had to stand aside while Pen moved in.

If Thackeray loads the scales severely against Pen, he yet makes him completely believable, and at the end he shows that while Pen has progressed somewhat in tolerance and understanding his faults of disposition are much what they were at first. 'Our endeavour,' says Thackeray, 'is merely to follow out, in its progress, the development of the mind of a worldly and selfish, but not ungenerous or unkind or truth-avoiding man.'

In this connection it is worth noting how Thackeray's desire for fidelity in characterization was thwarted by the prejudices of the reading public, whose taboos were inflexible. In the case of Becky Sharp he had been able to hint sufficiently well at what went on between the lines. But where the story demanded a detailed treatment of a passionate young man many of whose connections were broadly Bohemian, it was impossible to use convenient ellipses. Some compromise was inevitable if *Pendennis* were to be received into the Victorian home. The Victorian novelist treating of passion had to perform prodigious feats of virtuosity, had indeed to leap from floe to floe like a literary Eliza. Thackeray writhed, and conformed. In none of his novels is he more restive under the conventions which dictated exactly how much could be said, and in the preface he speaks his mind bluntly.

Even the gentlemen of our age—this is an attempt to describe one of them, no better nor worse than most educated men—even these we cannot show as they are, with the notorious foibles and selfishness of their lives and their education. Since the author of 'Tom Jones' was buried, no writer of fiction among us has been permitted to depict to his utmost power a MAN. We must drape him, and give him a certain conventional simper. Society will not tolerate the Natural in our Art. Many ladies have remonstrated and subscribers left me, because, in the course of the story, I described a young man resisting and affected by temptation. My object was to say, that he had the passions to feel, and the manliness and generosity to overcome them. You will not hear—it is best to know it—what moves in the real world, what passes in society, in the clubs, colleges, messrooms,—what is the life and talk of your sons. A little more frankness than is customary has been attempted in this story; with no bad desire on the writer's part, it is hoped, and with no ill consequence to any reader. If truth is not always pleasant, at any rate truth is best, from whatever chair . . .

As a contrasting device to bring out the character of Pendennis, Thackeray's creation of George Warrington was a technical triumph. Warrington is no mere lay figure, however. In spite of his somewhat 'worked-up' past, in which occurred the unfortunate marriage which keeps him from making love to Laura and commits him to a life of determined mediocrity, it is impossible to agree with the critics who find him colourless and two-dimensional. By a thousand little touches Thackeray makes him real and likable. We like his lack of affectation—

in his very black-whiskered uncouthness, Thackeray points out, there was a refinement which Pen's finery lacked. We like his cheerful good sense, his humour, his friendly caustic comments on Pen's laziness and dandyism. Indeed his affection for Pen makes us want to think better of that gentleman. And we write 'Aye!' in the margin each time the blunt dowager Lady Rockminster tells Laura that she prefers 'Bluebeard' to Pen as a suitor for Laura.

If we are to find something of Thackeray in Pendennis we must also see something of him in Warrington, who represents the other half of Thackeray's dualism. One can almost hear the dialogue between Thackeray's good and bad angels in the long important argument between Pen and George in Chapter 61—Pen's attitude of general scepticism and acquiescence in the world as it is versus Warrington's aggressive idealism (with Thackeray going out of the way to explain that in presenting Pen's worldly pococurantism he is speaking only dramatically!). Warrington accuses Pen of being merely a man of the world, and his uncle's pupil. Pen makes his defense, which runs to the effect that the world must be taken as it is and who is he to make it better? Men who begin with ideas of universal reform, he points out, give up their schemes after a few years of bootless talking.

Warrington replies:

If seeing and acknowledging the lies of the world, Arthur, as see them you can with only too fatal a clearness, you submit to them without any protest further than a laugh: if, plunged yourself in easy sensuality, you allow the whole wretched world to pass groaning by you unmoved: if the fight for truth is taking place, and all men of honour are on the ground armed on the one side or the other, and you alone are to lie on your balcony and smoke your pipe out of the noise and the danger, you had better have died, or never have been at all, than such a sensual coward.

To this Pen says, imperturbably: 'The truth, friend; where is the truth? Show it me. That is the question between us. I see it on both sides'—and he develops the idea in an eloquent passage. There is more of Pen than of Warrington in Thackeray, but neither puts the whole case for him. The truth of which Pen professed to be unaware lies perhaps somewhere between the two extremes. As for the battle that those extremes make in man's mind, Thackeray, like most people, declares a draw. There is nothing of the crusader in him, but nothing of the cynic, either. For the ideas whose potential creates religions and topples empires Thackeray had no aptitude; his muse is a plain one, but one to which nothing human is foreign.

For absolute precision of delineation the portrait of Major Pendennis is one of Thackeray's great successes—and one of the most memorable portrayals in English fiction. Here Thackeray traces without a single false touch the declining career of a superb old clubman and worldling—an old *habitué* of drawing-rooms who likes to tell Laura twaddling tales about great folks and to expound his view of morals, which, if not exactly sordid, is more than mildly utilitarian. He goes to church because 'every English gentleman does it,' but he is given to 'superannuated leers.' 'He was a very useful and pleasant personage in a country house,' where 'he had a word for everybody, and about everybody, and a little against everybody.' When Pen has decided to marry Blanche, the Major approves heartily of his technique of not committing himself on paper, of advancing 'under cover, with subterfuges, and securing a retreat behind him.' When Pen tells him finally that he has come to himself and refuses any longer to prostitute his honour for the sake of Blanche's money, the old man goes down on his knees to beg Pen to reconsider. In a word he is a corrupt, unregenerate worldling—and we love him. From the moment in the opening chapter when, brisk and spotless and dignified, he breezes into his club to open his mail and learn that his nephew threatens to marry an actress, he brightens every scene into which he comes and is a sheer intellectual delight.

He is possessed too of a sublime faith in the validity of the code of worldliness which governs him. Even when his plans collapse it never occurs to him that anything is wrong with his fundamental assumptions. We forgive him much, for he is very fond of Pen. As for his idols, he worships, as Thackeray says, 'the best thing he knows.' There is pathos in his decay, for the world is everything to him, and the day comes when he stands, be-corseted, in the light of the early morning after the ball at Gaunt House, and realizes that time has caught up with him.

There he stood, with admirable patience, enduring, uncomplaining, a silent agony; knowing that people could see the state of his face (for could he not himself perceive the condition of others, males and females, of his own age?)—longing to go to rest for hours past; aware that suppers disagreed with him, and yet having eaten a little so as to keep his friend, Lady Clavering, in good humour; with twinges of rheumatism in the back and knees; with weary feet burning in his varnished boots,—so tired, so, so tired and longing for bed! If a man, struggling with hardship and bravely overcoming it, is an object of admiration for the gods, that Power in whose chapel the Major was a faithful worshipper must have looked upwards approvingly upon the constancy of Pendennis's martyrdom.

There is more to the old boy, however, than decayed worldliness. He is stout-hearted and brave in a crisis, full of ingenuity and resource and strength of will. One of the best scenes in the novel is that in which he confronts and defeats his blackmailing valet, Morgan. Morgan knows that Blanche Amory's father is an escaped criminal and is not dead, as was supposed, but is really the mysterious Altamont who has been blackmailing Lord Clavering, Blanche's stepfather. He assumes that the Major, midstream in his negotiations to marry Pen to Blanche, will pay to keep those unpleasant facts concealed. Fortified with liquor, he confronts the Major, whom he has served discreetly and unobtrusively these fifteen years. Nothing could be more superb than the way in which that old war-horse sniffs the breeze, rises to the battle, and in a stormy scene completely cows the presumptuous valet.

Thackeray's picture of the Major, as sharp in its details as a Dutch *genre* painting, is hardly Victorian. Major Pendennis is of the brood of Regency men-about-town, like the Lord Steyne whom he admires and whose parties at Gaunt House he is proud to attend.[6] The women in *Pendennis,* on the other hand, help us to understand Thackeray's more conventional Victorianism as well as the degree of his emancipation from it. The Doras of Dickens and the Amelias of Thackeray lend support to the thesis that towards woman the Victorians were often irritatingly patronizing and unconsciously cruel. It was supposed to be one of the conventions of the time that she should not be too intelligent; indeed she was likely to be a little suspect if she were. She was to be sweet and simple and decorative. The home was to be her boundary, the yearly production of young Victorians her chief wifely occupation, and a shallow innocuous vapidity the measure of her temperament. At least so men liked to think of her; one suspects, however, even on the basis of Thackeray's novels, that she was not always such. Leaving aside Becky Sharp and Miss Crawley, consider the range of feminine characterization in *Pendennis.* Blanche Amory has been called a lesser Becky. She is no less a paragon of female wile, but the two have really very little in common. The Fotheringay is certainly no stereotyped Victorian maiden. Fanny Bolton, however much she flutters and sighs, is a congenital coquette. Lady Clavering, saddled with a husband who is pale, languid, and enervated, given to feeble hilarity, gambling, and strong drink, is herself uneducated and dull but good-natured and generous too, with a pleasant ungrammatical lack of affectation. She does not appear frequently, but one retains a clear and not unsympathetic impression of a woman neither conventionally sentimental nor conventionally grotesque.

When we come to Helen and Laura Pendennis, comparisons with *Vanity Fair* are more pertinent. Laura is much more than another Amelia. Hers is a rather thankless role: that of waiting

[6] In *Pendennis* Thackeray begins that interlocking of his novels by carrying over, briefly, the persons of one into the story of the next. Lord Steyne of *Vanity Fair* appears on the fringes of *Pendennis,* and there is reference to 'poor Rawdon Crawley,' now Governor of Coventry Island.

for two volumes while Pen makes up his mind to marry her. She shows sense enough, however, to become fond of George Warrington, however futilely, and in spite of her sweetness and compassion and in spite of the tears she weeps with Helen over Pen's vagaries, she has a good deal of spunk and courage. She can get angry with Pen: it is she who sees that he is wasting his time languishing at Fairoaks and lends him the money to go out and try to make something of himself. At the same time she is cheerful and kind and has a gift quite denied to Amelia— a sense of humour. And at the end when Thackeray, perhaps a little doubtful himself concerning the kind of a husband Pendennis will make, gives his blessing to the match, he admits that Laura sees Pen's 'faults and wayward moods—seeing and owning that there are better men than he,' and that she loves him in spite of that. 'His children or their mother,' says Thackeray, 'have never heard a harsh word from him; and when his fits of moodiness and solitude are over, welcome him back with a never-failing regard and confidence.' Certainly not a heroic or a notably 'Victorian' ending. Sentiment gives way to a quiet realism.

The case of Helen Pendennis is quite another matter; here realism is dissolved by sentiment. The parallel with Amelia Sedley is apropos in so far as it shows the conflict in Thackeray between heart and head. Once more the commentator contradicts the portraying hand. The characterization, taken at its face value, is one of Thackeray's finest. Helen is the all-absorbing mother, sincere and selfish, and wreaking all the more havoc because of her sincerity. Her devotion to her son is the one thing that lightens her habitual melancholy. From the beginning it is clear that she is marked for an early and an emotional death; she is one of the lost ones of the earth, intensely pious, worshipping Arthur and surfeiting him 'with sweet respect and submission.' She quarrels bitterly with Laura for turning Pen down after he had offered her a weary heart and had openly admitted that he was proposing only to please his mother. The comment here is firm: 'Helen could not pardon an act of justice in Laura.' She suspects the worst about Pen and Fanny Bolton and becomes cruel and inexorable when the latter's name is mentioned. When Pen falls ill she drives the others out 'and takes possession of her son.' Modern psychology has a name for all this engulfing emotionalism, and Thackeray does not flinch in recording the evidence. He is realistic in stating that Helen's idol-worship is the cause of much of Arthur's misfortune.

But against this remorseless case-history Thackeray sets some of his most ecstatic perorations about 'the sacred emotions of love and grief' and about Helen's sweetness and purity and dignity. Accesses of tenderness sweep him off his feet, until after Helen's death he can say: 'Pendennis's mother was worshipped in his memory, and canonised there, as such a saint ought to be. . . . That touching and wonderful spectacle of innocence, and love, and beauty.' No doubt it was in the light of such a mood as this that he identified Helen with his mother.

The curious contradiction remains, and baffles reasonable explanation. It is as if there were in Thackeray's mind two compartments, between which he could deny communication—the one creative and grimly faithful, the other passive and reverent, likely, however, to be set off into tangential ecstasies not unworthy in themselves but seemingly unconnected by logic or reason to the facts which the creative mind had set forth. Whatever the reason, Thackeray's art at such moments stumbles into irreducible difficulties.

Blanche Amory is another of Thackeray's very real women, this time presented unfalteringly. The reader delights in her while praying to be delivered from meeting any of her kind. Her stepfather Lord Clavering, who 'wished she were dead,' came close to the truth when he complained that she had the knack of making every one miserable. Pendennis met her shortly after his unhappy romance with the Fotheringay and for a time was taken in by her fair hair and brown eyes,[7] her sighs, and

[7] Becky Sharp was also blond. Thackeray's gentler heroines are always black-haired, a fact which would seem, however, to be without any particular scholarly significance.

her poems 'Mes Larmes' which she kept in her own dear little
book. She made Pen see that she was not appreciated at home,
that she had to live with her intellectual inferiors, that she was
a martyr who struck her lyre to the saddest of tunes. 'So "Mes
Larmes" dribbled out of her eyes any day at command: she
would furnish an unlimited supply of tears, and her faculty of
shedding them increased by practice.' Pen began to adapt for
her some of the poems he had written earlier for Emily Costigan. He could not see her being surly to her mother and cruel
to her brother—he saw only her distress when she thought how
lonely she would be after he was gone.

Thackeray makes from the self-indulgent sentimentalities of
this nefarious little creature some vastly amusing pages. Blanche
has indulged in false emotion for so long that she is incapable
of any true feelings, or indeed of caring whether she has any.
She had, says Thackeray, 'a sham enthusiasm, a sham hatred, a
sham love, a sham taste, a sham grief, each of which flared and
shone very vehemently for an instant, but subsided and gave
place to the next sham emotion.' The climax comes when Pen
writes to her explaining his poverty, reasserting, however, his
faithfulness to his promise to marry her. She replies in a very
hectic, sentimental letter—she has wept, prayed, passed sleepless
hours—she brings the gushing poesy of her being to him—'heed
not my bleeding heart,' etc. Whereupon Pen decides to call on
her, and finds her *tête-à-tête* with his infatuated friend Harry
Foker, a harmless youth who has recently inherited a fortune
which Blanche's sensibilities do not prevent her from perceiv-
ing.[8]

[8] In a letter to Mrs. Brookfield Thackeray describes a Blanche whom he
found in real life and incidentally shows how a novel was built under his hands:
'At the train whom do you think I found? Miss G[ore], who says she is
Blanche Amory, and I think she is Blanche Amory, amiable at times, amusing,
clever, and depraved. We talked and persiflated all the way to London, and the
idea of her will help me to a good chapter, in which I will make Pendennis and
Blanche play at being in love, such a wicked, false, hum-bugging London love,
as two *blasé* London people might act, and half deceive themselves that they
were in earnest.' (*Letters to Mrs. Brookfield*, p. 49.)

This then is Thackeray's second venture into the full-length novel in parts. He had done better in *Vanity Fair* and was to do better later; yet *Pendennis* carries its world on its own shoulders and needs no apology here. In addition to its autobiographical interest it is important because it shows Thackeray entering fully into the mood of mellow reminiscence which had already become his characteristic manner. As in all his work, its blemishes and its triumphs lie close together and it is frequently hard to disentangle them. But one thing is clear even to the casual reader: there are enough good things in *Pendennis,* and sufficient creative energy, to cut up into half a dozen stories for lesser novelists.

CHAPTER EIGHT

Henry Esmond

ANTHONY TROLLOPE, who liked to commend an edifying morality in other people's writing, declared that *Henry Esmond* was by far the best of Thackeray's novels. 'The lesson,' he said, 'is salutary from beginning to end. The sermon truly preached is that glory can only come from that which is truly glorious, and that the results of meanness end always in the mean.' [1] For that and other reasons he once told Thackeray that *Esmond* was so much his best work that there was none second to it. The latter replied, 'That was what I intended.' And although at certain other times Thackeray said that he believed *Vanity Fair* was his best work, he is also on record as saying that he was willing to let his reputation stand or fall by *Esmond*. It is to be doubted, however, that he liked it chiefly for its high morality, for he went on to tell Trollope, somewhat jokingly we may presume, that Henry was a prig. Nevertheless many subsequent critics have agreed with Trollope, and of all Thackeray's books *Esmond* has become required reading for school children. George Saintsbury allowed himself to be so transported with delight that he could declare: 'A greater novel than *Esmond* I do not know; and I do not know many greater books.' From this unequivocal praise it will be the duty of this chapter to dissent slightly. Yet if *Esmond* is not Thackeray's greatest novel it is

[1] *Thackeray (English Men of Letters)*, London, 1925 ed., p. 136.

his greatest work of art and certainly one of the best of all historical novels. He attempted a rare and difficult feat and he accomplished it triumphantly.

This triumph of art is the more surprising when one remembers that the novel was written while Thackeray was going through a great emotional catastrophe—the severing of his close relationship with Mrs. Brookfield. Hence perhaps the melancholy which gives its tone and colour to the story. In writing to his mother on 15 March 1852, he calls the book 'grave and sad . . . You will dislike it very much. It was written at a period of grief and pain so severe that I don't like to think of it yet . . .'[2] In another letter written a little earlier he had told her: 'I have nothing to say that is of use to anyone, to say or to hear, and though I could fill pages with blue devils, of what good would that be to anybody . . . so the griefs of my elderly heart can't be talked about to you and I must get over them as comfortably as I may . . .'[3] And to Lady Stanley about this time he wrote: 'I am writing a book of cut-throat melancholy suitable to my state . . .'[4]

So in spite of the fact that the events in *Esmond* are more than customarily dashing and exciting, the ground swell of the novel is sombre and its effect one of mitigated tragedy. The protagonists who survive at the end—Esmond, Rachel, even Beatrix—are weary before they are old. So much needs to be said. Yet the story is so full of good things, of crowded life and action and brilliant historical colouring, and the sadness is set off by such a counterpoint of lively intrigue that the reader remembers the action longer than the mood of melancholy. Such a person as the Dowager Viscountess Castlewood, for example—one of Thackeray's worldly ancient aristocratic females—does much to break up the gloom. She became devoted to Esmond and the only fault she found with him was that 'he was more sober than an Esmond ought to be; and would neither be carried to bed

---

[2] *Letters of Anne Thackeray Ritchie*, London, 1924, p. 37.
[3] Introduction to *Esmond, Centenary Biographical Edition*, p. xx.
[4] Ibid., p. xix.

by his valet, nor lose his heart to any beauty, whether of St. James's or Covent Garden.'

It was inevitable that Thackeray, who once thought seriously of continuing Macaulay's *History,* should one day write a Queen Anne novel. He had long steeped himself in the period. He loved not only the historical eighteenth century but also Fielding and Smollett and Goldsmith and Addison and Steele. He also had been 'living in the past century,' as he put it, in preparation for his lectures on the English humorists, and one hand helped to wash the other. In *Esmond* Thackeray was in a world of the imagination familiar and satisfying to him. He had strong theories, too, about what history should be, and those theories fitted comfortably the frame of the historical novel. Historians, he believed, cannot give the whole truth; as early as *The Paris Sketch Book* he had entered a whimsical defense of romance over history as giving the higher truth. It pleased him to see that the dignity of history diminishes 'as we grow better acquainted with the materials which compose it.' In the first chapter of *Esmond* Henry declares that history is court-ridden and has 'nothing to do with the registering the affairs of the common people . . . In a word, I would have History familiar rather than heroic: and think that Mr. Hogarth and Mr. Fielding will give our children a much better idea of the manners of the present age in England, than the *Court Gazette* and the newspapers that we get thence.'

In the larger sense *Esmond* does recapture the tone of a whole period, although like any historical novelist Thackeray rearranges history somewhat for his own purposes and at times even distorts it, consciously or unconsciously. Slight mistakes of detail are not infrequent. He boldly brings the Pretender to England at the time of Queen Anne's death, in violation of historical accuracy. In his chivalrous defence of his famous ancestor, General Webb, he does injustice to Marlborough, who is presented not merely as cold and ambitious but also as accepting bribes from the French and as wilfully cheating General Webb out of the credit for the victory at Wynendael. He is notoriously and savagely unjust to Swift. Richard Steele he presents sympathetically but somewhat patronizingly, emphasizing not his common sense and his courage but his amiable weakness for drink, his financial irresponsibility, and his sentimental inflammability. He has twisted fact in his portrayal of Lord Mohun. His greatest mistake is his presentation of the character of the Pretender, James Edward. Perhaps for lack of adequate information, perhaps because such a conception best fitted his plot for the last exciting volume, Thackeray shows him as a weak and self-indulgent libertine who had to be restrained from running after bar-maids and who barters his chance for a crown in order to pursue the slippery Beatrix. James Edward may have been ineffective; he certainly was not a drunken rake.[5] Yet however much all this may bother the historian, it does not invalidate Thackeray's fictional world, which is consistent and stable, nor does it obscure the uncanny skill with which he makes solid and three-dimensional a whole life and time. The Age of Anne is not a back-drop for the fictional passions of his characters; they are a part of each other. Compared with *Esmond,* most historical romances seem a masquerade of wig and silver buckle.

Thackeray's sensitiveness to the past reaches its full fruition in this novel; his love for the historical eighteenth century fuses with his other love for the personal and retrospective method of telling a story. Esmond is a Queen Anne hero telling the story of his youth long after the events described have taken place. The sense of years elapsed penetrates the story. Out of the whirlpool of the past, little eddies isolate themselves in time, and those spots of time become focal points for the moods of the narrative, arresting it and fixing it in memory with a graphic

[5] The only detailed and annotated edition of *Henry Esmond* is that by T. C. and W. Snow (Oxford University Press, 1915), which corrects Thackeray's chronology and points out some of his errors of fact. In a scholarly account of the lively career of Lord Mohun, Robert Stanley Forsythe shows how Thackeray twists his facts while still managing 'to obtain and preserve that verisimilitude, that plausibility, which makes *Henry Esmond* one of the most nearly perfect presentations in literature of the life and actions and thoughts of a past age.' (*A Noble Rake,* Cambridge, Mass., 1928, p. 251.)

pictorial power. Such scenes stand out: the boy Esmond looking adoringly at Rachel at morning prayers, remembering long
'how she looked and spoke kneeling reverently before the sacred
book, the sun shining upon her golden hair until it made a halo
round about her.' Still other spots of time: Esmond's return after
a year in prison for his implication in the duel in which Lord
Castlewood was killed by Mohun, and his coming out of the
winter night into Winchester Cathedral while the music was
playing, and finding Rachel there; the brilliant Beatrix, grown
a woman since Esmond last saw her, descending the stairs at
Castlewood; Esmond visiting his mother's grave in Brussels; his
return to Castlewood after an absence of fourteen years:

As for Esmond, he felt to be a hundred years old; his dear mistress
only seemed unchanged; she looked and welcomed him quite as of
old. There was the fountain in the court babbling its familiar music,
the old hall and its furniture, the carved chair my late lord used, the
very flagon he drank from. Esmond's mistress knew he would like
to sleep in the little room he used to occupy; 'twas made ready for
him, and wall-flowers and sweet herbs set in the adjoining chamber,
the chaplain's room . . . Mr. Esmond passed a part of that first
night at Castlewood, lying awake for many hours as the clock kept
tolling (in tones so well remembered), looking back, as all men
will, that revisit their home of childhood, over the great gulf of
time, and surveying himself on the distant bank yonder, a sad little
melancholy boy, with his lord still alive—his dear mistress, a girl
yet, her children sporting around her . . . All night long he was
dreaming his boyhood over again, and waking fitfully . . .

In *Esmond,* even more than in *Pendennis,* the story is seen
through a mellow autumnal haze of memory which captures
and fixes the mood of gentle melancholy.

It has always been recognized that *Esmond* is the best con-
structed of Thackeray's novels. It was the only one to be planned
and written as a whole before it appeared in the full dress of
three volumes. This helps to explain why it is only half as long
as *Vanity Fair, Pendennis,* and the later novels. It has fewer
characters and therefore less elaboration of minor collateral fig-

ures, as well as fewer loose ends. Nor does Thackeray indulge so freely in his customary whimsical digression and comment. Esmond tells his own story, and the point of view, which in the previous novels had suffered moments of uncertainty, is here steadily maintained. Although Esmond tells the story in the third person, the voice is unmistakably his throughout. Thackeray reminds us of this from time to time when with a cunning artlessness he makes Esmond drift easily into the first person. Any comments or philosophical or pious generalizations, therefore, appear to be Esmond's own. Although the melancholy hero has a definite infiltration of Thackeray's own temperament ('a handsome likeness of an ugly son of yours,' Thackeray told his mother), the disquisitions seem more natural because the showman is in the background.

Once again the plan is that of the memoir or 'history,' more sharply focused than previously. We see Esmond first during his wistful years as the supposedly illegitimate dependent of the house of Castlewood. Thackeray never wrote more poignantly than in those early chapters in which the lonely boy, who had known little happiness, expands in the atmosphere of love and kindness which comes to Castlewood with its new mistress. It is all seen through the boy's eyes: his dim understanding of the shame which haunts him when excited villagers shriek 'little Popish bastard' at him; his devotion to the genial plotting Jesuit, Father Holt, and his brushing the fringes of mysterious events without ever knowing what it is all about; his childish worship of the exalted lady who brought to him, for the first time in his life, pity and tenderness; the way in which he comes slowly to realize that Lord Castlewood and Rachel are not happy together; the former, careless and self-indulgent, becoming restless under the smothering absorption of Rachel's hero-worship and ultimately rebelling, as the lad sees, because he discovers that 'his slave and bed fellow . . . is his superior . . . So the lamp was out in Castlewood Hall, and the lord and lady there saw each other as they were.'

The dissipated Mohun comes into the picture and Castlewood

dies, jealous, under his sword. Rachel, not understanding Esmond's part in the affair, is estranged from him; and Esmond, after having spent a year in prison because he had acted as second to Castlewood, is taken in by the Dowager Lady Castlewood and later goes abroad to the Wars of the Spanish Succession. When he returns he finds that Beatrix has grown up, and the remainder of the story settles down to the complication of his hopeless love for her and the relation of Rachel to that suit. All this is worked out in the intervals of further battles, duels, and the final climactic intrigue in which Esmond becomes a leader in the ill-fated Jacobite plot to restore James Edward to the throne of his Stuart fathers. The climax of the intrigue and of Esmond's bootless chase of Beatrix comes simultaneously.

Subordinate to the personal history of Esmond and yet integral to it is the brilliant eighteenth-century background of literary and social London—Addison, Steele, Swift, *The Spectator,* the playhouse, the political jockeying, the whole spectacular panorama of a vanished century. Thackeray admits dramatic 'scenes' more frequently than is customary with him: such episodes as the duel between Mohun and Castlewood; General Webb's handing the offending *Gazette* to Marlborough on the point of his sword; Rachel making the haughty Duke of Hamilton recognize Esmond as the Marquis of Esmond. And best of all the final dramatic scene in which Esmond breaks his sword before the Pretender and the latter, impulsively repentant for his delinquencies, insists that he should be allowed to honour Esmond by formally crossing swords with him. All this is the very stuff of historical romance, and these bright-coloured threads weave warm scenes into the dominantly sad tapestry of Esmond's history. Thackeray shows himself a master of suspense and of rapid narrative action. The whole third book, with the Beatrix-Hamilton-Mohun imbroglio and the crescendo of excitement as the plot to enthrone the Pretender builds up and then collapses, is a swift and stirring sequence.

In spite of his dislike of the Georges, Thackeray was himself heartily Whiggish and a believer in the Hanoverian succession rather than in the cause of the Stuarts. For the purposes of romance, however, the Jacobite intrigues have always captured the imagination so completely that it is impossible to conceive of Thackeray's making Esmond anything but a supporter of James Edward. By the time Esmond came to write his memoirs he had seen the error of his ways, and he admits a great admiration for King William as well as a belief that the Stuarts fell through their own fault; 'were my time to come over again, I would be a Whig in England, and not a Tory.' Thus Thackeray gives his hero a delayed baptism into what seemed to the author intellectual truth, while retaining for the purpose of the story the imaginative sympathy by means of which the lost cause of the Jacobites has always conquered literature. Esmond, to be sure, doesn't think the problem out very clearly in his youth. He quite frankly takes the side of his family, in politics as in religion. When Father Holt tries to convert Esmond to Catholicism the latter replies 'that his church was the church of his country, and to that he chose to remain faithful'—with something of the logic of Hardy's rustic who declared: 'I hate a feller who'll change his old ancient doctrines for the sake of getting to heaven.'

Henry Esmond himself is quite properly the hero of the novel, and yet not quite all a 'hero' in the historico-romantic sense. He is brave, capable of quick and decisive action in a crisis, sensitive, a 'pattern of moral behaviour,' quixotically generous in his refusal to claim the title which was his by rights. His daughter, writing the preface to his memoirs, pictures him as a Virginia country gentleman who is a very paragon of courtesy and grace and refinement. Yet he is not good looking, is moody and lonely, and given to pious moralizing. Trollope called him 'a gentleman from the crown of his head to the sole of his feet,' and Thackeray wrote to his mother that the hero of his new novel was 'as stately as Sir Charles Grandison.' But he is capable, as Thackeray admitted, of being a most unheroic bore. His natural melancholy becomes at times merely a moody gloom; Beatrix calls him 'Don Dismallo' and he even refers to himself as the Knight of the Woeful Countenance. (Perhaps that is the reason the comedy he wrote ran only three nights and sold but nine copies.) His typical moods alternated between an exalted grief and a highly charged sentiment. The art comes, of course, in Thackeray's making Esmond thus reveal himself in his own words, and our impatience with Esmond cannot hide the fact that he is a real if sometimes irritatingly dreary person. There is little satire in *Henry Esmond,* but there is much of the deep irony which permeates Thackeray's best work—an irony blended with pity. It is not merely that we find a mixture of good and evil in all people, or that worldly persons are their own punishment. It is found in Esmond's tone of high regret and in the recognition of the irreconcilable contradictions of character in the noblest people. Of such contradictions Esmond has his share; the most intricate, however, belong to Rachel, Lady Castlewood.

Many readers have come away from *Esmond* feeling not a little uncomfortable about the relation between Esmond and Rachel. Rachel is sufficiently real—pious, tender, sweet, moving in an aura of sanctity and unpretentious benevolence. Esmond declares that she has great powers of intellect (which are not made clear in the novel) and that she is wittier than Beatrix (the only testimony for this being one sickly pun). When she was cheerful, says Esmond, she 'said the finest things.' It is our misfortune to see her when cheerfulness has difficulty creeping in. The fact is that she is too much like Esmond himself, stricken with a passionate sadness which envelops her and gives even her scenes of tenderness a curious hectic quality. She lives for affection, feeds on raptures, and is happiest when she can immerse herself in ecstasies of adoration or reconciliation. 'Don't raise me,' she would say to Esmond in a wild way, sinking to her knees, 'let me kneel, and—and—worship you.' There is, to be sure, nothing vulgar or offensive in Thackeray's presentation of this, nor is there any hint that Esmond is distressed by the highly charged sentiment. Quite the contrary. But Thackeray sets himself the hard task of showing, through Esmond's eyes, how this goddess is less than divine in her jealousy, which is just as passionate as her affection. She could be hard and un-yielding, relentlessly sinless and just as relentlessly stern—as for instance when she blames the lad Esmond for bringing small-pox into the house, or when she overwhelms him with recrimina-tions for not preventing Mohun from killing her husband, though Esmond has really tried to avert the quarrel.

This phase of her character is pointed up sharply in her daugh-ter's preface to the book, which represents, presumably, Thack-eray's final reflections on the people he had created. There Ra-chel is shown to have been so insistent, as long as Esmond lived, upon absorbing every bit of his love that she was jealous of his fondness for their own daughter; and Esmond, under her watch-ful eye, was unable to express his real fondness for the child. It is not much wonder that the earlier Lord Castlewood tired of such adoration; it took a Henry Esmond to live with it and like it.

Now it is not impossible that a woman of Rachel's high-strung and devotedly passionate temperament, whose idolization of her coarse husband was just as unreasoning as was her later devo-tion to Esmond, should after her husband's death transfer her affection to the lad whom she had protected. Nor is it unlikely that she would be jealous of Esmond when he is mooning after her daughter Beatrix. This is all within the bounds of human probability and need be neither ridiculous nor repugnant; al-though one feels a little uneasy at the spectacle of the mother who, as Mrs. Jameson put it, 'for years is the confidante of a man's delirious passion for her own child, and then consoles him by marrying him herself!' But we watch the love grow until Thackeray's comment, when he was taken to task for marrying them at the end, is perfectly plausible: 'I didn't make them do it; they did it themselves.' [6] Very credible, too, is Ra-chel's wavering between instinctive jealousy and a determined

---

[6] One wonders, however, why Thackeray dismisses in a hurried and per-functory passage on the last page of the novel the event towards which the whole creation of the book has been moving.

martyrdom. At one moment she will warn Esmond against Beatrix, saying that the man who marries Beatrix will never be happy. But at another time she tells Esmond: 'I wish she would have you,' and Esmond, at the height of his lovesickness, reposed all his dreary confessions with his 'dearest mistress' Rachel, 'who never tired of hearing him and pleading for him.'

The difficulty with a situation like this is that its delineation requires an absolute certainty of touch, and it is at just such moments that Thackeray is likely to be confused by conflicting impulses. We are never sure, during the growth of this strange affection, just what it means at any given moment. It is not improbable that Rachel and Esmond themselves should at certain stages be uncertain of the exact nature of their feelings for each other, but certainly Thackeray should know, and it is not clear that he did.

The relationship begins with a generous protective impulse on the part of the young wife towards the lad who is seven or eight years her junior, and with a rapt worship of his benefactress on the part of the lonely Esmond. His sustained tone is one of awed rapture that such a pure devotion as Rachel's should be poured out on him. A little later young Frank Castlewood tells Esmond bluntly that his mother is in love with him, but the word 'love' is a confusing one in this book, and Esmond seems not to get the full significance of Frank's remark. After a year's separation Esmond returns home and 'his mistress . . . was his dearest mistress again . . . 'Twas happiness to have seen her: 'twas no great pang to part; a filial tenderness, a love that was at once respect and protection, filled his mind as he thought of her; and near her or far from her, and from that day until now, and from now until death is past, and beyond it, he prays that that sacred flame may ever burn.' Come now, Esmond, *what* flame? Your 'filial tenderness,' long before this writing, must have been sublimated at the marriage altar. And in that famous scene in which Esmond returns home to Rachel, 'bringing his sheaves with him,' and swears eternal devotion to her, he is a confused blend of son and lover. Rachel, for her part, speaks 'with a mother's sweet plaintive tone and look.' But here is what she *says:* 'Yes, there is no sin in such a love as mine now; and my dear lord in heaven may see my heart.'

Still later, when Esmond has been pouring out to Rachel his love for Beatrix, she says: 'I am your mother, you are my son, and I love you always'; and Esmond's comment is on 'that amazing and constant love and tenderness with which this sweet lady ever blessed and pursued him.' It is impossible to tell at what point, or even how, this attachment turns into what it ultimately becomes. All we know is that immediately following the *débâcle* of the Pretender episode and Esmond's sudden wonderment, as he looked at Beatrix, that he could ever have loved her, comes the record of Rachel's marriage to Esmond, amid some supercharged transports of wonder and gratitude.

One comes to the conclusion that his perplexity as far as *Esmond* is concerned stems, as in previous instances, from Thackeray's inability at certain times to reconcile and justify the characterization and the comment on the characterization. Here, to be sure, Esmond is making the comments, but it is clear that Thackeray does not sense the strange mixture of feelings. Esmond is by no means blind, for example, to Rachel's hard jealousy. 'If my mistress was cruel,' he says, 'at least she never could be got to own as much. Her haughtiness quite overtopped Beatrix's, and, if the girl had a proud spirit, I very much fear that it came to her by inheritance.' Against such passages as these one has to set off the 'devotional ceremonials' which would indicate that Rachel is almost too fragile a spirit to endure the terms of our mortality. The reader retires in some confusion.

It is altogether likely that Thackeray's uncertainty here is a reflection of the tangled state of his own heart at the time, and that in the exalted passages of adoration, at least, Rachel Castlewood became for him Jane Brookfield. The writing of *Esmond* succeeded, we remember, the crisis of the Brookfield business. Thackeray's correspondence at this time echoes the same intense and worshipful tones that we find in *Esmond*. Writing as late as December 1853 to Kate Perry, he says: As for J O

B[rookfield]—I remember a passage of a novel called Esmond which says when Mr. E. thought of the splendour and purity of his dear Mistress's love, the thought of it smote him on to his knees.' Castlewood, as Lady Ritchie points out in her introduction to the novel, was Clevedon Court in Somersetshire, the paternal home of Mrs. Brookfield.

There is no such uncertainty in the characterization of Beatrix. As Rachel is to Amelia Sedley, so Beatrix is to Becky Sharp; and Beatrix, like Becky, would save any novel. So far does she cast her shadow over *Henry Esmond* that it is hard to believe that the story is half over before we see her in anything except occasional flashes. The explanation is, of course, that it takes her 250 pages to grow up. Yet from almost the beginning she is the vivacious bright-eyed coquette—pert, vain, bright, mischievous—who makes eyes at Esmond, and who, indeed, would make eyes at anything in breeches. Her haughty beauty captivates Esmond as it captivated her long line of devotees from the Marquis of Blandford to Lord Ashburnham to the Duke of Hamilton to the Pretender. Esmond knew her faults well, knew that she was imperious, light-minded, flighty, false, and he loved her with a humiliated desperation. She is blandly unmoved by his protestations. Even her delight in conquest and her passion for admiration, so primary in her nature, could not keep her from being fatigued by the raptures of the noble but dullish young man. 'She was a princess, though she had scare a shilling to her fortune; and one of her subjects—the most abject and devoted wretch, sure, that ever drivelled at a woman's knees—was this unlucky gentleman; who bound his good sense, and reason, and independence, hand and foot; and submitted them to her.' She once explains to Esmond that he might have fared better if he had not been so humble and down on his knees.

Thackeray makes of this character, however, more than a brilliant coquette. Behind her magnificent vanity was a hard ambitious purpose which she confessed to with a worldly cynicism: she wanted a wealthy husband and she knew that her face was her fortune. She demanded what Esmond could not give her—

flattery, compliments, diamonds, a coach-and-eight. But as Charlotte Brontë pointed out,[7] Beatrix is pursued by a terrible destiny. Her suitors die, or are killed, or drop away from her. Her heart had not been touched by any of them, and at length this dazzling creature discovers that she shares the fate of all such worldlings: she no longer has any heart to be touched. In a terribly candid and self-revealing passage she tells Esmond that had she found the man she could love 'I would have followed him in rags had he been a private soldier, or to sea, like one of those buccaneers you used to read to us about when we were children . . . I was frightened to find I was glad of his [her betrothed, Lord Hamilton's] death; and were I joined to you, I should have the same sense of servitude, the same longing to escape.' Her last game at high stakes was to lure the impressionable Pretender away from Kensington to Castlewood at the time when he should have been active in the plot for the throne. At this point Esmond's love dies within him, and he is free.

One of Thackeray's greatest successes in this novel of eighteenth-century England is the aptness of his prose style. A discussion of this invites a preliminary consideration of Thackeray's prose style in general—an important subject. Certainly no small share of his fame rests on the felicity with which he said what he had to say. There were few contemporary authors who could have drawn as much praise as Thackeray did from two such widely separated stylists as Matthew Arnold and Thomas Carlyle. Arnold said: 'Thackeray is not, I think, a great writer, but at any rate his style is that of one.' Carlyle said: 'Nobody in our day wrote, I should say, with such perfection of style.' When such strange bed-fellows unite in a chorus of praise it is time to see what they meant.

The seeming effortlessness of Thackeray's writing should not hide the fact that he knew exactly what he was doing and took

[7] In a letter to the publisher George Smith (10 November, 1852), (*Life and Letters of Charlotte Brontë*, IV, 19.) Smith had sent her the manuscript of the first two volumes of *Esmond* as they had come from Thackeray's hands.

a quiet pride in his accomplishment. In one of his letters he makes a humorous reference to Dickens's recent simplification of his style and his overcoming the use of 'fine' words. 'By this the public will be the gainer,' he writes, 'and *David Copperfield* will be improved by taking a lesson from *Vanity Fair*.' Yet no style could seem less conscious of itself than Thackeray's. Like all great narrative styles it is simple in vocabulary and structure. The right word is always there, set plainly into its context without tortured effort or puzzle-headedness. The sentences slip along with an almost colloquial ease, flowing into every curve of the author's thought—idiomatic, strong, and sure. For all its subtlety of rhythm and its hint of distant harmonies it is sinewy and clean. No extravagant words, a minimum of set rhetorical device, and yet a sense of happy abundance—the lucid outpouring of a mind in which word and idea are one.

Thackeray seemed not to have to labour for the luminous clarity which is the hall-mark of his writing. The style of his important novels has a richer texture, a warmer, more flexible adaptability than that of his early work; but from the very beginning, in his sprightly and facetious attempts as in his more pedestrian reviewing, there is the same transparent idiomatic lucidity. To take a passage at random from one of the early tales: in the *Fitz-Boodle Papers* he is describing Ottilia, an early incarnation of Blanche Amory.

Ottilia was pale and delicate. She wore her glistening black hair in bands, and dressed in vapoury white muslin. She sang her own words to her harp, and they commonly insinuated that she was alone in the world,—that she suffered some inexpressible and mysterious heart-pangs, the lot of all finer geniuses,—that though she lived and moved in the world she was not of it,—that she was of a consumptive tendency and might look for a premature interment. She even had fixed on the spot where she should lie: the violets grew there, she said, the river went moaning by; the grey willow whispered sadly over her head, and her heart pined to be at rest. 'Mother,' she would say, turning to her parent, 'promise me—promise me to lay me in that spot when the parting hour has come!' At which

Madame de Schlippenschlopp would shriek, and grasp her in her arms; and at which, I confess, I would myself blubber like a child.

This is humorous burlesque, to be sure, but even here the style coils itself around the thought and the mood, spontaneously immediate.

Thackeray's is an intensely personal style—in the best sense of that word. It is urbane and civilized, but its good breeding is not colourless nor its simplicity monotonous, and its colour is that of Thackeray's own rich and varied personality. It is useless to try to trace its sources in detail, for there is nothing synthetic about it; but one thinks of what Herbert Read calls Charles Lamb's 'sense of selfhood,' of the warmth of Goldsmith and Steele, and of Sterne's perverse and captivating discursiveness. As has often been pointed out, the kinship of Thackeray's style is with the eighteenth century—with Fielding's fine free strength and still more with the meditative, genial, ruminating eloquence of the essayists, with Addison particularly. From these come, perhaps, the haunting musical cadences which play through the lines of both his novels and his essays—for Thackeray is as much the essayist turned novelist as he is the novelist who diverges into the essay.

It is a remarkably even style. If there are few purple patches there are few stylistically monotonous ones. As Chesterton put it: 'Thackeray is always interesting, even in the passages which are bad.' He does not have the same exuberant energy and bounding spirits which get Dickens safely over many hurdles of bad writing; but the level passages, those descriptive or expository sections which hold a novel together, are in Thackeray of a steady excellence. Even in what Professor Elton calls his 'choric' moods, Thackeray never writes merely to exercise his pen, although his habit of chatty, confidential familiarity sometimes makes him garrulous. Occasionally we wish to prune him because he goes into unnecessarily long-winded detail, but never because he is in the slightest degree artificial or affected.

In spite of this embroidery of comment, however, Thackeray

often approximates the naked purity of Swift. He might have been describing qualities of his own style when he said of Swift: 'His statement is elaborately simple . . . he never indulges in needless extravagance of rhetoric, lavish epithets, profuse imagery. He lays his opinion before you with a grave simplicity and a perfect neatness.' This simplicity of Thackeray's is capable, however, of a wide range of effects. It can be trenchant as well as meditative, hilarious as well as pensive. It bends metaphor to its will. At its best it has a homely felicity shot through, as often as not, with a familiar humour which builds a paragraph to a climax and then guides it down to a smooth conclusion. One example of this: Philip Firmin has just been told by the cousin with whom he is in love that she is engaged to be married to another man.

The pier tosses up to the skies, as though it had left its moorings —the houses on the cliff dance and reel, as though an earthquake was driving them—the sea walks up into the lodging-houses—and Philip's legs are failing under him: it is only for a moment. When you have a large, tough double-tooth out, doesn't the chair go up to the ceiling, and your head come off too? But, in the next instant, there is a grave gentleman before you, making you a bow, and concealing something in his right sleeve. The crash is over. You are a man again. Philip clutches hold of the chain-pier for a minute: it does not sink under him. The houses, after reeling for a second or two, reassume the perpendicular, and bulge their bow-windows towards the main. He can see the people looking from the windows, the carriages passing, Professor Spurrier riding on the cliff with eighteen young ladies, his pupils. In long-after days he remembers those absurd little incidents with a curious tenacity.[8]

The qualities of style which have been noted above, avoiding as they do sublimity on the one hand and commonness on the other, are those which bring Thackeray so much within the range of the eighteenth century that when he came to write *Henry Esmond* he had only to adapt that style a little to give

[8] This passage is cited also by Raymond Las Vergnas in his excellent discussion of Thackeray: *W. M. Thackeray—l'homme, le penseur, le romancier*, Paris, 1932.

it a surprising Queen Anne authenticity. Nevertheless it is surprising to find how little the style of *Esmond* differs in arrange-
ment and substance from Thackeray's normal style and how
completely, at the same time, he seems to have identified himself with a memoir-writer of the eighteenth century. There is
only a patina of archaisms, a few sprinkled 'hath's' and 'saith's'
and ' 'twas's,' and a fairly frequent use of 'says my lord' and
'says she.' The difference does not lie chiefly in vocabulary; more
general and characteristic is the sort of loose-knit, rambling sentence which seems to the unpedantic reader the manner in which
a colonel of Queen Anne's day might have written his history.

Thus: 'Esmond was especially amused with the talk of one
long fellow, with a great curling moustache, and blue eyes, that
was half a dozen inches taller than his swarthy little comrade
on the French side of the stream, and being asked by the Colonel to salute him said that he belonged to the Royal Cravats.' [9]
And again:

When they got to their second bottle, Harry Esmond used commonly to leave these two noble topers, who, though they talked
freely enough, Heaven knows, in his presence (Good Lord, what a set
of stories, of Alsatia and Spring Garden, of the taverns and gaming-
houses, of the ladies of the Court, and mesdames of the theatres, he
can recall out of their godly conversation!)—although I say they
talked before Esmond freely, yet they seemed pleased when he went
away, and then they had another bottle, and then they fell to cards,
and then my lord Mohun came to her ladyship's drawing-room;
leaving his boon companion to sleep off his wine.

The purest distillation of this sort of thing comes, of course,
in the famous parody of a *Spectator* paper, which is convincing
enough to have been written by Steele himself. No wonder Beatrix was taken in. But for the most part the sentence texture,
the broad rhythm of thought in *Esmond* is not consciously or
closely imitative at all; it is soaked so thoroughly in the atmosphere of a period that it becomes a sort of re-creation, even

[9] See the preface to T. C. and W. Snow's edition of *Esmond* for a discussion
of the language used.

to the extent of obscuring to the average reader the many places, both in conversation and in disquisition, where Thackeray expresses ideas that are not of the eighteenth century in tones that are modern. Over the whole book, however, eighteenth century or not, lies a heavy brooding sense of time past; it is steeped in a nostalgic recognition of the hurrying years. 'They passed thence through the music-gallery, long since dismantled, and Queen Elizabeth's rooms, in the clock-tower, and out into the terrace, where was a fine prospect of sunset, and the great darkling woods with a cloud of rooks returning; and the plain and river with Castlewood village beyond, and purple hills beautiful to look at . . .' 'We rode over Castlewood Downs before the breaking of dawn. We passed the very spot where the car was upset fourteen years since; and Mohun lay. The village was not up yet, nor the forge lighted, as we rode through it, passing by the elms, where the rooks were still roosting, and by the church, and over the bridge. We got off our horses at the bridge and walked up to the gate.' And sometimes Thackeray freezes in words a scene which has the plastic charm of a Gainsborough painting:

There was in the court a peculiar silence somehow; and the scene remained long in Esmond's memory;—the sky bright overhead; the buttresses of the building and the sundial casting shadow over the gilt *memento mori* inscribed underneath; the two dogs, a black greyhound and a spaniel nearly white, the one with his face up to the sun, and the other snuffing amongst the grass and stones, and my lord leaning over the fountain, which was plashing audibly. 'Tis strange how that scene and the sound of that fountain remain fixed on the memory of a man who has beheld a hundred sights of splendour, and danger too, of which he has kept no account.

Henry Esmond is not, in spite of its many delights, 'the greatest of all novels.' It is not even Thackeray's best or most penetrating. But it has warm brilliant spots and it tells a rattling good tale. It is more than a *tour de force;* it is a great artistic achievement.

CHAPTER NINE

Lectures: *The English Humourists* and *The Four Georges*

EVER SINCE his severe illness in 1849 Thackeray had been oppressed by the belief that he had few years left him, and he felt that he must somehow provide a competence for his daughters in the event of his death. As his fame increased his letters were filled with his relief that he need no longer worry about the financial future. During his first lecture visit to the United States in 1852-3 he watched the 'dollars roll in' with unfeigned delight; and during his second trip in 1855-6 he wrote back gleefully: 'I shall make all but £1000 in 5 weeks.' Still later, when he was taking *The Four Georges* up and down the English countryside he wrote to friends in America:

Think that at the end of next year if I work I shall be worth £20,000! It's as much as I want—10,000 apiece for the girls is enough for any author's daughters . . . I have taken shares in the *Transatlantic Telegraph*—I feel glad somehow to contribute to a thread that shall tie our two continents together—for though I don't love America I love Americans with all my heart.

And indeed Americans—if not America—had done well by him. He was fêted, applauded, and well paid. New York, Boston, Philadelphia, Baltimore, Savannah received him with unbounded enthusiasm. Thackeray, for his part, weary as he was of the turmoil and confusion and the uncomfortable travelling conditions which beset lecturers in the United States in the mid-nineteenth century, was genial and appreciative and made friends everywhere. Unlike Dickens who, after he had returned from a successful lecture tour of the States, had pilloried his hosts in *American Notes,* Thackeray refused to write a book about America. 'No man should write about the country under 5 years of experience, and as many of previous reading.' In this attitude Thackeray remains almost, if not quite, unique among his lecturing fellow countrymen before or since.

The first series of lectures, which he later took abroad, was *The English Humourists of the Eighteenth Century.* These were first given in London, in the spring and early summer of 1851, to brilliant and fashionable audiences. Thackeray was very nervous about his abilities as a lecturer and was somewhat dazed by his initial success. People like Macaulay, Carlyle, Wilberforce, Lord and Lady Ashburton, Hallam, Dickens, Doyle, Cruikshank, Harriet Martineau came to Willis's Rooms to hear him. Charlotte Brontë was there, and wrote to her father afterwards:

I have now heard one of Mr. Thackeray's lectures and seen the great Exhibition. On Thursday afternoon I went to hear the lecture. It was delivered in a large and splendid kind of saloon—that in which the great balls of Almack's are given. The walls were all painted and gilded, the benches were sofas stuffed and cushioned and covered with blue damask. The audience was composed of the *élite* of London society. Duchesses were there by the score, and amongst them the great and beautiful Duchess of Sutherland, the Queen's Mistress of the Robes. Amidst all this Thackeray just got up and spoke with as much simplicity and ease as if he had been speaking to a few friends by his own fireside. The lecture was truly good: he had taken pains with the composition. It was finished without being in the least studied; a quiet humour and graphic force enlivened it throughout.

In the series of six lectures Thackeray discussed Swift, Congreve, Addison, Steele, Prior, Gay, Pope, Hogarth, Smollett, Fielding, Sterne, and Goldsmith. He approaches them as humorists, under his own definition of a humorist, who becomes a writer to 'awaken and direct your love, your pity, your kindness . . . He takes upon himself to be the weekday preacher, so to speak.' This, together with Thackeray's announced purpose of treating the men and their lives rather than their books, gives the clue to the lectures. Within the limits of this approach and within the limits of Thackeray's own prejudices, Addison, Steele, Gay, Fielding, and Goldsmith would be likely to receive one kind of treatment; Swift, Congreve, and Sterne quite another. We find a small amount of literary criticism here, and a good deal of moralizing; a penetrating and sympathetic evaluation of character when Thackeray approved of his man, and much perverse and brilliantly wrong-headed diatribe when he could not. The lectures tell us by indirection a good deal about Thackeray. His portraits are those of a novelist rather than of an historian—underlining eccentricities, sharpening contrasts, highlighting the roughnesses. What we get at last is Thackeray's impression of these men, candid and clear, but so carefully selected and bent so by sympathy or lack of it that sometimes even when he speaks truth he gives a total effect of something less than truth. The fragility of his touchstone is seen in the test that he proposes early in his first lecture: 'Would we have liked to live with him? That is a question which, in dealing with these people's works, and thinking of their lives and peculiarities, every reader of biographies must put to himself.' No test could be simpler and no test could be less likely to lead a prejudiced biographer towards the light.

Nevertheless if one corrects, as he reads, some of the extravagances of the text, these lectures are still attractive and rewarding. Never had Thackeray written more easily or crisply. Within the range of his information and his predilections he is vigorous, trenchant, even brilliant. His discussion of Congreve is a good example of his eloquence. Compared with Macaulay, Thackeray is tender with the gaiety and youth of that vanished day, and he sees clearly that Congreve's comedy was a pagan protest against 'the new, hard, ascetic, pleasure-hating doctrine.' But Restoration comedy to him is a dead muse, even though he does not belabour it like Macaulay. He sees the passing of its youthfulness rather than feels its joys.

Congreve's comic feast flares with lights, and round the table, emptying their flaming bowls of drink, and exchanging the wildest jests and ribaldry, sit men and women, waited on by rascally valets and attendants as dissolute as their mistresses . . . [Congreve's comedies] are full of wit. Such manners as he observes, he observes with a great humour; but ah! it's a weary feast, that banquet of wit where no love is.

Addison, on the other hand—the Addison of *The Tatler* and *The Spectator*—not only makes us laugh but also leaves us good and happy, says Thackeray, and he honours him for his kind, serene impartiality. In an artificial age he 'began to speak with his noble, natural voice.' Thackeray admits his coldness and his lack of depth, 'his cheerful selfishness,' but he is a gentle satirist 'who hits no unfair blow.'

With a wealth of excellent detail and much brilliance of background Thackeray makes the Age of Anne live again when he comes to Richard Steele. Here again he repeats his concept of true historical writing: to become acquainted with the life and being of the time rather than the political transactions and the characters of the leading public men. What character of what great man, he asks, is known to us? 'In common life don't you often judge and misjudge a man's whole conduct, setting out from a wrong impression?'—a statement which we might well write in the margin against his denunciation of Swift. About Steele, however, Thackeray writes *con amore*. Out of the rapid, rattling, potpourri scene of the daily life of the time—churches, coffee-houses, chairmen, footmen, coaches, inns, highwaymen— comes the rollicking convivial Dick Steele, always sinning and repenting, 'deep in debt and in drink and in all the follies of the town' while writing the ardent devotional work *The Christian Hero*. Thackeray likes Steele's respect for women and his tenderness towards children, the sweet naturalness of his writing and his reckless good humour. There is, however, something a little unconsciously condescending in his praise of Steele. He delights to honour him but he finds it necessary to excuse him at length. He gives us too much of the 'poor Dick Steele' business, too much kindly emphasis upon his 'wild and chequered life,' his improvidence and weakness. Thackeray had no intent to damn by faint praise, nor does he, but he almost damns by forgiveness.

In quite a different manner he subdues the acidity and bitterness of Pope. He admits the unpleasant gallantry of Pope's letters to women but is able to find the rest of that doctored correspondence 'cheering and ennobling.' He grants that Pope established the Grub Street tradition and revelled in base descriptions of poor men's want, making generations believe 'that author and wretch, author and rags, author and dirt, gin, cowheel, tripe, poverty, duns, bailiffs, squalling children and clamorous landladies were always associated together.' Yet Pope's love for his mother excused, for Thackeray, almost everything else in his character. As for his opinion of Pope's literary powers, he calls him 'the greatest literary *artist* that England has seen.'

One would expect Thackeray to do full justice to Goldsmith, and he does, in his praise of Goldsmith's sentiment, his friendliness and compassion, his humble confession of faults and weaknesses, his pleasant little vanity, his gentleness and generosity. One would expect him to do less than justice to Sterne, and he does, peppering his pages with a fine disgust at the unregenerate clergyman, and writing half a lecture about him without mentioning my Uncle Toby. He has no patience with the 'cheap dribble' of Sterne's sentimentality, and less with his 'nasty humour,' his 'latent corruption,' his 'dreary *double-entendre*.' Only a small part of that looseness will Thackeray attribute to the times, so much freer than those of the Victorian ladies and gentlemen who were listening to the lecture. There is no doubt that much of Thackeray's horror is justifiable according to the standards of 1851, or that Sterne, in his letters, gave the moralist many openings. There was much that was peculiarly unpleasant in Sterne's personality. It is characteristic, however, that Thackeray should be so blinded by the ecstasy of his rage that he found it impossible to admire even where admiration would seem inevitable. Yet nowhere has Thackeray written in more pungent vein than in his desperate irritation with 'this actor, this quack.' Here again Thackeray is not untrue, but not all true.

The lectures on Swift and on Fielding are the most famous of all, and in each case Thackeray helped to set the tone which was to remain fixed in the public mind and to be the admiration and despair of subsequent judicial critics who set out calmly to correct error and recover truth.

The attack on Swift is the most damaging. He admits that Swift is 'the greatest wit of all time' and then sets out to make of him a demoniac, titanic creature almost outside the human family. Not quite outside, however. Thackeray looks on him as a highwayman in politics, a man servile, bitter, insulting, a gross bully, 'an awful, an evil spirit.' Yet he grants Swift's magnificent and dazzling genius, which could 'flash upon falsehood and scorch it into perdition, to penetrate into hidden motives, and expose the black thoughts of men.' And Swift's love for Stella becomes for Thackeray 'the pure star in that dark and tempestuous life.' The infinite pathos of Swift's frustrate love touches Thackeray, and he speaks nobly of it. He is curiously contradictory, however, concerning Swift's religion. In one place he says that 'Swift's was a reverent, was a pious spirit—for Swift could love and could pray,' and again he says that Swift 'suffered frightfully from the consciousness of his own scepticism, and that he had bent his pride so far down as to put his apostasy out to hire.'

Thackeray's general tone, however, is one of awed and fearful wonder at 'the great sufferings of this great man . . . He goes through life, tearing, like a man possessed with a devil. Like Abudah in the Arabian story, he is always looking out for the Fury, and knows that the night will come and the inevitable hag with it. What a night, my God, it was! what a lonely rage and long agony—what a vulture that tore the heart of that

giant!' Now this is very well for the Cambyses vein, and moreover it is undeniably Swift, if Swift a little out of focus. But
when Thackeray comes to judge his most characteristic writing
he cuts loose from all sane critical moorings. He acknowledges
the surprising humour and the honest satire of *Gulliver's Travels*
—'truth topsy-turvy, entirely logical and absurd'—yet goes on
to call the moral of *Gulliver* 'horrible and shameful, unmanly,
blasphemous.' Then this Jeremiah pronounces his considered
judgment: 'And giant and great as this Dean is, I say we should
hoot him.' Even more incredible is Thackeray's purblind rage
against *The Modest Proposal*. If ever a piece of writing showed
a lacerated tenderness it was this annihilating *reductio ad absur-
dum* of man's inhumanity to man. One wonders by what perverse misunderstanding Thackeray saw in it only the savagery
of a man who 'enters the nursery with the tread and gaiety of
an ogre,' exposing 'the unreasonableness of loving and having
children.' Here is real irony: the great satirist of the eighteenth
century stupidly misread by the great Victorian satirist!

Thackeray's treatment of Swift arouses one's critical curiosity,
the more so because it is easy to point out parallels between the
two men. Thackeray is in some ways a paler Swift, less misanthropic, less bitterly satirical, less given to dwelling upon the
emblems of mortality; but also lonely and melancholy (like most
satirists). Thackeray had also watched one who was dear to him
go down, as Swift had gone, into the darkness of an unbalanced
mind. James Hannay once told Thackeray that he and the Dean
of St. Patrick's had a great deal in common and 'resembled each
other in certain important points more than we should find many
humorists do if we viewed them in couples.'[1] Here may lie
part of the answer. In the lecture on Congreve Thackeray says
that Swift is a humorous philosopher whose truth frightens one.
'Frightens one'! Is this the reason Thackeray was so hard on
Swift? In his early years Thackeray had done his share of cutting
and slashing, penetrating the follies and hypocrisies of men less

[1] 'Thackeray on Swift,' *Temple Bar*, 1867. Thackeray's reply is not recorded.

mordantly than Swift but with a similar disillusion. Now he had mellowed, and the native benignity and the relish for life which had never been Swift's portion had softened the satirist. But it is possible that he had a dim, almost unacknowledged recognition of at least a potential kinship with Swift and that the latter led him to brinks towards which his own inclination had drawn him in dark hours, but of which what was mild and healthy in his nature did not approve.

With Fielding, Thackeray was on much happier ground. The links with Swift are tenuous and difficult; there is no doubt of Thackeray's clear comradeship, temperamentally and artistically, with Fielding. He loved the eighteenth-century novelist's 'vast health and robust appetite, his ardent spirits, his joyful humour, and his keen and healthy relish for life,' just as he scorned Richardson, the 'puny cockney bookseller, pouring out endless volumes of sentimental twaddle.' Like Fielding Thackeray described what he knew and saw, and like Fielding he was fond of virtue, despised meanness, and was gentle with honest frailty. Like Fielding the novel was to him a personal art form, meant to present average people not too depraved and not too noble. Moreover, Thackeray could declare with Fielding: 'I intend to digress through this whole history, as often as I see occasion, of which I am myself a better judge than any pitiful critic whatever.' [2] Nevertheless it is not surprising that Thackeray liked Fielding's *Amelia* (where Fielding least follows his own theories) the best of his novels, and convinced himself, on the principle that 'human nature is always pleased with the spectacle of innocence rescued by fidelity, purity and courage,' that we ought to like Captain Booth better than Tom Jones—that the former is the better hero. Thackeray can't quite forgive Fielding the Lady Bellaston episode in *Tom Jones,* in spite of the fact that he is fully aware that the morality of the eighteenth century was not that of the nineteenth. Nor does he think he ought to approve of Fielding's 'evident liking and admiration for Mr. Jones.'

[2] *Tom Jones,* Bk. I, ch. 2.

Thackeray indulges in some casuistry about Tom's right to clas-
sify as a 'hero' in the Victorian sense, a position which Fielding
would never have claimed for Tom and which the author of
'a novel without a hero' should have known better than to
demand.[3] 'I protest,' says Thackeray, 'even against his being
considered more than an ordinary young fellow, ruddy-cheeked,
broad-shouldered, and fond of wine and pleasure. He would not
rob a church, but that is all . . . But a hero with a flawed reputation . . .' etc., etc. Of all writers it is strange to see Thackeray
choking so alarmingly over the title of 'hero' or 'non-hero.'

But these collateral swim-bladders of morality which Thackeray throws out do not hide his relish for Fielding's art. 'What
an admirable gift of nature was it by which the author of these
tales was endowed, and which enabled him to fix our interest,
to waken our sympathy, to seize upon our credulity, so that we
believe in its people—speculate gravely upon their faults or their
excellences . . . What multitudes of truths has that man left
behind him! What generations he has taught to laugh wisely
and fairly!'

Thackeray's picture of the man Fielding, however, has caused
much head-shaking among subsequent biographers who have
had to devote no little space to correcting the impression which

---

[3] Coleridge knew better, and the note from Coleridge which corrects Thackeray is inserted at the foot of the page in the printed edition of the lectures.
(James Hannay had been commissioned to add the notes.)

'Manners change from generation to generation, and with manners morals
appear to change—actually change with some, but appear to change with all
but the abandoned. A young man of the present day who should act as Tom
Jones is supposed to act at Upton, with Lady Bellaston, &c., would not be a
Tom Jones; and a Tom Jones of the present day, without perhaps being in
the ground a better man, would have perished rather than submit to be kept
by a harridan of fortune. Therefore, this novel is, and indeed pretends to be,
no example of conduct. But, notwithstanding all this, I do loathe the cant which
can recommend *Pamela* and *Clarissa Harlowe* as strictly moral, although they
poison the imagination of the young with continued doses of *tinct. lyttæ,* while
Tom Jones is prohibited as loose. I do not speak of young women; but a young
man whose heart or feelings can be injured, or even his passions excited by this
novel, is already thoroughly corrupt. There is a cheerful, sunshiny, breezy spirit,
that prevails everywhere, strongly contrasted with the close, hot, day-dreamy
continuity of Richardson.' (*Literary Remains,* II, 374.)

Thackeray gives of a genial wine-bibber, wild and dissipated in his youth, accustomed to being carried home on the shoulders of watchmen. Thackeray spares the moral lash here, and it needs to be said that in so doing he was ahead of his time, but he makes his case the more damagingly plausible by his frank apologies, and by identifying Fielding unjustifiably with the heroes of his books. 'Why hide his faults? . . . Why not show him, like him as he is . . . with inked ruffles, and claret stains on his tarnished laced coat, and on his manly face the marks of good fellowship, of illness, of kindness, of care, and wine.' Subsequent investigation has shown, of course, that Thackeray's facts, gathered from erroneous tradition, were wrong—and that he was also inclined to touch up the picture with something of a novelist's licence. Nevertheless, as Professor Cross admits, Thackeray 'intended no harm. His appreciation of Fielding's novels was whole-hearted and sincere; it gave Fielding a higher place in the republic of letters than he had enjoyed at any time since his death.'[4]

These thumb-nail biographies of eighteenth-century humorists are arranged with a shrewd feeling for effect, are vigorous and lively and for the most part appreciative. So superb is the style in which they are couched that they are impressive even where distorted in interpretation. Thackeray is most in error when his prejudices or his misinformation lead him astray; he is most happy when an admiration for an author blends with a sympathy for his misfortunes and a tolerance for his more gracious human weaknesses, as in the case of Goldsmith and Fielding. One concerned for the welfare of Thackeray's critical reputation would wish he had blotted many a line. What would then remain, however, we should not willingly lose.

Thackeray's lectures on the Four Georges were first delivered in the United States; they were the occasion of his second visit there, in 1855-6. He spoke to crowded houses, who received him

4 Wilbur L. Cross: *The History of Henry Fielding,* 3 vols., New Haven, 1918, III, 226.

even more enthusiastically than on his earlier visit. At first there was some doubt about the success of the lectures. 'The people did not know,' Thackeray wrote, 'what to make of George I and his strumpets. Morality was staggered. But they liked better and better with each lecture, and now they're done and the success of the affair beyond a question. Last night at Brooklyn there were twenty-five hundred persons at the lecture.' [5] The audiences liked the lecture on George III best, said Thackeray, 'on account of the pathetic business.'

On his return to England in the spring of 1856 Thackeray repeated the lectures in London, to the confusion of some critics who had declared that he would not have the courage to attack the Hanovers on their own ground. Later he took the lectures through the provinces, going as far north as Edinburgh. There he found it necessary to defend himself against the charge of disloyalty. This he did by referring to his warm praise of the Queen in the lecture on George IV and by pointing out that 'in speaking the truth as we hold it of a bad sovereign, we are paying no disrespect at all to a good one.'

Thackeray's severe criticism of the Georges had been foreshadowed in 1845, when he had printed in *Punch* a series of acid epitaphs on those monarchs. In like manner the paper 'The Snob Royal' in 1846 was a vitriolic preliminary dissection of George IV—'the first gentleman of Europe' as Thackeray liked to call him. This sketch ended: 'Out of Court, out of Court, fat old Florizel! Beadles, turn out that bloated pimple-faced man! —If Gorgius must have a statue in the new Palace which the Brentford nation is building, it ought to be set up in the Flunkeys' Hall.' Ten years later Thackeray was no less severe if more polished in his excoriation.

Thackeray is as much concerned in these lectures with giving the portrait of an age as with the kings themselves. He culls

---

[5] Letter to Frank Fladgate, 14 November 1855. See J. G. Wilson: *Thackeray in the United States*, I, 214. Charles Pearman, Thackeray's valet, put it more bluntly in his diary: '. . . he was welcomed heartily; the lecture was too smutty for the fair sex.'

from the memoir writers many anecdotes and bits of local colour
and social history, and is eager to recapture the feeling of the
times. In the case of the first two Georges particularly, much of
the material relates not specifically to the kings but rather to
their intellectual, social, and moral *milieu*. George I appears as
a shrewd, selfish ruler, insulated from the flow of English life
by his German court and his ugly mistresses. Yet he did, Thackeray acknowledges, keep his compact with his English subjects,
preserving and transmitting their liberties. In the lecture on the
second George, Thackeray sketches in briefly the picture of the
choleric little sovereign who cracked ribald jokes at bishops, who
was homesick for Hanover and kept returning there without
being in the least missed by his English subjects. Thackeray's
real purpose is to bring back the flavour of a corrupt and selfish
age; so we get a great deal about Horace Walpole and Lady
Suffolk and old Peterborough, about the games the people
played, the bottles of wine they drank, the poems they wrote,
the life they lived in London and in the country towns. All
social England appears, from the Pump Room at Bath to the
inns and fairs of the villages. This is the kind of history that
Thackeray could write well, and the descriptions sparkle.

In similar fashion he constructs vividly the riotous, hard-drinking, hard-living society of George III, a world extravagant beyond measure, surrounding the exemplary, frugal, and pious
young king with 'a court society as dissolute as one country
ever knew.' Against the picture of the Marches, the Selwyns, and
the Chesterfields Thackeray threw the shadow of the real giants
of the age—Johnson, Burke, Garrick, Goldsmith, Reynolds. 'It
is to the middle class,' said Thackeray, speaking to the middle
classes, 'we must look for the safety of England.' George III,
'simple, stubborn, affectionate, bigoted,' he treats with more pity
than contempt, particularly as he appeared in his last years,
sightless and mad and deaf—a story 'too terrible for tears . . .
All history presents no sadder figure than that of the old man,
blind and deprived of reason, wandering through the rooms of
his palace, addressing imaginary parliaments, reviewing fancied

troops, holding ghostly courts.' In general, Thackeray throws the spotlight on George's homely virtues and on the pathos of his decline rather than on his dullness and obstinacy.

In the opening lines of his last lecture Thackeray expresses bluntly and scathingly his contempt for George IV—'a worn-out voluptuary, a great simalacrum.' In extenuation he admits that this royal debauchee 'had more temptations than most.' 'He was kind to his servants,' says Thackeray, searching to see what good might be said of the prince. The brilliant part of this lecture, as of the others, is the background description of the period—the dissipations and reckless high jinks of the Regency days, the open vice and corruption of the court of George IV. At the end, and not insincerely, Thackeray throws into effective contrast the elaborate, pretentious decorations of Carlton House at the time of George's twenty-first birthday, and the dignified resignation speech, in the same year, of George Washington.

The style in these lectures is easily conversational, but not too familiar; eloquent, but not oratorical. In the end it is an artistic product that he presents, painting in the lights and shadows boldly, as a popular lecturer must. His synthesis has all the composition of a consciously shaped creation: vivid, lively, full of sharp contrasts, emphasizing the depravity of eighteenth-century fashionable life, but playing off against that another world of humility and dignity and worth—a world usually represented, it is interesting to note, by literary figures.

CHAPTER TEN

The Newcomes

THE BIRTH of one of Thackeray's novels is usually marked in his letters by a trail of groans and laments, for literary generation came hard to him. This was particularly true of *The Newcomes,* begun at Baden in July 1853, and finished at Paris in June 1855, having been issued in twenty-four monthly parts. Much of it he wrote in actual physical pain, in the intervals of recurrent seizures which left him weak and helpless.[1] More and more frequently we find Thackeray referring to himself as an old man, ready at 43 to close his accounts. Writing to Libby Strong in 1854 he says:

As in the railroad tunnels (unknown in your free country) we get deeper and deeper plunging into the dark and the bright spot we set out from grows fainter and fainter till it winks out invisible . . . Something dismal must be in the air for instead of writing gaily to a young lady on her birthday see the page is full of darkness, death, weariness of soul, failing memory, advancing decrepitude, speedy departure.[2]

While writing No. 2 of *The Newcomes* he told his mother:

[1] Clean-cut medical diagnoses are infrequent in Victorian memoirs, but it is pretty clear that Thackeray suffered from stricture, and at one time contemplated an operation. One of the books in his library at the time of his death was Thompson's *Pathology and Treatment of the Stricture of the Urethra.*
[2] *Letters to an American Family,* pp. 189, 191.

I can't but see it is a repetition of past performances, and think that vein is pretty nigh worked out in me. Never mind; . . . this is not written for glory, but for quite as good an object, namely, money, which will profit the children more than reputation when there's an end of me, and money and reputation are alike pretty indifferent . . . One of Dickens's immense superiorities over me is the great fecundity of his imagination.

About the same time he wrote to the Baxters: 'I'm in low spirits about The Newcomes. It's not good. It's stupid. It haunts me like a great stupid ghost. I think it says why do you go on writing this rubbish? You are old, you have no more invention, &c.' [3] Out of all this pain, despair, and fear of failing powers came what is in many ways the richest of all his novels, the complete realization of his talent for seizing upon a whole society and fixing it in words. As time went on Thackeray was inclined to repeat his characters and situations; none knew that better than he. In some ways even *The Newcomes* is just a better *Pendennis,* but it is so much better that it stands, in its scope and variety, with *Vanity Fair* at the head of all the novels. Never had Thackeray's grasp of character been firmer, his observation shrewder, his satire sharper, or his humanity deeper. There is in *The Newcomes* a balance of all that is best in Thackeray and least of that with which it has been necessary for us to find fault. Nor is there, for this reader at least, any discernible weariness of hand. It would have been better, doubtless, if he had shortened and tightened the novel—the story drags in the middle—better if he had shown less tenacity in the development of some minor incidents. Nevertheless the effect here, as in any great novel of manners, is partly cumulative. If the pity and terror of the last hundred pages seem too long-drawn-out it is only because the suffering of Clive and his father in the hands of the relentless Campaigner seems almost too real for fiction, and the death of Colonel Newcome a too long-delayed release from the rack of a world of nightmare hideousness.

[3] Ibid., p. 89.

Thackeray had never worked on a broader canvas or with more technical skill. In none of his novels is there a larger *dramatis personæ,* yet each is sharply defined and all fit into the mosaic which makes up the memoirs of 'a most respectable family.' One admires Thackeray's deftness in weaving the thread of his story in and out of his crowds of people, avoiding confusion, connecting tangential groups logically and credibly, maintaining always a delicate sense of the relation of the individual to the larger family units whose history is the theme of the novel. The plot, as always, is slight, but the number of people who have to be manœuvered is so great and the interwoven actions so potentially complicated that Thackeray's control here is beyond praise.

The device of having Pendennis record the story seemed to give Thackeray a good deal of satisfaction. 'By the help of this little mask,' he wrote to Mrs. Baxter, 'I shall be able to talk more at ease than in my own person. I . . . am immensely relieved by adopting it.' He makes a good deal of effort to keep the point of view consistent, and the use of Pendennis gives the story the air of actuality which comes with an eye-witness report. It suits Thackeray's objective method, which reports the feelings of his people largely on the basis of what can be seen and heard, without trying to get too deeply into their streams-of-consciousness.[4]

The impression, too, of a whole fictional society is increased by Thackeray's genial habit of re-introducing characters from past novels. Not only the Pendennises appear. George Warrington, living in the Temple with Pen, is given some typically forthright speeches. Blanche Amory is mentioned. In the very first chapter Captain Costigan comes into the Cave of Harmony,

---

[4] Thackeray supplements this objective approach, of course, by his own, or Pendennis's, interpretations. Pen himself is unobtrusive enough, particularly before his marriage, but in the latter part of the book one gets a little weary of Laura's chirping domesticity, her too-sweet serenity and her smug assurance. Her sympathies are generous, but we would appreciate her more if Pen were less insistent upon what Laura would doubtless have called their 'connubial bliss.'

drunk, and sings a bawdy song which so angers Colonel Newcome that he makes an angry speech and stalks out with Clive.
Dobbin appears at one of Colonel Newcome's dinners; Rawdon
Crawley is discussed, as well as Rebecca Sharp in her later
incarnation: the one 'who wrote the hymns, you know, and
goes to Mr. Honeyman's chapel.'

Chesterton called Thackeray 'the novelist of memory, that is,
of the emotion of experience.' In *The Newcomes,* as in *Pendennis*
and *Henry Esmond,* the author resurrects the scenes and feelings
of his youth, treating with a loving tenderness those reminiscences of the past to which he was always so sensitive. The whole
Anglo-Indian background had been Thackeray's own. Clive, like
Thackeray, had been born in India and had come to England
as a boy, stopping at St. Helena on the way to see Napoleon's
tomb. The Miss Honeyman who took charge of young Clive in
England was Thackeray's great-aunt Becher. Both lads (like so
many of Thackeray's characters) went to school at Grey Friars.
Clive became an artist; like Thackeray, he was not a particularly good artist and knew it. But Clive, like Thackeray, loved
to paint, and the author enters with high zest into the descriptions of artists and their labours, their haunts, and their pleasures.
When Clive describes ecstatically the beauty of Ethel he does
so in painters' terms of colour and line. His letters from Rome
on art and artists sound like one of Titmarsh's travelogues—as
indeed they are. Thackeray in his student days must have ex-
perienced, as Clive did, some of the scorn felt for the artist's
profession by many respectable snobs. Even Colonel Newcome
is not too happy about Clive's desire to be an artist, although
he wants to be pleased by what pleases Clive. There is another
connection, too, between Thackeray and his hero, which opens
vistas of speculation. James Russell Lowell says that once Thackeray, when reading aloud one of the Campaigner's worst tirades,
interrupted himself to say: 'That's my she-devil of a mother-in-
law, you know, whom I have the good fortune to possess still.'[5]

---

[5] *Thackeray in the United States,* I, 327-8. Letter written to Charles Eliot
Norton, 11 August, 1856.

This helps to illuminate those biographically dim years of Thackeray's early married life and to explain the terrifying veracity of the Campaigner's portrait.

Thackeray's early experiences, however, are only a background for the families whose story the novel reveals. It is, by and large, a slow-moving story. Very little happens during the first 250 pages. It takes that long to get the characters introduced and to set at work the delicate forces of attraction and repulsion which create the tensions for the later crises. Yet there is a lot of minor if not of major action, and it is all good humoured and interesting, accompanied by much lively and penetrating characterization. Stroke by stroke, in conversation and description, Thackeray brings out the subtle differences which make individuals of his people. Few novelists can immerse the reader as completely in the satisfactions that come from learning to know people, so that he forgets to ask after the plot. Thus we meet Fred Bayham, blustery, voluble, with a gargantuan humour and a harmless grandiloquence: 'a man very easily moved—as it were, a softened sinner'; Paul de Florac, kindly, gay, and impeccably French; Lord Farintosh, an offensive sprig of decayed nobility, and Lord Kew, wayward but generous, sensible and unaffected; Rosey Mackenzie, with her pretty face and sweet manners, which contrast so sharply with the ultimate stark tragedy of her pathetic career under the almost hypnotic control of her mother—but the list is too long for more than an indication here of its variety.

The contemporary reviewers liked to point out what is quite true: that *The Newcomes* has more honest and amiable people than we find in any of Thackeray's previous novels; that against Barnes and the Campaigner and Mrs. Hobson Newcome and Lady Kew can be set off a whole galaxy of 'good' people—the saintly artist J. J. Ridley, Colonel Newcome, the Countess de Florac, Ethel, Clive, Miss Honeyman, and the immaculate Mrs. Laura.[6] At the same time it needs to be remembered that evil

---

[6] One reviewer, however, found occasion to lament that in spite of Ethel's attractiveness and brilliance 'we would rather not have our daughters resemble

appears here in its worst form—not villainy on a heroic scale, but malignant and hard, the resultant of the cumulative little hatreds which are the hardest of all to live with.

The Newcomes themselves are of course the center of the story. Sir Brian, the mildest of the lot. His wife, Lady Ann, who indulges in flighty disconnected monologues and who is overcome by the weariness of her life with a husband whom she married from a sense of duty, and whom she despises. Lady Kew, the antique tyrannical grandmother who takes control of Ethel's career and rules the family with an iron hand—the best of all Thackeray's masterful, strong-willed, worldly, elderly matriarchs. She is a fitting companion piece for Lord Steyne, her brother. Hobson and Mrs. Hobson Newcome—the former horsey, cold-hearted, selfish, and successful, the latter meanly jealous of her sister-in-law, Lady Ann, believing in her own superiority, not only envious but proud of her envy, mistaking it for 'honesty and public spirit.'

And in the midst of this merry crew Ethel and Clive and the Colonel—and Barnes, too, as believable a villain as Thackeray ever conceived. Barnes is a mean-spirited little snob, impudent, clever, and cowardly. He has a standing feud with Clive and the Colonel. He marries the spiritless Lady Clara for her rank and then abuses her until she runs away with a former suitor. After this catastrophe come the precious divorce-court scenes, with Barnes, who had previously ruined and deserted a poor young girl, dragging the family name farther into the mud. Later, in his campaign for a seat in Parliament, he tries the religious dodge and gives two lectures on 'The Poetry of Childhood' and 'The Poetry of Womanhood, and the Affections.' Here this 'scrupulously whited sepulchre' reaches his apotheosis.

The theme of *The Newcomes,* repeated as it is in a variety of ways by parallel situations, emerges with perfect clarity. Its

this young lady . . . If this [picture of her] is not good morals, it is still less good art. Providence has exempted woman from the grosser temptations, and romance has gifted her with a more ethereal life.' (*Blackwood's Magazine,* January 1855, p. 95.)

social world is that of the borderline between the upper middle classes and the aristocracy, with all the tawdry ambitions and mean envies which afflict those with wealth who are eager to marry their children to titles, and those aristocrats willing to dilute their noble blood in order to make their fortunes. Thackeray is on his familiar hunt for pretension and greed. The career of Ethel Newcome is a battle against her family's—and particularly Lady Kew's—insistence that she do the proper thing and marry title and money. Her match with Lord Kew does not come off, and she escapes Lord Farintosh only when the defection of Barnes's wife makes her see the shamefulness of the worldly marriages to which her society is devoted. Thackeray is very bitter against such made-marriages; the book is an exposition of the grief and despair which come in their wake. His outburst against the domestic bargainings which he observes at Baden is typical: 'What is shame? Virtue is very often shameful according to the English social constitution, and shame honourable . . . Ah! yes; all stories are old. You proud matrons in your Mayfair markets, have you never seen a virgin sold, or sold one?' [7] He pretends to be very much discouraged with Ethel's acceptance of her family's iron tradition:

A girl of great beauty, high temper, and strong natural intellect, who submits to be dragged hither and thither in an old grandmother's leash, and in pursuit of a husband [Lord Farintosh] who will run away from the couple, such a person, I say, is in a very awkward position as a heroine; and I believe if I had another ready to my hand (and unless there were extenuating circumstances), Ethel should be deposed at this very sentence.

The full force of Thackeray's irony is employed in his description of the outcome of this way of life as seen in the Newcome Divorce Bill in the House of Lords, where the whole shabby business of Barnes's loveless marriage is laid before the British

[7] One just criticism of the book is that Thackeray, in the person of author, keeps reminding us too frequently of his angry point of view here. The repetition would doubtless have been less noticeable had one been reading the novel in monthly instalments.

public. Thackeray is very stern with the laws which would put money into Barnes's pocket for having trampled on his wife 'and scorned her, and driven her to ruin . . . O Hymen, Hymenæe! The bishops, beadles, clergy, pew-openers, and other officers of the temple dedicated to Heaven under the invocation of St. George, will officiate in the same place at scores and scores more of such marriages: and St. George of England may behold virgin after virgin offered up to the devouring monster, Mammon (with many most respectable female dragons looking on) . . .'

He works in a great deal of incidental glancing satire, too, such as his comment on social decorum: 'Backbiting is all fair in society. Abuse me, and I will abuse you; but let us be friends when we meet'; or his whimsical elucidation, in respect to Lady Kew, of the advantages which a furious temper brings: such a person gets what she wants. 'Whereas for you and me, who have the tempers of angels, and were never known to be angry or complain, nobody cares whether we are pleased or not.' Yet there is little distortion of characterization in the novel for burlesque effect. Trollope complained that Charles Honeyman was not a real clergyman (certainly he never came from Barsetshire) and perhaps Honeyman is too broadly sketched to be true. Nevertheless there is a curious elaborate authenticity about him —his banal oratory, his high-flown cant, his lazy luxuriousness. He was inclined to cry a good deal in his sermons; no one understood the handkerchief business better than he. When this fashionable preacher's debts caught up with him, Clive interviewed 'the slippery penitent' in the sponging house and Colonel Newcome insisted on settling his debts, though he sickened of Honeyman's 'expressions of rapturous gratitude.' Better days return to Honeyman when he livens up his church service by means of shrewd if questionable publicity. Thackeray's satire is not on the cloth so much as on the dupes taken in by such roguery. He had for Honeyman the amused appreciation of one who can admire a skilful sinner without loving the sin.

One of the criticisms brought against *The Newcomes* is that

Thackeray is unable here, indeed is unable in any of his work, to enunciate great truths; that at most he generalizes on his social observation; that he never draws a man of strong convictions or of thoughtful mind; that his insight is delicate rather than profound; in short, that he lacks *ideas* in the larger sense. The charge is serious enough to merit close consideration. Certainly Thackeray's approach was not patently intellectual or philosophical in the sense that Charlotte Brontë's or George Eliot's or Meredith's was. It is not hard to list his chief ideas in *The Newcomes:* the Peerage is the Bible of English society; marriages made for money are not likely to be happy; not all poor men are honest; the way to get ahead in society is to push yourself forward; every one has a skeleton in his closet; hearts do not break for love; innocent old gentlemen are likely to be imposed on. But to say that such a body of statement catches the main drift of a Thackeray novel is as ridiculous as to say that Shakespeare wrote *King Lear* to prove that old men had better not divide their kingdoms before they die; that ungrateful children are likely to fight among themselves, and that bastardy is a social handicap. To be sure, Thackeray does rely more on his intuition than on his reasoning power to approach truth, and his best ideas are expressed concretely through character rather than through exhortation. Profundity, however, is a matter of relative definition, and Thackeray's deep and sensitive intuitions coupled with his microscopic observation give him a grasp of those borderline suggestions of character which are not pure idea, or yet pure feeling, but which probe and illuminate facets of human nature sometimes hidden from the philosopher. 'I have no head above my eyes,' he said, and some people have taken him at his word. Critics have carped at his pin-hole view of English society, and it is only fair to say that he ignored many of the aspects of his contemporary civilization which filled the pages of his fellow novelists. But it is uncritical to complain of what Thackeray did not do instead of inspecting the quality of his perception within his acknowledged range. There one finds a subtlety and incisiveness which in their sharpness and understanding approximate if they do not constitute profundity.

All this brings up again the quality of Thackeray's asides and comments. It has not been sufficiently noted that often his comments are merely a means of oblique characterization. He frequently implies in these commentaries qualities of character which are hard to put into words. Out of a seeming irrelevance, or what appears to be an unnecessarily detailed parenthesis of illustration, Thackeray often draws allusively an implication which, more bluntly presented, would be misunderstood. Again, he tempers his severity and at the same time gives universal scope to the peccadilloes of his characters by referring their individual aberrations to a larger scheme of human frailty. As Chesterton puts it, Thackeray says easily that all is vanity so as not to say that Ethel Newcome was vain. The whimsical humour of his parentheses is likely to obscure the fact that they are more than amusing: they give an artistic extension to what we may speak of boldly as his idea.

An illustration of this. Thackeray wants to say that 'Charles Honeyman, the beloved and popular preacher . . . who melts, rouses, terrifies in the pulpit; who charms over the tea-urn and the bland bread-and-butter: Charles Honeyman has one or two skeleton closets in his lodgings, Walpole Street, Mayfair.' The statement is clear and seemingly sufficient. But Thackeray also knows that he is on the fringe of a disturbing speculation which applies to others as well as to the egregious Honeyman. So he elaborates an aside in which a seemingly fanciful imagination plays over the surface of a frightening truth.

The writer of these veracious pages was once walking through a splendid English palace standing amidst parks and gardens, than which none more magnificent has been since the days of Aladdin, in company with a melancholy friend, who viewed all things darkly through his gloomy eyes. The housekeeper, pattering on before us from chamber to chamber, was expatiating upon the magnificence of this picture; the beauty of that statue; the marvellous richness of these hangings and carpets; the admirable likeness of the late Marquis, by Sir Thomas; of his father the fifth Earl, by Sir Joshua, and so on; when, in the very richest room of the whole castle, Hicks—such was my melancholy companion's name—stopped the cicerone in her prattle, saying in a hollow voice, 'And now, madam, will you show us the closet *where the skeleton is?*' The scared functionary paused in the midst of her harangue; that article was not inserted in the catalogue which she daily utters to visitors for their half-crown. Hicks's question brought a darkness down upon the hall where we were standing. We did not see the room: and yet I have no doubt that there is such a one; and ever after, when I have thought of the splendid castle towering in the midst of shady trees, under which the dappled deer are browsing; of the terraces gleaming with statues, and bright with a hundred thousand flowers; of the bridges and shining fountains and rivers wherein the castle windows reflect their festive gleams, when the halls are filled with happy feasters, and over the darkling woods comes the sound of music;—always, I say, when I think of Castle Bluebeard, it is to think of that dark little closet, which I know is there, and which the lordly owner opens shuddering—after midnight—when he is sleepless and *must* go unlock it, when the palace is hushed, when beauties are sleeping around him unconscious, and revellers are at rest. Oh, Mrs. Housekeeper, all the other keys hast thou; but that key thou hast not!

Have we not all such closets, my jolly friend, as well as the noble Marquis of Carabas? At night, when all the house is asleep but you, don't you get up and peep into yours? When you in your turn are slumbering, up gets Mrs. Brown from your side, steals downstairs like Amina to her ghoul, clicks open the secret door, and looks into *her* dark repository. Did she tell you of that little affair with Smith long before she knew you? Psha! who knows anyone save himself alone? Who, in showing his house to the closest and dearest, doesn't keep back the key of a closet or two? I think of a lovely reader laying down the page and looking over at her unconscious husband, asleep, perhaps, after dinner. Yes, madam, a closet he hath: and you, who pry into everything, shall never have the key of it. I think of some honest Othello pausing over this very sentence in a railway carriage, and stealthily gazing at Desdemona opposite to him, innocently administering sandwiches to their little boy—I am trying to turn off the sentence with a joke, you see—I feel it is growing too dreadful, too serious.

All this to explain Charles Honeyman!—and yet not all Charles Honeyman. Here is a quality of apparently casual arm-chair imagination, pleasantly garrulous, which is in truth disguised artistry of a high order.

Sometimes the ironic implications are conveyed in direct description, as in the episode of Lady Kew's funeral, with its griefless mourners.

Leave we yonder velvet-palled box, spangled with fantastic heraldry, and containing within the aged slough and envelope of a soul gone to render its account. Look rather at the living audience standing around the shell:—the deep grief on Barnes Newcome's fine countenance; the sadness depicted in the face of the Most Noble the Marquis of Farintosh; the sympathy of her Ladyship's medical man, (who came in the third mourning carriage) . . . The ceremony over, the undertaker's gentlemen clamber on the roof of the vacant hearse, into which palls, tressels, trays of feathers, are inserted, and the horses break out into a trot, and the empty carriages, expressing the deep grief of the deceased lady's friends, depart homeward.

Or again, in the brevity of a single sentence, 'The true pleasure of life,' he says quietly, 'is to live with your inferiors.' No, to underestimate the potency of Thackeray's irony is to miss one of the main clues to his greatness.

At the center of the manifold and shifting lines of tension in *The Newcomes* is Ethel Newcome. She is unequivocally Thackeray's greatest heroine, with the wit and intelligence and verve of Becky or Beatrix but with a gentleness and sympathy denied those brilliant adventuresses. For once Thackeray has been able to draw a girl whom we can respect as well as admire, who in spite of her waywardness has genuine intellectual and emotional integrity. She has none of the fluttering softness of Amelia or Laura or Rachel, and Thackeray finds it possible to admire her without indulging in the wheezy genuflections with which he bent before the altar of femininity in his description of those earlier heroines. We get angry with Ethel, but we know that she can be angry with herself, and we never lose our respect for her. She is high-spirited without being hard, warm without being spongily soft. To put it bluntly, Ethel, after she has been ripened by chastening experience, is almost the only heroine of Thackeray's with whom the modern reader would want to take a matrimonial plunge. She would neither poison his punch *à la* Becky nor water it with Sedleyan tears of sensibility. She is simply a superb creation, and in spite of the contemporary reviewer's opinion quoted above, one could do worse than to have daughters like her.

We like Ethel from the first moment we see her, when, contrary to the convention of her family, she gives her uncle the Colonel her immediate affection. We like her when she irritates Clive by making fun of his artist's mustachios and that sensitive young gentleman sets her down as a very haughty, spoiled, aristocratic young creature. She is fond of Clive, however, and battles Barnes and Lady Kew on his behalf. Quick to detect affectation or insincerity, as Thackeray points out, impatient of dullness or pomposity, scornful of flattery or meanness, she despises not only her brother Barnes but also most of the circle in which she moves. She is not popular with women. She falls in love with Clive but will hardly admit it, for under the influence of the wily Lady Kew she has been forced into the grooves of the family tradition which demands that she should marry for wealth and social position. Not that she is unambitious herself; she discovers that she can tolerate admiration and luxury. Thackeray makes it clear, however, that this proud-spirited young woman is torn by conflicting impulses. Her better self is contemptuous of the great world which she nevertheless accepts. It is true that one can never be sure how much her refusal of Clive and her successive engagements to Lord Kew and Lord Farintosh are due to a fatalistic resignation and how much to her own ambition, although the former motive is stronger than the latter. There is plenty of evidence that she is disgusted with her own compliant worldliness and that she conducts herself 'as a most reckless and intrepid young flirt' because of an unhappy bitterness with her lot.

At the art exhibit Ethel tells Lady Kew that 'we young ladies in the world, when we are exhibiting, ought to have little green tickets pinned on our backs, with "Sold" written on them; it would prevent trouble and future haggling, you know. Then at the end of the season the owner would come to carry us home.' Lady Kew says shortly, 'Ethel, you are a fool,' and is infuriated when that night at dinner Ethel appears before the assembled Newcome family and Lord Kew with a bright green ticket pinned on her frock.

Yet in spite of her high-tempered revolt she bows her head to the seemingly inevitable. Kew, when she dismissed him, was generous enough not to want Ethel to marry without love. He knew that she loved Clive, who, he said, 'is a thousand times cleverer and better than I am.' But later she tells Clive, kindly and affectionately, that whatever their feelings may be, neither of them can alter their conditions. She must be obedient, she says, to her parents.

It takes the horrible object lesson of Barnes's domestic collapse to bring Ethel to her senses. By that time Clive is on the verge of marrying the placid and docile Rosey Mackenzie, and Ethel and Clive have to wait beyond the last page of the novel for the reunion which all sympathetic readers desired for them. Thackeray cleared the way for such a 'happy ending' by killing off Rosey, but he seemed reluctant to give his explicit benediction to the match, and hints at it only indirectly in a postscript. Something in his artistic conscience shied away from such a pat conclusion. Lowell once complained that his marrying Clive and Ethel was an artistic blunder. 'He acknowledged that it was so,' says Lowell, ' "But then, you see, what could a fellow do? So many people wanted 'em married." ' [8] Indeed it takes a severely critical reader, after those last hundred pages of the novel, to want to deny Clive and Ethel a peaceful harbour after such stormy seas. Thackeray had to cut the knot of Clive's marriage rather than to untie it, but these people are so real and likable that it is easy to be uncritical for the moment necessary to

[8] Letter to Norton cited previously.

indulge one's humane desire for their well-being. Certainly Thackeray does not blink the tragedy of their previously tangled lives.

And tragedy much of the latter part of the book is. There is none of Thackeray's mild and tranquil melancholy here; he is unsparing in those relentless chapters in which Clive and his father are helpless sufferers under an intolerable persecution. Financially dependent, bound by domestic responsibility to protect Rosey, they are hag-ridden by one of the most intolerably real shrews in all fiction.

Mrs. Mackenzie, whom Warrington calls 'an ogling, leering, scheming, artful old campaigner,' appears first as a brisk, jovial, alert creature given to interminable monologues and obvious flatteries, always fluttering about her dear child Rosey, chattering about the girl's angelic temper and sweet looks—a bore, but as yet nothing sinister. She sees a great deal of merit in Clive since the Colonel has become rich, and she conspires with the old man to marry Rosey and Clive. Because Clive has lost all hope of securing Ethel and because, generously weak, he wishes to please his father, the match takes place. Then comes the crash of the Bundelcund Bank which wipes out the Colonel's fortune, and the small family comes under the domination of the Campaigner, who reveals herself as a literal hellion. Sour to her were the uses of adversity. She turns cruel, rapacious, bitter, encased in an impregnable armour of self-righteousness and scattering pain and dismay wherever she goes. In the midst of this ghastly domestic scene Clive sometimes wonders how his suffering father can live under the woman's taunts and jibes. All efforts to get rid of her are in vain, until that final climactic scene in which Clive, at last in possession of money through the tactful generosity of Ethel, beats off her passionate recriminations and declares himself and his father free. By this time the Campaigner has worked upon poor Rosey's jealousy and ill health and has driven her into a fatal illness. Nothing could be more horribly real than that dreadful cacophony of screams and tantrums which is the last thing Rosey hears before she dies.

Thackeray's pen is absolutely merciless here, presenting without a quiver each sordid detail of the whole frightening episode.

Clive is a more likable if somewhat less real hero than Pendennis had been; his weaknesses are of a different order. He is conceited at first and given to harmless magnificent airs—not strong, but good-tempered, manly, affectionate, with an obstinate habit, inherited from his father, of telling the truth. There is touching reciprocal love between the father and son, and each has great pride in the other. Clive admires his father's goodness and suffers when he is hurt. We seldom see the young man happy. No sooner does he recover from the moody gloom which cloaks him during his baffled pursuit of Ethel than he is plunged into the worse fate of marriage with Rosey. The strife which springs up between Clive and his father at this time distresses both greatly. '. . . It seemed as if there were anger on Thomas Newcome's part, because, though come together again, they were not united, though with every outward appearance of happiness Clive was not happy.' This lost sympathy was not recaptured until the two made common cause against the Campaigner and the Colonel began to see 'that he had pressed him too hastily in his marriage.'

Colonel Newcome takes his place in a long traditional gallery of similar portraits. He is one with Don Quixote, Sir Roger de Coverley, Dr. Primrose, Parson Adams, Uncle Toby, Samuel Pickwick—innocents all. One wonders just what strange fascination these simple souls have had for successive generations of novel readers. In whatever age, such characters have always been anomalies. They are all incredibly naïve idealists, with a child-like goodness and trustfulness which confound the average sensual man. They beam with benevolence; they are the soul of honour and simplicity. It is clear that they live not by their intellect but by their heart. Some people might find them boring companions on a week-end party, yet to learn of them is to think better of the dignity and worth of mankind. One is led to hope that there is yet room in this world for gentleness and kindness and truth and honour and simplicity—great words

which men are periodically forced to forget but of which the
continuity of letters constantly reminds us.

As far as Colonel Newcome's being a bore is concerned,
Thackeray here sets out a man who in real life would be confessedly dull, perhaps, yet he reveals him so convincingly and
sympathetically that we are drowned in intellectual delight, and
forget to be bored. Of Colonel Newcome, then, as an artistic
creation—with his foibles and eccentricities, his gracious stupidi-
ties and his blundering good-will, his tiresome absurdities and
his great capacity for affection, this chapter can say little but
good.

Nevertheless it is clear that Thackeray never meant him to
be a paragon of virtue, and he is careful to delineate his weaknesses. Out of the excess of his great desire for Clive's happiness
he well-nigh ruins that happiness. When Ethel refuses to marry
Clive he displays an unreasoning hostility towards the girl of
whom he had been so fond. His dealings with Barnes show him
capable of a vindictiveness unexpected in a man so natively
generous. In the time of his prosperity, after he had built the
ornate house in Tyburnia and felt it his duty to live in the
midst of splendour, he becomes slightly ostentatious. Once when
Thackeray was writing the novel someone asked him if he had
had a good night, and he replied: 'How could I, with Colonel
Newcome making a fool of himself as he has done?'

'But why did you let him?'

'Oh, it was in him to do it. He must.'

The Colonel's weaknesses, however, are in a sense accidental to
his character. They make him seem less of a saint without can-
celling the total effect of his pure warmth and benevolence.[9]

Thackeray treats with great understanding the scenes in which

---

[9] Thackeray had been reading *Don Quixote* and the *De Coverley Papers* as he
was writing *The Newcomes*. He told an American friend that Colonel Newcome was a blend of Sir Roger and the Don. 'I tried to make the Colonel a
creation of my own,' he said, 'but I was conscious all the while that my beloved old heroes were blending in my mind.' (*Thackeray in the United States*,
II, 92.)

It was always assumed, too, in the Thackeray family, that Thackeray had used

Clive and his father, who 'loved each other so that each was afraid of the other,' drift apart for a time in their sympathies. The Colonel had returned from India with great plans for the future—'how he would read, work, play, think, be merry together with his boy.' But as one could have foretold, Clive developed new ideas and occupations, and acquired friends in whom the older man could take no interest, whose waggeries and jests he could not even understand. He was sad at heart when he saw that his presence fell like a shadow across their gaiety. 'Together they were, yet he was alone still.' After Clive's marriage their relationship was still further strained. Rosey began to come between them. And so ' "My boy's heart is gone from me," thinks Colonel Newcome. "My wife appeals to my father," thinks Clive.' Clive told Pendennis: 'We fight mute battles, don't you see? and our thoughts, though we don't express them, are perceptible to one another, and come out from our eyes, or pass out from us somehow, and meet, and fight, and stroke, and wound.' All this underground unhappiness Thackeray traces with delicate yet incisive skill.

Colonel Newcome's death, coming after the long bitter struggle with Mrs. Mackenzie and softened by his reconciliation with Ethel, is one of the best examples we have of Thackeray's ability to treat a death-bed scene (there are not many such scenes in his novels) without breaking over the uncertain line which divides pathos from mere maudlin emotion. He succeeds here by virtue of a controlled straightforwardness—a direct objective reporting without distortion or comment—and by the strength of a brilliant reminiscent connotation expressed in a prose style of unadorned, quiet simplicity. Of all the pages that Thackeray wrote this needs quoting least, and must inevitably be quoted.

his old Anglo-Indian stepfather, Major Carmichael-Smyth, as a model. If that is the case some of the Colonel's dullness, as well as his beneficence, must have come from the stepfather, for in an unpublished letter written to Mrs. Elliot in 1856 he is obviously fed up with the old man's tediousness (he was 76), his caring for no amusement but to sit by his fireside and harangue the others with stupid talk out of the newspapers.

At the usual evening hour the chapel bell began to toll, and Thomas Newcome's hands outside the bed feebly beat time. And just as the last bell struck, a peculiar sweet smile shone over his face, and he lifted up his head a little, and quickly said 'Adsum!' and fell back. It was the word we used at school, when names were called; and lo, he, whose heart was as that of a little child, had answered to his name, and stood in the presence of The Master.

It is difficult to compare *Vanity Fair* and *The Newcomes*. Each is great in its own way, for similar and for different qualities. Thackeray never went higher than the former, nor deeper than the latter. Together they stand at the head of his performance. Now the slow descent begins; at forty-four, old before his time, Thackeray felt with some justice that he had exhausted his creative vein. But many pages, by no means all dull, were to come from his pen before he laid it aside.

CHAPTER ELEVEN

Last Novels: *The Virginians; Philip; Denis Duval*

ALTHOUGH Thackeray wrote no fiction between the last number of *The Newcomes,* in August 1855, and the first number of *The Virginians,* in November 1857, the interim had been a busy one. He had seen through the press the thirteen volumes of his *Miscellanies,* a collection of earlier ballads, sketches, and stories. He had made his second visit to the United States and had also carried the lectures on the Four Georges up and down the length of England and Scotland. And quite aside from his business of authorship, he had made his brief and amusingly quixotic stand for election to Parliament in July 1857.

There has been a general impression, supported by Lady Ritchie in her 'Biographical Introductions' to her edition of the *Works,* that Thackeray was not much interested in politics. It is true that the novels do not touch on political themes, and his youthful spree of campaigning for Charles Buller and Reform in 1832, as well as his appeal to the electorate in 1857, do not in themselves indicate any strenuous preoccupation with practical politics. Nevertheless his letters and more particularly his anonymous contributions to *Punch* show an active concern with political questions of the day. Because it is impossible to know Thackeray's mind without knowing something of what he thought about contemporary issues, it would be well to examine parenthetically here his attitude towards the political scene. He did not stand apart from it even though he did not turn it to fictional use.

He remained always a liberal in politics, with radical sympathies, striking out indignantly against oppression of all kinds. His friend Buller, the friend too of Grote and John Stuart Mill, was one of the younger Philosophic Radicals. As late as 1840 Thackeray writes to his mother about the 'two humbugs,' the 'rascally Whigs and Tories.' But

I'm not a Chartist, only a Republican. I would like to see all men equal, and this bloated aristocracy blasted to the wings of all the winds. It has been good and useful up to the present time, nay, for a little longer, perhaps—just up to the minute when the great lion shall shake his mane and scatter all these absurd insects out of it . . . I see how in every point of morals the aristocracy is cursing the country. Oh for a few enlightened Republicans, men to say their say honestly, and dare to do and say the truth.[1]

In *Going to See a Man Hanged* (*Fraser's*, August 1840) he digresses into what he calls 'an unconscionable Republican tirade.' 'Populus' has been growing in wisdom he says, 'and there are ten million of him, to whom we give—exactly nothing.' He favoured the ballot and universal suffrage (in 1848 he wrote an open letter in *Punch* to Joseph Hume approving his principles) but frowned on the Chartists with their threats of force; the bigotry 'of the present Chartist leaders is greater than the bigotry we suffer under.' The extreme radical, he believed, was the Conservative's best friend.

Thackeray was for the most part a supporter of policies rather than of parties or even of men. Although, as Lady Ritchie has indicated, Thackeray's left-wing liberalism sometimes gave offence to female friends of the family, it was no pose with him but a part of his deep belief that the government owed to the welfare of the people a debt it had not been paying. He was

[1] Biographical introduction to *Barry Lyndon*.

perfectly willing to take pot-shots at either side, Whig or Tory, if it seemed to him to be making political capital of human suffering. Nor did his patriotism have in it any taint of jingoism. Thackeray lived into the days when the excitement of Empire began to pulse in English veins, and England, typically thrifty, came to see that colonies which had been more or less of a political liability might be made into a national asset. The song of the white man's burden had no charms for him, and with almost a Shavian pertinence he attacked 'Colonial land-grabbing conducted by the British Propaganda under the cloak of religion and missionary work.' [2]

To say, therefore, that Thackeray was not interested in the political currents of his time is to do an injustice to his active and inquiring mind. It would be foolhardy, however, to declare that his political opinions were always pertinent or ever really profound. In politics he was always more or less the big, beaming, enthusiastic outsider, with liberal instincts and a judgment guided by a warm and sympathetic heart rather than by a clear political head. The best that Thackeray had to say to his generation cut across political lines and went much deeper than party affiliations.

After his defeat at Oxford Thackeray laid active politics aside and in the fall of 1857 began to write his next novel, *The Virginians*. The subject of this sequel to *Esmond* had been in his mind as early as 1853, when he had written to Miss Lucy Baxter during his tour in the United States: 'Tomorrow I shall pass down the Potomac on which Mrs. Esmond-Warrington used to sail with her 2 sons when they went to visit their friend Mr. Washington. I wonder will anything ever come out of that preface, and will that story ever be born?' The preface mentioned was that to *Henry Esmond,* purporting to be signed by Esmond's daughter, Rachel Esmond Warrington, and dated 'Castlewood, Virginia: November 3, 1778.' As *Esmond* followed upon Thackeray's studies for the lectures on the English humor-

---

[2] M. H. Spielmann: *Hitherto Unidentified Contributions of W. M. Thackeray to Punch,* 1899, p. 131.

ists, so *The Virginians* came out of his visits to America and the lectures on the Four Georges. During his second trip to the United States Thackeray told John Esten Cooke: 'I shall lay the scene in Virginia during the Revolution. There will be two brothers who will be prominent characters; one will take the English side of the war, and the other the American, and they will both be in love with the same girl.' [3] This plan changed under his hand; the scenes in Virginia came to occupy a relatively small place in the whole, and instead of making both his heroes fall in love with the same girl he created two English sisters for the two American brothers.

As so often happens in the world of letters, Thackeray was paid best for the work which has added little stature to his reputation. Bradbury and Evans offered him £300 for each number, of which monthly amount Thackeray drew only £250 because, as he said, the novel did not do 'so very well as expected.' But this gave him £6,000 for the twenty-four monthly parts (November 1857-October 1859), as compared with the £2,000 he received for *Vanity Fair*. The lectures on the Georges had netted him £9,500, so that he was now beyond the reach of financial worry. He talks much in his letters of this period about his desire to leave a comfortable fortune for his daughters, and with transparent delight he sees that fortune accumulate.

At the same time, for a variety of reasons, writing was becoming increasingly difficult for him. The attacks of 'spasms' were sending him to bed more and more frequently, and the monthly numbers were often received by the printer at the last possible moment, after the delay caused by his illnesses and by his native habits of procrastination had made necessary a frenzied burst of activity. Late in 1857 he wrote to Dr. John Brown: 'I read no new books, only Newspapers and Magazines of 1756, get out my numbers with extraordinary throes and difficulty—am as one distraught while the process is going on, and if I don't do that, am for days without ability to do anything else.' The next sum-

---

[3] Wilson, *Thackeray in the United States*, I, 264.

mer he wrote to the Baxters: 'I am constantly unwell now—a fit of spasms—then get well in about 5 days; then 5 days grumbling and thinking of my work; then 14 days work and spasms da capo—and what a horribly stupid story I am writing! Don't tell me. I know better than any of you. No incident, no character, no go left in this dreary old expiring carcass.' A little earlier he had written: 'The book's clever but stupid, that's the fact. I hate story-making incidents, surprises, love-making, &c more and more every day; and here is a third of a great story done equal to two thirds of an ordinary novel—and nothing has actually happened, except that a young gentleman has come from America to England.' As he told Brown: 'I dawdled fatally between [numbers] 5 and 10.'

Certainly Thackeray, weary and ill,[4] was his own most remorseless critic. Tandem to the recurring seizures of pain ran the spectre of creative decay. He was beginning to imitate himself, and he knew it. 'I have exhausted all the types of character with which I am familiar,' he wrote, 'and it is very difficult to strike out anything new.' As his energy weakened, the narrative faults which had been subdued in the earlier novels were suddenly magnified. Too often he not only refuses to get on with the story but even seems to forget that he is telling a story. Chapters of pure padding begin to appear. What had earlier been discursiveness shades off into garrulousness. He moralizes more frequently and less effectively. He gets hold of an idea and shakes it, terrier-like, long after its life has departed. One becomes aware that his parenthetical comments are more than mere echoes; they are a complete repetition of past performances, and not always his best performances. Not that his comments, one by one, are less freshly stated than before; the difficulty is that often they are of the kind that will not bear exces-

---

[4] His letters show how tired and old he felt. Writing to Dr. Brown concerning the death of Brown's father he said: 'Next comes our little turn to pack up and depart. To stay is well enough, but shall we be very sorry to go? What more is there in life that we haven't tried? What that we have tried is so very much worth repetition or endurance?' Thackeray was forty-eight years of age at this time.

sive restatement. Thus the skeleton-in-the-closet dissertation re-
appears, a little wanly. When he finds it necessary to equivo-
cate about the life which Harry Warrington and other young
bucks of fashion led in eighteenth-century London, he complains
again about the restraints laid upon the modern novelist—the
unpleasant necessity of draping the statue. Still more frequent
are the melancholy 'time-past' musings. And these too have
undergone a subtle change. In the great novels such passages
had a certain mellow validity; he made us enjoy his nostalgia.
Here the nice balance of humour and sadness gives way to a
bleak, resigned weariness, only slightly disguised by drollery.
'I know it is an old story,' he once turns on himself to say, 'and
especially that this preacher has yelped vanitas vanitatum five
hundred times before.' It is a sad spectacle, this intensification of
old debilities, this progressive hardening of the artistic arteries.
Some writers, by means of a technical dexterity, can coast for
a long time on a declining inspiration; Thackeray's faults were
such that when the old creative zest dwindled the seams of his
fictional structure gaped.

The Virginians is the story of twin brothers, grandsons of
Henry Esmond, who, after relinquishing his claim to the title,
had migrated with Rachel Esmond to Virginia and had there
taken possession of the family estate. His daughter had married a Warrington, for whom she apparently had little respect;
the implication is that he led a hen-pecked life. He died soon
after the marriage, and his widow reassumed the name of Esmond, of which she was very proud. The history of the two
sons, Harry and George, unlike in disposition but devoted to
each other, forms the backbone of the story, which includes
also the later chronicle of the house of Castlewood. As a matter of fact the Virginian part of the story is little more than a
background for the adventures of the two boys in English society. By the convenient device of supposing George killed, early
in the story, in the Braddock expedition against the French and
Indians, Thackeray is able to focus the first part of the book on
Harry. Later, when George escapes from capture and comes to

London, the story belongs to him; indeed he tells the last fourth of the story in his own words. Only one-fifth of the book, roughly, is occupied with the American scene, and the events of the American Revolution, with the brothers fighting on opposite sides, are compressed into the last sixty pages.

The major portion of the novel, then, is devoted to the alternate experiences of the twins in England: Harry's falling into love (and out again) with his predatory cousin, Lady Maria Esmond, twenty years older than he; his acquaintance with the Lambert family and his interest in Hetty Lambert; his gay reckless life in London. George turns up just in time to keep his brother out of debtors' prison. Harry joins the military, and that keeps him conveniently out of the way in France and America (he goes with General Wolfe on the expedition against Canada). Thus Thackeray can concentrate on George's career in England: his playwriting; his falling in love with the cheerful, lovable Theo Lambert; Madame Esmond's opposition to the match, and the ultimate reconciliation after a great deal of distress all around. Then, hurriedly, at the end, the whole business of the American revolt, with the brothers on opposite sides; and afterwards George settling down to the comfortable life of a country gentleman in England; Harry marrying, against his mother's wishes, Fanny Mountain, the daughter of Madame Esmond's companion, and continuing to live in America on the family estate.

For narrative effectiveness the American chapters are by all odds the most lively. The large middle portion of the book has a certain factitiously interesting eighteenth-century colouring, but the story itself runs in grooves too long familiar to Thackeray. There are some interminable Tunbridge-and-London chapters in which, with an almost wilful perversity, Thackeray writes a great deal about nothing at all. It is not merely that the book moves sluggishly—it sometimes turns back and swallows itself.

There is, to be sure, a clear effort to gain historical authenticity, and the narrative takes on some light and colour through the introduction of historical personages. Ben Franklin is seen briefly, shrewd and facetious. Samuel Richardson and David Garrick and Lord Chesterfield walk across the scene. Dr. Johnson drinks 'pailfuls' of tea with the Lamberts, and advises George on his playwriting in good stout Johnsonian diction. General James Wolfe is presented briefly but sympathetically. Most interesting of all, however, is the characterization of George Washington. Thackeray is very generous to Washington. He appears first as a friend of the Warringtons, but George and Harry are so fearful that this young Colonial wants to marry their widowed mother that they try to force him into a duel. This is avoided just in time by the arrival of word which convinces the brothers that Washington has quite other marriage plans. Later on Washington appears as the grave, dignified leader of the Continental Army. Thackeray's sympathies were wholly on the side of the Americans in the dispute, and he makes clear his belief that England's petty tyrannies and her insolence and imperious domineering spirit brought on the Revolution. He describes Washington as 'all mankind's superior' —'a character to revere and admire; a life without a stain, a fame without a flaw.'

When planning *The Virginians* Thackeray told Canon Elwin that he wanted 'a cheerful hero, though this is very difficult, for a cheerful character must have some deeper element to give sufficient dignity and interest. It is hardly possible to have a hero without a dash of melancholy. I think the cheerful man must be the second character—a good-humoured, pleasant rogue. But people are always complaining that my clever people are rascals, and the good people idiots.' On this basis George would be the titular hero, for Harry is the good-humoured, pleasant rogue, energetic, warlike, and noisy—with good instincts, but generously weak. He was just the sort of debonair young rascal of whom Thackeray was always very tolerant, for he himself had heard the chimes at midnight. George, on the other hand, is marked by the Thackerayan melancholy which possessed Pen and Esmond and Clive. He was peaceful and studious, generous and gentle—much like his grandfather, and like him fond of gloomy introspection. Like Pen and Clive he had artistic instincts. He writes plays. *Carpezan,* a wild and murderous tragedy produced at Covent Garden by Rich, succeeds; *Pocahontas* is a failure in spite of its production by Garrick. Like most of Thackeray's heroes George suffers poverty for a time but comes at last into financial bliss and the haven of a happy marriage with the adoring Theo Lambert.

We see a great deal of the Lambert family, who are uniformly sweet and wholesome and are thrown into contrast with the self-seeking Castlewoods. Thackeray presents them with a favourable flourish. Colonel (later General) Lambert has a pleasant waggish humour and a high sense of honour and duty. Mrs. Lambert is kind-hearted and sentimental. Hetty and Theo are solid, ruddy, lively girls. The family goes to Tunbridge; the family goes to Court; the family goes to the theatre. We like them and feel a bit ashamed of ourselves for finding them dull. Our excuse perhaps is that Thackeray, concerned with adorning a tale which has a low narrative potential, lingers too long and lovingly over the interminable Lambert family chit-chat and intersperses with it too much of his own lesser chatter.

The Castlewood outfit is on quite a different level. Here is seen Thackeray's old skill in catching all the nuances of sordid motives as he describes the banked fires of mutual suspicion behind which the greedy Castlewoods watch each other jealously. They are obsequious to their aunt, Madame Bernstein, because she has money. They are all inordinately fond of cards and gambling, and the present Earl of Castlewood takes his kinsman Harry Warrington into his toils and fleeces him. William, Castlewood's half-brother, is a quarrelsome offensive brute, surly when he is drunk, and drunk most of the time. Lady Maria, Castlewood's unmarried sister, with a doubtful past and a still more doubtful age, whose heart was a territory 'like the Low Countries, accustomed to being conquered, and for ever open to invasion,' works vehemently to catch Harry in the bonds of matrimony. Her interest drops off when she learns that he is no longer heir to the Virginia estate. In describing these people

Thackeray traces all the undercurrents of family tension—how they attempt always to read the truth behind each other's words. The proper hell for this family comes at the time of Madame Bernstein's death, which they had been awaiting with ill-concealed impatience. George tells the story: 'But when she was gone, and we descended to the lower rooms after all was over, we found Castlewood with his white face, and my Lady from Kensington, and Mr. Will, already assembled in the parlour. They looked greedily at us as we appeared. They were hungry for the prey.' And then they discovered that the old lady had left everything to Harry!

Not quite so unpleasant is Madame Esmond-Warrington, Henry Esmond's daughter and the mother of Harry and George. We see little of her, but she sticks in the memory as a distinctly unlikable person—good to the poor and self-consciously pious, 'for ever applying to the Sacred Oracles,' and accommodating their sentences to her purpose, passionately calling upon heaven for its interference in her family quarrels—but also uniformly despotic and domineering, stubborn and haughty, ruling with a rod of iron every one who came under her control. Both Harry and George finally marry against her wishes—and she deserves such a fate.

Undoubtedly the most brilliant portrait in the book is that of Madame Bernstein, who had been the Beatrix of *Henry Esmond*. She appears here as an old lady, having grown old not too gracefully after a battered career first as the wife of Bishop Tusher and finally as Baroness Bernstein. But by a thousand little touches of remembrance—the Kneller picture of Beatrix in her beauty, which watched over the bed of Bernstein when she was dying; her praise of Henry Esmond, whom she had sent away, and her passionate affection for his grandson as shown in the ruthless energy with which she rescues Harry's letters from Maria; the frequent references to her ruined beauty; her brilliant sarcastic wit and malice—by all these Thackeray bridges the years and makes Bernstein that rare thing in fiction: a believable sequel to herself. Thackeray does not soften the picture. The Baroness is as worldly and fickle as she had been in the days of her triumph, loving cards and shady stories to her unregenerate end, impatient to the last of doctors, whether of medicine or divinity. In her last delirium she relives the scenes of her youth, labouring always under the same delusion, that George, who was at her side, 'was the Henry of past times, who had loved her and had been forsaken by her, whose bones were lying far away by the banks of the Potomac.' The characterization of her who had been Beatrix Esmond does much to redeem the faltering narrative of *The Virginians.*

To write about *The Virginians* is to discover much that must be said unfavourably, and yet to say only that would be uncritical. The book is not as bad as criticism has to make it seem. One inevitably refers it to the series of great novels which preceded it and so is tempted to pay more attention to the decline than to the absolute accomplishment. Yet if Thackeray's invention flagged, his portraying, characterizing hand was still firm, and there is a host of good things to set off against the growing weakness. Always, as ever, there is the prose style, which is unfailingly felicitous, helping to carry the reader across the shallows of narrative uncertainty and even making garrulity bearable. Thackeray could sometimes be trivial and loquacious, but he could be absolutely dull only with great difficulty.

Philip, Thackeray's last complete novel,[5] comes naturally into comparison with *Pendennis* and *The Newcomes,* for like them it is a picture of mid-nineteenth-century English society. And the story of Philip, like that of Pen and Clive, is in many places a rearrangement of the early career of William Makepeace Thackeray himself. To say that it is less good than either of the others is to indicate that the thread of Thackeray's narrative

[5] It ran serially through 1861 and the first half of 1862 in the *Cornhill Magazine,* of which Thackeray was currently the uneasy editor (see the next chapter). In July 1862, it appeared in the full dress of three volumes with the following title: *The Adventures of Philip on his way through the world, shewing who robbed him, who helped him, and who passed him by.*

invention was becoming more and more tenuous. His own criticism of the book was that it 'had not enough story.' Never greatly concerned with plot, he was coming more and more to depend upon prolixity rather than creation. The *Roundabouts,* which were running concurrently with *Philip* in the *Cornhill,* laid their chatty discursiveness upon the novel and graceful little humorous essays twist the stream of the story into pleasant but distracting eddies. Thackeray muses upon the mutations of fashion. He moralizes upon the example of love and honour which parents should set for their children. He digresses, like a weary old man, to lament the novelist's necessity for describing the moonlight raptures and passionate outpourings of young love; although elsewhere he looses a flood of sentiment upon the subject of happy young marriage. With a sprightly melancholy he meditates on the celerity with which men are forgotten when they are dead. Like old friends reappear the Skeleton-in-the-Closet and the familiar indictments of snobbishness and of mothers who 'bring their virgin daughters up to battered old rakes . . . ready to sacrifice their innocence for fortune or a title.' Thackeray was again listening to himself.

He was tired, and it was so much easier to repeat old situations than to create new ones. His allusive tangential manner, so pleasing as an *apéritif,* begins to overflow into an uncomfortable loquaciousness—as in the section dealing with the life of the Baynes family in the Paris boarding house, an episode which yields a great deal of second-degree chatter. Details begin to overcome him. The story bogs down, and the reader is almost as grateful as Thackeray must have been when he comes to the perfunctory and fortuitous ending in which Philip, by accident, recovers the lost will of Lord Ringwood which insures him and his family the fortune of which they are so much in need.[6]

[6] This device by means of which the gods deliver a happy ending on the last page of the book has been condemned as a weak trick. It illustrates well the difference between fact and artistic truth, for Thackeray had entered carefully into his note-book the account of the event in real life which served as the basis of the episode.

Like *Pendennis* and *The Newcomes*, *Philip* is penetrated by
the reminiscent vein which came so easily to Thackeray. The
reader is told not to worry, that this will be no 'pulmonary romance'; although the events described took place some fifteen
years ago, Philip is alive and happy today. 'So, young gentleman, if you are for melancholy, despair, and sardonic satire,
please to call at some other shop.' The manner is once again
that of the mellow old gentleman telling the tale from his arm-
chair. At its best this quality of ruminating retrospection had
given a certain personal richness to Thackeray's novels; in *Philip*
the excess of this quality is more apparent. As in a dream one
sometimes moves slowly through a recognizable distortion of his
daily life, and the events of the waking existence become in
sleep caricatures of themselves, so the weakening of Thackeray's
creative energy allowed the diffuseness which was always at his
heels to assume exaggerated proportions. The story somehow
gets itself told, but, as it were, in spite of Thackeray.

This much must be said in criticism of the tissue of the narrative as a whole, its structural amorphousness, its repetitiousness,
its reiterative musings. That it is still a solid and considerable
book—better in some ways than *The Virginians*—is testimony
that Thackeray's eye and hand had by no means lost all their
cunning. Buttressing the weaknesses are many pungent and a
few brilliant scenes. These range from the powerful chapter in
which Philip for the first time penetrates the secret of his father's
past—that terrible meal over which the greasy chaplain Hunt
leered and winked 'as he gave it his sinister blessing'—to the
lusty comedy of the boarding-house scene in which General
Baynes almost but not quite fights a duel with Colonel Bunch.
Behind this last bit of comedy, however, is a great deal of very
pertinent characterization. General Baynes is angry with his
old friends because he knows they are right in condemning his
severity towards his daughter Charlotte and Philip. All the General's blustering and swearing hide a very tender heart, and a
deep unhappiness with his wife. 'I don't think,' says Thackeray, 'poor General Baynes ever had a proper sense of his sit-

uation, or knew how miserable he ought by rights to have been.' Then Thackeray gives us that deeply bitten scene of Baynes and his wife lying silent beside each other in bed, awake in the darkness; the father remorseful and grief-stricken because of his daughter's misery; the mother planning how she will marry Charlotte to the right wealthy suitor—each alone beside the other, consumed silently by bitter thoughts. It is impressively clear that the decline of Thackeray's narrative power brought with it little weakening of his amazing ability to catch in words that abundant sense of reality in characterization which is his great contribution to fiction. These are for the most part people seized firmly in a great creative imagination and given there an independent life.

This quality of perceived reality has little relation to the 'pleasantness' or 'unpleasantness' of the people depicted. Philip himself is a good case in point. He has more vitality, perhaps, then either Clive Newcome or Pendennis,[7] but he is an irritating sort of hero, who is betrayed into happiness more by good luck than by native merit. He is good-hearted and honest, a hater of shams and hypocrites, but he is afflicted with a boisterous bumptiousness and an arrogant quick temper. Thackeray meant him to be likable in spite of his weaknesses of head and heart, yet it is difficult to sympathize with his rudeness or his swagger. 'As nature made him,' says Thackeray, 'so he was. I don't think he tried to improve himself much. Few people do . . . Philip roared his griefs: he shouted his laughter: he bellowed his applause: he was extravagant in his humility as in his pride, in his admiration of his friends and contempt for his enemies: I dare say not a just man, but I have met juster men not half so honest; and certainly not a faultless man, though I know better men not near so good.'

Philip is a continuation of *A Shabby Genteel Story,* written twenty years earlier at the time when Thackeray was suffering

---

[7] Pendennis is the narrator of Philip's history, and we see a good deal of the assorted Pendennises, whose married felicity we are again forced to admire a little too frequently.

great domestic grief, and broken off abruptly when *Fraser's Magazine* showed little desire to continue publication of the story. A comparison of the two makes clear how Thackeray's art had matured in the interim. *A Shabby Genteel Story* has more gusto but far less richness and subtlety of detail than *Philip*. It is a mixture of the romantic-farce-tragedy kind to which Thackeray was given in those years, and, as sometimes happened, Thackeray failed to integrate his materials. It will be remembered that the shabby-genteel side of the story concerns the Gann family, honestly and unostentatiously vulgar: old Gann, lazy, boastful, and boozy; and his shrew of a wife, who had a taste for cheap finery and whose chief occupation was taking medicines. Their daughter Caroline (the Little Sister of the later *Philip*) is a pale, thin, shy, affectionate girl who acts as a household drudge in the Gann establishment. Into this Eden comes the dissolute young man who calls himself George Brandon (his real name, as he appears later in *Philip,* is George Brand Firmin). Caroline discourages his dishonourable advances but is persuaded into a marriage ceremony which ultimately proves to be fraudulent, performed by the reprobate clergyman Thomas Tufthunter (the Reverend Thomas Hunt of *Philip*). Here the story breaks off, on a note of tragedy. But there has been much vigorous action by the way, a great deal of it furnished by the fantastic bewhiskered young painter Andrea Fitch, drawn in Thackeray's best early rollicking manner. The story could never have come to much, and when Thackeray picked it up again he did well to start it off on a new tack.

The central characters reappear in *Philip*. Firmin, now a fashionable society doctor, had married long since, and his son Philip had been nursed through a severe childhood illness by the former Caroline, who still calls herself Mrs. Brandon. Philip is thenceforth devoted to her, and she to him. Dr. Firmin has developed into a sinister sort of rascal who loses his own fortune by speculation and illegally dissipates Philip's inheritance by perpetrating a fraud on the trustee, General Baynes. He finds it advisable to move to New York, and even at that distance he gets Philip into trouble by forging his name to a note. Tufton Hunt, now a besotted creature 'stained with crime, drink, debt,' had tried to blackmail Dr. Firmin, and when he gets hold of the forged note tries to threaten Philip with it. In one of the big scenes of the book the Little Sister, as courageous as she is constant and gentle, gets Hunt tipsy, chloroforms him in what must be one of the earliest fictional uses of that anæsthetic, and burns the forged document.

The greater part of the book is devoted to Philip himself. It takes him through his early journalistic career; his initial and fortunately frustrate love affair with his cousin Agnes Twysden; his marriage after many tribulations to the beautiful and worshipping Charlotte Baynes; his subsequent financial difficulties, for he had an unfortunate habit of insulting his employers and getting discharged; and the ultimate goal of financial security reached through the discovery of the lost will.

The story keeps Philip himself somewhat too pertinaciously in the foreground, yet there comes into it a whole Thackerayan gallery of minor figures. Twysden, a most respectable snob and intolerable old bore. His daughter Agnes, who, with her eye on the main chance, marries the stingy Mr. Woolcomb and his moneybags and reaps a miserable reward for her selfish ambition. Lord Ringwood, another cynical nobleman of Thackeray's Regency breed, rude and brutal to those who fawn upon him but possessing a shrewd sardonic humour. Ringwood Twysden, Philip's snobbish cousin, an offensive young toady whom Philip, at the Embassy Ball, throws into a fountain. And the ineffable but likable self-made Mugford, owner of the *Pall Mall Gazette* and Philip's employer, who is greatly amused at those who scorn him for his lack of gentility.

Here too Thackeray indulges for the last time his whim of introducing casually characters from previous novels. The ubiquitous Pendennises are much in evidence.[8] J. J. Ridley, now an

---

[8] It gave Thackeray a sense of freedom to pretend to have someone else tell the story, even though he makes little effort to maintain the first-person point of

honoured R.A., comes out of the pages of *The Newcomes* to become Philip's friend.[9] Clive Newcome and Fred Bayham appear briefly, and the Campaigner is mentioned as Clive's mother-in-law. Finucane and Captain Shandon are translated from *Pendennis*. The Ravenswing (*Men's Wives*), now Mrs. Woolsey, sings at one of Mugford's parties, to be treated there by Philip with an insolent ill-humour. By such cheerful homely links Thackeray tied his novels together. He liked the people he had made and it pleased him to think of them as continuing on, crossing the lives of still newer creations.

None of the novels, not even *Pendennis* or *The Newcomes,* is more reminiscent than *Philip* of Thackeray's own past. A composite biography of Thackeray might be written, a little dangerously, to be sure, on the basis of the novels. Philip was the last of a long line of heroes to attend the Grey Friars-Charterhouse school.[10] Like Thackeray, Philip left college early, for Philip was an idle student, perhaps not unlike the young Thackeray. Both read law, not too seriously. Both in their adventures skirted Bohemia—

A land over which hangs an endless fog, occasioned by much tobacco; a land of chambers, billiard-rooms, supper-rooms, oysters; a land of song; a land where soda-water flows freely in the morning; a land of tin-dish covers from taverns, and frothing porter; a land of lotus-eating (with lots of cayenne pepper), of pulls on the river, of delicious reading of novels, magazines, and saunterings in many studios . . . I have lost my way to Bohemia now, but it is certain that Prague is the most picturesque city in the world.

Nor is it difficult, from what we know of Thackeray, to discover something of his likeness in his description of Philip:

view. 'I should like to make Mr. Pendennis the author of my story,' he wrote concerning *Philip,* 'and let him walk through it. He can talk more freely than Mr. Thackeray.' (Biographical Introduction, p. i.)

[9] Thackeray thinks wistfully of his ambition, years earlier, to be a painter. 'To be a painter,' he says, '. . . I hold to be one of life's *summa bona.'*

[10] 'Be not angry, patient reader of former volumes by the author of the present history, if I am garrulous about Grey Friars, and go back to that ancient place of education to find the heroes of our tale. We are young but once.'

He had a childish sensibility for what was tender, helpless, pretty, or
pathetic; and a mighty scorn of imposture, wherever he found it.
He had many good purposes, which were often very vacillating, and
were but seldom performed. He had a vast number of evil habits,
whereof, you know, idleness is said to be the root. Many of these
evil propensities he coaxed and cuddled with much care; and though
he roared out *peccavi* most frankly when charged with his sins, this
criminal would fall to peccation very soon after promising amend-
ment. What he liked he would have. What he disliked he could with
the greatest difficulty be found to do. He liked good dinners, good
wine, good horses, good clothes, and late hours; and in all these
comforts of life (or any others which he fancied, or which were
within his means) he indulged himself with perfect freedom. He
hated hypocrisy on his own part, and hypocrites in general. He said
everything that came into his mind about things and people; and,
of course, was often wrong and often prejudiced, and often occasioned howls of indignation or malignant whispers of hatred by his
free speaking.

Like Thackeray Philip inherited a fortune, lost it, and then
turned to journalism. The letters which Philip sent home from
France to the *Pall Mall Gazette* must have been much like the
letters which young Thackeray wrote for the *National Standard*
and for the *Constitutional*. Philip also wrote articles for the *European Review;* Thackeray, articles for the *Foreign Quarterly Review*. Philip's weekly letters to the New York journal *The Gazette of the Upper Ten Thousand* are reminiscent of Thackeray's contributions to N. P. Willis's New York paper *The
Corsair*. It is probable that Thackeray, like Philip, did not receive his promised pay for the transatlantic letters. Finally, both
hero and author married on £400 a year, and went through
days of pain and gloom and poverty.

Lady Ritchie says that she can remember Thackeray's saying
how much of his own early life was written down in the pages
of *Philip,* and she hints that Charlotte Bayne may be identified
with the Isabella Shawe whom Thackeray married. Thackeray
had written to George Smith: 'Philip is unfortunately going
into Poverty and Struggle, but this can't be helped, and as he

will—*entre nous*—take pretty much the career of W.M.T. in the first years of his ruin and absurdly imprudent marriage, at least the portrait will be faithful.' As Thackeray thought tenderly of his own 'imprudent' marriage so he approved of the match between the penniless Philip and the penniless Charlotte. 'In love, somehow, one is pleased that young people should dare a little.'

There is, too, one biographical link which throws some light on Thackeray's antipathies to mothers-in-law and helps to explain such portraits as those of the Campaigner and Mrs. Baynes. Charlotte's mother, says Philip, had promised her a 'little portion of fifty pounds a year, which had never been paid since the second quarter after their marriage.' And Thackeray, in describing his own 'early and imprudent marriage' to John Eliot (see p. 16 *supra*) said that part of his means were '50£ a year promised by her mother, and paid for 2 quarters, since which (1837) I have received exactly 10£ on account.' And one of Mrs. Baynes's subsequent payments to Charlotte and Philip was a ten-pound note! It is not likely that Thackeray would hold a £50 hatred long, but the analogies, plus the clear indications elsewhere that Thackeray and his wife's mother had some bitter differences of opinion, give a lively biographical interest to the studied malevolence of Thackeray's pictures of mothers-in-law.

It is characteristic of Thackeray that in this last full novel he should weave himself so fully back into his own past. His illnesses were steadily becoming more severe; he was tired and sad, but nowhere has this most reminiscent of novelists been tenderer to the follies and hopes and struggles of youth. The weariness of a premature old age and the progressive drying up of his fecundity led him to make up by discursiveness what he lacked in creative energy. But this final novel, uneven as it is, is far from being an exhibition of senility. It has many rewarding chapters, and to emphasize too much its symptoms of decay would be to do injustice to a narrative and characterizing art which is inferior only when thrown against the background of Thackeray's own greater work.

Two pieces of fiction remain to be considered in the pattern of Thackeray's achievement: the one a short novel in six chapters written hurriedly for the new *Cornhill Magazine* and furnishing something less than exciting reading; the other, a fragment of the novel upon which he was engaged when he died. 'Yet a few chapters more,' he wrote, 'and then the last: after which, behold Finis itself come to an end, and the Infinite begun.'

The first of these stories, *Lovel the Widower,* antedates *Philip* slightly in point of time, having been published in the *Cornhill* from January to June 1860. It is an extended and novelized form of a two-act play, *The Wolves and the Lamb,* which Thackeray had written some time before and which had been rejected in 1855 by Alfred Wigan of the Olympic Theatre. Thackeray was greatly disappointed that it did not reach production, and he consoled himself by giving it an amateur presentation in his new house at Palace Green, Kensington. It seems to have been enjoyed by the family, but as a play it is incredibly bad, turgid and stiff and dull, past being saved even by occasional flashes of Thackerayan humour or by a Thackerayan butler who drops his 'h's' but reads Montesquieu and Helvetius. The plot deals with a widower who is tyrannized over by a household of termagant females—his mother and his mother-in-law—and who at last saves his sanity by marrying his children's governess and driving the others out of the house. It is all pretty inferior and would not need to be mentioned here if Thackeray, with typical thrift, had not decided to turn the play into a novel.

The best that even the optimistic George Saintsbury, incurably generous towards Thackeray, could say of *Lovel the Widower* was that it 'has, I think, very few thoroughgoing partisans.' That is a masterpiece of understatement. The story furnishes, however, an interesting study in literary method, for we see Thackeray taking the bones of the plot and the characterizations from *The Wolves and the Lamb* and clothing them with the amplitude of comic characterizing detail which came so easily to his pen. Too easily—for not even a plethora of shrewd whimsical touches can make malleable so dull a plot and such colourless characterizations. The satire always just misses fire. One feels that Thackeray is shadow-boxing with himself, that he knew he was being a bore. There are some pages which hold turns of phrase or flashes of perception that could belong only to Thackeray, but there are few pages which make the reader want to turn on to the next. *Lovel the Widower* was a literary indiscretion, and those who love Thackeray will not want to linger long here.

Denis Duval is quite another matter. It is impossible to judge it satisfactorily, for we have only eight chapters out of what was planned as a full-length novel. Yet it would seem that in the midst of the pain which was now his constant companion and was making increasingly difficult the task of writing,[11] Thackeray had caught somehow a second wind. Certainly the fragment of *Denis Duval* is as fresh and athletic as anything he ever did. Even Charles Dickens, who always found it difficult to be generous to Thackeray, wrote of *Denis* after its author's death: 'In respect of earnest feeling, far-seeing purpose, character, incident, and a certain loving picturesqueness blending the whole, I believe it to be much the best of all his works.'[12]
Much of the renewed vigour in *Denis Duval* stems from

[11] In May 1863, Thackeray writes to Mrs. Ritchie, the widow of his cousin William Ritchie: 'If I haven't written to you sooner, be pleased to know that for the last ten days I have been almost *non compos mentis*. When I am in labour with a book I don't quite know what happens. I sit for hours before my paper, not doing my book, but incapable of doing anything else, and thinking upon that subject always, waking with it, walking about with it, and going to bed with it. Oh, the struggles and bothers—oh, the throbs and pains about this trumpery!'
The eight finished chapters were published in the *Cornhill Magazine,* March-June 1864.

[12] There is some irony, doubtless unconscious, in Dickens's identification of a fragment of an uncompleted novel as Thackeray's greatest achievement.

Thackeray's deliberate choice of subject, which called for action
and adventure rather than retrospective philosophizing. Denis
tells his own story in good easy racy narrative style, and the very
materials of the tale keep it clear of the reflective disquisition
which had been bringing Thackeray's mellowness close to over-
ripeness. He knew that *Philip* had not had enough story and
he was determined, as his daughter says, 'that the new book
must be a success if he could make it so.' With his favourite
Henry Esmond in mind he turned to his familiar and beloved
eighteenth century—the days of the American and French Revolutions this time, rather than to the Age of Anne. Denis was
born in 1763. Once again (with a difference) Thackeray began
a historical romance which caught delicately the flavour of a
past age. The difference is that Denis is not afflicted by the
gloomy morbidity which haunted the moralizing Esmond. Even
as a lad—for we see him only as such—he lives a life of crowded
action, in which so much happens that there is little time for
reflection.

These few chapters hold as much adventure as half a dozen
Philips and *Pendennises*. Denis, a boy living on the Sussex
coast with his mother and grandfather, who are of a French
Protestant refugee family, takes innocent part in a series of
smuggling operations; witnesses a domestic intrigue which leads
to a fatal duel; shoots and wounds a highwayman who turns
out to be a neighbour and who thenceforth makes life dangerous for the lad; discovers by accident, after the French Wars
have begun, some treasonable correspondence; and in general
makes enough enemies to provide potential dramatic conflict
for three crowded volumes. As the novel breaks off Denis has
been pressed into His Majesty's navy and is listening to the
broadside which marks the beginning of the battle between
the *Serapis* and the ships of the 'renegade Briton' John Paul
Jones. Already, too, he has fallen in love with Agnes de Sa-
verne, a Catholic girl who is the ward of the family whence
came the highwayman into whose face Denis had fired his brass
pistol. As in *Henry Esmond,* such exciting events, plots and

counter-plots, are seen realistically through the eyes of a boy who is aware that he is living on the fringes of great events, but who is vague about the meaning of it all. The narrative is rapid, objective, and sure.

We learn from the careful notes which Thackeray had prepared that much of the subsequent action of the novel was to take place at sea—a new *milieu* for Thackeray—and with his passion for fidelity he was spending much time in mastering the technical details of an unfamiliar nautical setting. 'Why,' he asks in a letter to Dr. John Brown, 'am I not writing the history of Denis Duval, Esq., Admiral of the White Squadron? Because I don't know anything about the sea and seamen, and get brought up by my ignorance every other page.' In another letter he tells humorously how he 'learned to scuttle a marlin-spike, reef a lee-scupper, keelhaul a bowsprit as well as the best of them.' It is pleasant to find Thackeray writing, during these last days, in the full glow of his best narrative manner, untouched by any symptoms of artistic decrepitude. As he laid down the gold pen for the last time he was living in an Indian summer of his literary career.

CHAPTER TWELVE

Roundabout Papers; Ballads

EVER SINCE the days of the ill-fated *National Standard* and *Constitutional* Thackeray had longed to edit a magazine. Ainsworth, Jerrold, Hood, and Dickens had each established a periodical, with varying degrees of success, and the journalistic virus was likewise deep in Thackeray's veins. Therefore when the publisher George Smith proposed to found a shilling monthly and asked Thackeray to be its editor as well as its chief contributor, the old war-horse took one sniff of printers' ink and pranced into editorial battle. Smith had agreed to pay £350 for each monthly instalment of a novel by Thackeray as well as £1,000 a year for the editorship.[1] The first issue of the *Cornhill Magazine* appeared in January 1860.

Most of the famous names of the day found their way into the magazine during Thackeray's editorship: Trollope, Father Prout, Milnes, Landseer, Sala, Tennyson, Ruskin, Hood, Lever, Matthew Arnold, Elizabeth Barrett Browning. It was to contain something for everybody. 'There is hardly any subject we *don't* want to hear about,' wrote Thackeray, 'from lettered and instructed men who are competent to speak on it'—but fiction was to be its staple. From the first the *Cornhill* sold hugely, 100,000 copies a month at first. Thackeray was as exuberant

---

[1] This latter sum was doubled as soon as it became clear that the magazine was headed for a great success.

as a boy over its success, and he plunged energetically into the business of issuing prospectuses, soliciting contributions, and reading manuscripts. 'We've got two horses in our carriage now,' he wrote. 'The magazine goes on increasing and how much do you think my next twelve months' earnings and receipts will be if I work? £10,000! Cockadoodleoddloodle. We are going to spend four thousand in building a new house on Palace Green, Kensington.' At the same time he was writing the novels and essays which appeared under his name. *Lovel the Widower, The Four Georges,* and *Philip,* as well as the *Roundabout Papers* were all printed during the period of his editorship.

Soon, however, the drudgery of editing began to pall on him. Temperamentally he was unfitted to grapple with insistent would-be contributors. It hurt him to turn down the bushels of worthless junk sent him by importunate authors who accompanied their manuscripts with descriptions of their poverty and illness. 'No day passes,' he wrote, 'but that argument *ad misericordiam* is used.' He would spend hours composing gentle rejections, only to be bombarded in turn by vitriolic letters of abuse. In one of the *Roundabout Papers* he described ruefully these thorns in the cushion of the editorial chair.

Out of mere malignity, I suppose, there is no man who would like to make enemies. But here, in this editorial business, you can't do otherwise: and a queer, sad, strange, bitter thought it is, that must cross the mind of many a public man: 'Do what I will, be innocent or spiteful, be generous or cruel, there are A and B, and C and D, who will hate me to the end of the chapter—to the chapter's end— to the Finis of the page—when hate, and envy, and fortune, and disappointment shall be over.'

Thackeray's sensitiveness and his desire for the good opinions of others were too keen to let him be comfortable under such stresses. He would leave unopened for days a letter from a friend whose manuscript he had found it necessary to reject.

Unhappy with the responsibilities of his position and suffering from increasingly severe ill-health he finally resigned his editorship in March 1862. He continued, however, as contributor: *Denis Duval* was in the course of publication at the time of his death and the *Roundabouts* had been appearing regularly month by month since the first issue of the magazine.[2]

The *Roundabout Papers* are the distillation of those moods and attitudes which give the clue, not to Thackeray as a novelist *per se*—that is, as a creator of scene and character—but to that individuality of manner and treatment and way of thinking which is almost as much a part of the novels as their plots or their people. If behind the novels there is a quality of mind Thackerayan as distinct, say, from Dickensian or Trollopian, that quality is beautifully fixed in the essays. They are the logical fruit of that reflective retrospective tone which is so strong in the novels. Here he is freed from the necessity of feeding his reflections into the interstices of a novel, free to be as discursive as he chooses and as frankly egoistic as a good familiar essayist must be. Here he can turn easily from subject to subject and let his vastly allusive mind play freely over both the contemporary scene and the past, bathing each in the warm afternoon glow of his rich personality. Whim, fancy, jocularity, sympathy, respect for goodness and simplicity and honesty, occasional reproof for meanness and injustice—all and more are here. He is still perceptibly the satirist of Vanity Fair and the moralist of the week-day sermons; but he is the satirist softened and the moralist mellowed. Benignity envelops him without dulling the edge of his humour. To be sure, the actual stuff of which the essays are made is of uneven excellence. He sometimes seizes upon material which not all his powers of fancy or imagination can refine. But in no similar number of pages is his personality so characteristically displayed. When he does get hold of a felicitous topic he adorns it not only with his gracious chatty fireside manner but also with his canny insight into motive and with his wide sympathy with human weakness and frailty—including his own frailty! FitzGerald said that the *Roundabouts*

[2] For the *Roundabouts* he received an extra payment of twelve guineas a page.

sounded like Thackeray talking. If that is true, he must have been one of the best talkers in the world.

The *Roundabouts* are in the great tradition of the familiar essay, from Montaigne down through Addison and Steele and Goldsmith to Leigh Hunt, Lamb, and Hazlitt. At their best they are perhaps closer to Elia than to any of the others. Thackeray's direct simplicity kept him away from the conscious old-world quaintness which Lamb delighted in. Yet there is in both much of the same love of the fantastic, the same frank admission of prejudices and weaknesses, the same rich allusiveness, literary and otherwise, and the same delicate embroidery of a whim or elaboration of an idea which unfolds into manifold connotations, beginning with almost nothing and proceeding like a train of Greek fire round a whole periphery of related suggestions. But when one gets through with a *Roundabout* he realizes that Thackeray, like Lamb, has made a central point neatly and that there is a unity to the thing after all. Thackeray also wraps his ideas in the humour which is perhaps the central quality of the best of such writing, sometimes a little wistful or rueful, but just as likely to be extravagant or robust—a humour saltier and more worldly than Lamb's. Above all, Thackeray sticks close to common things and like Lamb loves 'sun, and sky, and breeze, and solitary walks, and summer holidays, and the greenness of fields and the delicious juices of meats and fishes, and society, and the cheerful glass, and candlelight, and fireside conversations.'

Like so many great familiar essays the best of the *Roundabouts* are reminiscent and autobiographical. 'I should like,' says Thackeray (*On Two Children in Black*), 'to touch you sometimes with a reminiscence that shall waken your sympathy, and make you say, *Io anchè* have so thought, felt, smiled, suffered. Now, how is this to be done except by egotism? *Linea recta brevissima.* That right line "I" is the very shortest, simplest, straightforwardest means of communication between us, and stands for what it is worth and no more.' As always, Thackeray looked back tenderly on his own childhood. *On a Lazy Idle*

Boy tells of the novels he read as a lad—Dumas particularly. *Tunbridge Toys* is a charming recollection of his own school-boy days and a trip he made from London to Tunbridge Wells. *On Being Found Out* describes the horrors of his first private school: 'cold, chilblains, bad dinners, not enough victuals, and caning awful!' This thought of the master and the cane carries him into a contemplation of 'what life would be if every rogue were found out, and flogged *coram populo!* What a butchery, what an indecency, what an endless swishing of the rod!' He develops this idea in vast humorous detail: what if the master were whipped as well as the student, the bishop as well as the clergyman, etc.

De Juventute is another delightful essay written as by an old man remembering the days of his youth and commenting on the changes that have occurred since that time, perfectly aware, however, that it is not the times that have changed so much as he himself. The quiet humorous irony here fuses with a warm and personal sentiment to create a poignant perception of time and change, of the sort which comes home to the bosoms of all mature people.

We who lived before railways, and survive out of the ancient world, are like Father Noah and his family out of the Ark. The children will gather round and say to us patriarchs, 'Tell us, grandpapa, about the old world.' And we shall mumble our old stories; and we shall drop off one by one; and there will be fewer and fewer of us, and these very old and feeble. There will be but ten præ-railroadites left: then three—then two—then one—then o!

He contemplates the more recent past, too, how 'in former days, I too have militated; sometimes, as I now think, unjustly; but always, I vow, without personal rancour. Which of us has not idle words to recall, flippant jokes to regret?' But 'it is wonderful how gallantly one bears the misfortunes of one's friends.' He muses on the life of Thomas Hood, which was 'even better than his books, and I wish with all my heart, *Monsieur et cher confrère,* the same could be said for both of us,

when the inkstream of our life hath ceased to run.' Many of
the essays flow thus in a mood of past experience, of summa-
tion. 'The writer,' he says, 'belongs to the old-fashioned classes
of this world, loves to remember very much more than to
prophesy . . . he sits under Time, the white-wigged charioteer,
with his back to the horses, and his face to the past, looking at
the receding landscape and the hills fading into the grey distance.' As has been pointed out, young poets from Dante down
through Shakespeare and up to T. S. Eliot have assumed this
same manner. This mood was not an affectation with Thackeray; he really felt old.

All is not reminiscence, however. We learn about Thackeray's
favourite authors, that Montaigne and Howell's *Letters* are his
bedside books and that he loves Don Quixote and Goldsmith
and Boswell and Fielding and Rabelais and Burton and Lamb
and Scott. He treats topical subjects in *Nil Nisi Bonum,* written
when Washington Irving and Macaulay died within the month,
and in *On Half a Loaf,* dealing with imminence of war between
Britain and the United States in 1862. He travels: *A Missis-
sippi Bubble* tells of his experiences in the States and *Notes of
a Week's Holiday* is a congenial and appreciative travel sketch
of a trip to Belgium and Holland. He gives us literary criticism too, tells us how well he knows the sound of his characters' voices, and how strangely they seem to assume an independent life and to tell him what to write. In one essay he holds
an imaginary conversation with the shade of Laurence Sterne.

Occasionally the edge of satire breaks through these benignant
musings, but even there Thackeray hastens to cry *mea culpa*
while he strikes home. We are all weak brethren and one man
is as good as another and a great deal better, as the Irish philosopher said. The lies that people tell stir Thackeray to criticism
(*On a Hundred Years Hence*):

Gracious goodness! how do lies begin? . . . I look back at some
which have been told about me, and speculate on them with thanks
and wonder. Dear friends have told them of me, have told them to
me of myself . . . We somehow greedily gobble down all the stories

in which the characters of our friends are chopped up, and believe wrong of them without inquiry . . . *O mea culpa, mea maxima culpa!* But though the preacher trips, shall not the doctrine be good? Yea, brethren! Here be the rods. Look you, here are the scourges. Choose me a nice long, swishing, buddy one, light and well-poised in the handle, thick and bushy at the tail. Pick me out a whip-cord thong with some dainty knots in it—and now—we all deserve it— whish, whish, whish! Let us cut each other all round . . . Certain it is that scandal is good brisk talk, whereas praise of one's neighbor is by no means lively hearing. An acquaintance grilled, scored, devilled, and served with mustard and cayenne pepper, excites the appetite; whereas a slice of cold friend with currant jelly is but a sickly un-relishing meat.

Not infrequently he turns moralizer and lays his finger, more gently than in the early days, and with an ironic and humor-ous return upon himself, upon the follies and vagaries and meannesses of men. Taking as his text 'all claret would be punch if it could' (*Small Beer Chronicle*) he rings the changes on the theme of man's pretence and self-seeking.

How much claret that would be port if it could is handed about in every society! In the House of Commons what small-beer orators try to pass for strong! Stay; have I a spite against any one? It is a fact that the wife of the member for Bungay has left off asking me and Mrs. Roundabout to her evening parties. Now is the time to have a slap at him. I will say that he was always overrated, and that now he is lamentably falling off even from what he has been . . . Have I any little literary animosities? Of course not. Men of letters never have. Otherwise, how I could serve out a competitor here, make a face over his works, and show that his would-be port is very meagre ordinaire indeed! Nonsense, man! Why so squeamish? Do they spare *you?* Now you have the whip in your hand, won't you lay on? You used to be a pretty whip enough as a young man, and liked it too. Is there no enemy who would be the better for a little thong-ing? No. I have militated in former times, not without glory; but I grow peaceable as I grow old. And if I have a literary enemy, why, he will probably write a book ere long, and then it will be *his* turn, and my favourite review will be down upon him.

With a disarming frankness this moralizer pleads guilty to the charge his critics bring against him. In *De Finibus* he has been talking about Dr. Firmin in *Philip*. He had planned to drown him but relented before the end and gave him a small chance of repentance.

I wonder whether he *did* repent when he found himself in the yellow-fever, in Virginia? The probability is, he fancied that his son had injured him very much, and forgave him on his death-bed. Do you imagine there is a great deal of genuine right-down remorse in the world? Don't people rather find excuses which make their minds easy . . . ? Nay (for I am making a clean breast, and liberating my soul), perhaps of all the novel-spinners now extant, the present speaker is the most addicted to preaching. Does he not stop perpetually in his story and begin to preach to you? When he ought to be engaged with business, is he not for ever taking the Muse by the sleeve, and plaguing her with some of his cynical sermons? I cry *peccavi* loudly and heartily. I tell you I would like to be able to write a story which should show no egotism whatever—in which there should be no reflections, no cynicism, no vulgarity (and so forth), but an incident in every other page, a villain, a battle, a mystery in every chapter. (*De Finibus*)

One more example by way of showing how Thackeray could elaborate an ironic idea, keeping the ball in the air with an inventive fertility. He is saying that many people have little sense of humour:

Raillery in writing annoys and offends them. The coarseness apart, I think I have met very very few women who liked the banter of Swift and Fielding. Their simple tender natures revolt at laughter. Is the satyr always a wicked brute at heart, and are they rightly shocked at his grin, his leer, his horns, hoofs, and ears? *Fi donc, le vilain monstre,* with his shrieks, and his capering crooked legs! Let him go and get a pair of well-wadded black silk stockings, and pull them over those horrid shanks; put a large gown and bands over beard and hide; and pour a dozen of lavender-water into his lawn handkerchief, and cry, and never make a joke again. It shall all be highly-distilled poesy, and perfumed sentiment, and gushing eloquence; and the foot *shan't* peep out, and a plague take it. Cover it up with the surplice. Out with your cambric, dear ladies, and let us all whimper together. (*Thorns in the Cushion*)

The temptation in discussing the *Roundabout Papers* is that of quoting them entire, for they are as original and amusing as they are honest. What brings it all home, of course, is the style, which never was more nearly right than in these essays. It has that sense of abundance and effortless ease which gives validity to this kind of writing. Unrhetorical, loose in structure, it can be eloquent, and is always precise in its effects. What language can do in the way of fusing word and idea, thought and feeling, Thackeray makes it do in the prose of the *Roundabouts*. It is as transparent and clean as it is subtle in its seemingly uncalculated rhythms. If the *Roundabout Papers* seem old-fashioned today it is because that sort of thing has gone out of fashion. The present in which Thackeray lived has become our past, and in our new society the familiar essay itself, rooted in easier times, grows vestigial. Thackeray might have something to say on the subject (doubtless something very realistic and 'twentieth-century') if we could hold converse with his shade as he did with Sterne's. Failing that, we can only let Carlyle's 'impenetrable time-curtains' rush down, and return the *Roundabouts* to the bosom of the nineteenth century, whence they will continue to be resuscitated by those in any age who love the kind of excellence of which Thackeray was one of the great English masters.

Thackeray's verses are to poetry much as his illustrations are to art. What they can do they do well. For what they do not pretend to do they cannot be criticized. The 'ballads,' as he called his rhymes, vary greatly in quality. At their infrequent worst they are compounded of rather sterile sentiment in the 'Keepsake' manner, or of unlicked humour. At their best they bubble with a sprightly and buoyant gaiety crossed, however, by frequent touches of pathos. Typically they combine sentiment and humour—and sometimes indignation—in a merry-sad brew of

Thackeray's own peculiar tap. The analogies of his verse are with Béranger, whom he adapted, with Prior and Gay and Praed, and above all with his favourite Horace, whom he imitated and whose spirit pervades his thinking.

If Thackeray did not exactly breathe in numbers he yet began to versify early. By no means the worst of his attempts was the pseudo-prize poem *Timbuctoo* which he wrote at Cambridge in 1829 and published in *The Snob*. As noted earlier this was a playful burlesque of the stilted pretentious poetizing about strange and distant lands and carried an elaborate appendage of explanatory and self-commendatory footnotes as amusing as the conscious dullness of the poem itself. This gift for parody and burlesque was to remain central in his later ballads.

Poetic composition came hard to him, in spite of the seeming spontaneous ease of his versification. When he was labouring with *The Chronicle of the Drum* in 1841 he wrote to Mrs. Procter: [3]

It is the deuce, that poetry—or rhymes—and never was an unfortunate fellow so plagued. For a whole week you would have fancied me a real poet, having all the exterior marks of one—with a week's beard, a great odour of tobacco, a scowling, ferocious, thoughtful appearance. I used to sit all day meditating, nail-biting, and laboriously producing about twenty lines in twelve hours. Are all poets in this way?

Certainly none of these labour-pangs appears in the sparkling brightness of his published verses. If they are sometimes dull it is because their topical implications no longer interest us—many of them were occasional pieces—or because the brogue of *Lyra Hibernica* or the grotesque misspellings of Policeman X do not carry today quite the load of wit which Thackeray meant for them. It must be remembered, too, that many of the ballads were turned out on schedule for *Punch* and that Thackeray frequently had to be funny while the printer's boy was waiting in the hallway for the copy.

[3] Biographical Introduction to *Barry Lyndon*, xvii.

With a few exceptions the ballads are on a poetically low level, *vers de societé* or mere humorous doggerel. He does not attempt the higher flights; his muse was a homely one and he recognized it for such. His emotion is tender and warm rather than ecstatic or inspired. At the same time one can learn from his more serious verse something about his philosophy of life. In *The Pen and the Album,* for example, he shows us how he liked to think of himself as the jester with the tragic face behind the mask. The gold pen is speaking:

> I've help'd him to pen many a line for bread;
> To joke, with sorrow aching in his head;
> And make your laughter when his own heart bled.
>
> * * *
>
> Nor pass the words as idle phrases by;
>   Stranger! I never writ a flattery,
> Nor sign'd the page that register'd a lie.

The same theme is touched in *The End of the Play,* in which much of his habitual temper is seen:

> A moment yet the actor stops,
>   And looks around, to say farewell.
> It is an irksome word and task;
>   And, when he's laughed and had his say,
> He shows, as he removes the mask,
>   A face that's anything but gay.

The secret is to be gentle and honest and kindly, to cultivate a stoic resignation to the 'inscrutable design,' which sometimes decrees that

> The strong may yield, the good may fall,
>   The great man be a vulgar clown,
> The knave be lifted over all,
>   The kind cast pitilessly down.

His anti-militarism comes as a pungent, direct blast against the so-called glories of war, described in *The Chronicle of the Drum:*

And ever since historian writ,
   And ever since a bard could sing,
Doth each exalt with all his wit
   The noble art of murdering.

* * *

Take Doctor Southey from the shelf,
   An LL.D.,—a peaceful man;
Good Lord, how he doth plume himself
   Because we beat the Corsican!

* * *

Your orthodox historian puts
   In foremost rank the soldier thus,
The red-coat bully in his boots,
   That hides the march of men from us.

* * *

Go to! I hate him and his trade:
   Who bade us so to cringe and bend,
And all God's peaceful people made
   To such as him subservient?

Thackeray once said that *The Cane-Bottomed Chair* was his favourite. Few today would rate it so high, but the statement shows how he treasured his reminiscent, wistful moods of mingled sentiment and pathos. Of the poems in this vein the famous *Ballad of Bouillabaise* and *The Mahogany Tree* are by all odds the best. The Mahogany Tree was the old initialed table around which the editorial board of *Punch* used to gather.

Here let us sport,
Boys, as we sit;
Laughter and wit
Flashing so free.
Life is but short—
When we are gone,
Let them sing on,
Round the old tree.

Evenings we knew,
Happy as this;
Faces we miss,
Pleasant to see.
Kind hearts and true,
Gentle and just,
Peace to your dust!
We sing round the tree.

Care, like a dun,
Lurks at the gate:
Let the dog wait;
Happy we'll be!
Drink, every one;
Pile up the coals,
Fill the red bowls,
Round the old tree!

His best effects, however, are humorous ones. He can turn an amusing verse with neat skill, the rhymes—including the ingenious double and triple ones—falling exactly right, the whole tone bright and glancing. Such a piece is the burlesque *Sorrows of Werther*,[4] or *The Willow Tree*, where he writes a yearning

[4] Werther had a love for Charlotte
Such as words could never utter;
Would you know how first he met her?
She was cutting bread and butter.

Charlotte was a married lady,
And a moral man was Werther,
And, for all the wealth of Indies,
Would do nothing for to hurt her.

So he sighed and pined and ogled,
And his passion boiled and bubbled,
Till he blew his silly brains out,
And no more was by it troubled.

Charlotte, having seen his body
Borne before her on a shutter,
Like a well-conducted person,
Went on cutting bread and butter.

An amusing footnote to this poem appears in an unpublished letter of Thackeray's now in the Huntington Library. He is drafting a letter, evidently, to an

romantic ballad too good to be mere parody, only to turn and
rend it in extravagant burlesque. Again, he elbows aside a pretty
lyric sentiment in *Mrs. Katherine's Lantern* with a wilfully
comic parenthesis:

> And a man—I let the truth out,—
> Who's had almost every tooth out,
> Cannot sing as once he sung,
> When he was young as you are young,
> When he was young and lutes were strung
> And love-lamps in the casement hung.

Commanders of the Faithful has all the easy rollicking felicity
of his best humour:

> The Pope he is a happy man,
> His Palace is the Vatican,
> And there he sits and drains his can:
> The Pope he is a happy man.
> I often say when I'm at home,
> I'd like to be the Pope of Rome.
>
> And then there's Sultan Saladin,
> That Turkish Soldan full of sin;
> He has a hundred wives at least,
> By which his pleasure is increased:
> I've often wished, I hope no sin,
> That I were Sultan Saladin.
>
> But no, the Pope no wife may choose,
> And so I would not wear his shoes;

editor in whose columns a correspondent has complained that the closing line
of the poem is 'a falsification.' 'What is there in Goethe's text,' asks Thackeray, 'to show that after young Werther's suicide Charlotte did *not* continue
to cut bread and butter? "They feared for Lotty's life" I take to mean that
she was at one time much affected by Mr. Werther's demise, but that she sur-
vived the circumstance: in which case as a good housewife, she would certainly resume those operations in which she was so charmingly employed when
Werther first beheld her.

'Otherwise—I should probably have written Charlotte *left off cutting bread
and butter*,—a fine line too, but not so pathetic, I still humbly think, as that
which has the misfortune to displease your correspondent . . .'

> No wine may drink the proud Paynim,
> And so I'd rather not be him:
> My wife, my wine, I love, I hope,
> And would be neither Turk nor Pope.

Although Thackeray's ballads are among the best of their kind, no one would pretend that their kind was the best. Nevertheless they are of a piece with his other work, warmed by the same sunshine and darkened by the same shadows. In his rhymes as in his novels and essays he is the hater of shams and affectations, literary or social; the brisk, tolerant sceptic with a tear in his eye; the lover of laughter and the wistful observer of evanescent happiness. No one could misread here the tenderness which informs the gentle melancholy of a man hungry for affection. Yet he likes fun as well as sentiment and is courageous as well as kind.

At last 'the end of the play' came. The puppets were laid aside and the puppet-master bade farewell to the life of which he had become so weary and which he had at the same time loved so much. Thackeray died in his sleep the day before Christmas, 1863, in the fifty-third year of his life. For another Christmas, fifteen years earlier, he had written a valedictory:

> My song, save this, is little worth;
>   I lay the weary pen aside,
> And wish you health, and love, and mirth,
>   As fits the solemn Christmastide.
> As fits the holy Christmas birth,
>   Be this, good friends, our carol still—
> Be peace on earth, be peace on earth,
>   To men of gentle will.

Index